# *Terrified*

The heartbreaking true story of a girl nobody loved
and the woman who saved her

ANGELA HART

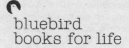

bluebird
books for life

First published 2016 by Bluebird
an imprint of Pan Macmillan
20 New Wharf Road, London N1 9RR
Associated companies throughout the world
www.panmacmillan.com

ISBN 978-1-5098-0551-8

1 3 5 7 9 8 6 4 2

A CIP catalogue record for this book is available from the British Library.

Typeset by Ellipsis Digital Limited, Glasgow
Printed and bound by CPI Group (UK) Ltd, Croydon, CR0 4YY

Visit **www.panmacmillan.com** to read more about all our books
and to buy them. You will also find features, author interviews and
news of any author events, and you can sign up for e-newsletters
so that you're always first to hear about our new releases.

# 1

## *'What have we done?'*

'Shall we have a Chinese tonight?' I said to my husband, Jonathan.

'Definitely,' he replied. 'I think we've earned it.'

It was 5.20 p.m. on a balmy Friday evening in July 1989 and we were shutting up our florist shop. As usual it had been an exhausting week and it wasn't over yet; Saturday was always our busiest day.

'Perhaps we could rent a video?' I said as I swept the floor and pulled down the shutters. 'What would we all like, do you think?'

As Jonathan listed a few of the recent releases, like *A Fish Called Wanda* and *My Stepmother Is An Alien*, the phone rang. It was Tricia, the social worker we'd dealt with ever since we started fostering two years earlier.

'Hi Angela, sorry to call you on a Friday evening, but I wondered if you'd be interested in taking in a girl of thirteen?'

'When were you thinking?'

'Tonight, actually. Just a short-term placement. She's been living with her sister, but the sister needs a break, because she's heavily pregnant. I thought of you because you're doing so well with Michelle.'

Michelle had recently turned fourteen and had been with us for two years. She was a quiet, sweet-natured girl who was always very welcoming to other children who came to us for short stays. It was nice of Tricia to acknowledge our success with Michelle, and I felt my energy levels lift as I asked the social worker to hold the line for a moment while I swiftly relayed the request to Jonathan. He smiled instantly, and I knew he felt the same way as I did, and was more than happy to help.

Jonathan and I had been together for sixteen years, since meeting in our teens in the early seventies, and for as long as I can remember we have had an almost telepathic understanding of one another. We swapped animated glances, and I told Tricia we'd be delighted to accept the placement.

'Fantastic! Thanks, Angela. We'll be with you within the hour, if that's all right. She's with me at the office now. Her name's Vicky.'

I had a spring in my step as I finished lifting the flowers into the cold storage room at the back of the shop. In the relatively short time we'd been fostering I'd come to know this feeling quite well. Waiting to meet a new foster child is always very exciting and nerve-racking.

We lived in a large town house attached to the shop, with three bedrooms and a bathroom on the top floor, the lounge and our bedroom and bathroom on the middle floor, and the kitchen and dining room sharing the extended lower floor with the shop. This meant I had enough time to quickly nip up to my bedroom to get changed, tell Michelle about Vicky's imminent arrival and then open the windows in the bigger of our two spare bedrooms at the top of the house. As the room aired, Michelle offered to help me put fresh covers on the bed, choosing a pink and white duvet set with candy canes on that had just been washed. It was Michelle's favourite bedding; she loved anything pretty and pink.

'I think Vicky will like her room,' Michelle said, looking round approvingly. Sunlight was beaming through the window, reflecting dancing squares of light off the shiny lampshade and onto the freshly painted white walls. 'Do you think she'll be into Whitney Houston?'

'I don't think she'll have any choice, will she?' I smiled.

Michelle blushed. She seemed younger than her years and was a naturally shy girl, but she loved music and we'd had one or two run-ins about the volume dial on her stereo, particularly when she blasted out her all-time favourite, Whitney's 'So Emotional'.

We had no set house rules in those days; now, with nearly thirty years of fostering experience under our belts, we have a list of rules designed to work in everybody's favour, but back then it was a case of using our common sense and tackling issues as best we could, as and when they came along. With Michelle's music, we'd mutually agreed that she had to keep the volume at number six or below on the dial. It was easy to reason with her, and in many ways we'd struck lucky having Michelle as our first placement.

'Lulled into a false sense of security, more like!' Jonathan used to joke, and that's not far from the truth. Michelle was incredibly willing to please and hardly ever challenged us.

'Can I help?' was typically the first thing she said to me when I came through to the kitchen from the shop after work to set about preparing the dinner. 'Well yes, that would be great. Now let me see . . .'

Michelle would invariably pick up the potato peeler or begin to put dishes away off the draining board before I'd even finished my sentence.

'Are you doing anything later, Michelle?' I'd often ask, though the answer was usually the same each night.

'Not really,' she'd shrug. 'I've already done my homework. Do you want to watch telly later?'

'I'd love to, sweetheart,' I nearly always replied.

Michelle had a small but close circle of school pals who were all as polite and unassuming as she was, though she rarely went out. The two of us enjoyed watching the soaps together, and we had been glued recently to a *Coronation Street* storyline involving Rita Fairclough's foster daughter Jenny Bradley, whose father, Alan, had been killed by a tram in Blackpool.

'It must be terrible for poor Jenny, losing her dad like that,' Michelle had commented.

The plot had struck a chord with both of us. The teenage

character's father had let her down in so many ways and had even tried to kill Rita but, just as Michelle behaved with her own dad, Jenny was very loyal to Alan and supported him unconditionally. Michelle's father didn't live very far away and she saw him two or three times a week. He had behaved very irresponsibly in the past and now refused to have his daughter living with him, but Michelle was very forgiving and never critical.

'I wonder if Vicky is into the soaps?' she said cheerfully as we finished making the bed. 'I hope so!'

Before I had chance to reply we were interrupted by Jonathan calling up from the kitchen.

'They're here!' he yelled, his voice sounding surprisingly urgent.

'That was quick!' I said.

'Yes it was! I think I'll wait up here for a bit,' Michelle replied.

With that she scampered off to her bedroom along the landing, while I ran down the two flights of stairs to the ground floor as quickly as possible. I found Jonathan rooted to the spot and staring out of the kitchen window, with a horrified expression on his face.

'Oh my God!' he said. 'Look out there!'

I followed his gaze and saw two figures in the distance, walking down the public passageway that ran adjacent to the left hand side of our house. One was clearly Tricia; you couldn't mistake her mass of dark, permed hair and curvaceous figure. The other had to be Vicky.

'Oh my God!' I said, eyes darting back to Jonathan. 'What have we done?'

Vicky was dressed in a dark purple tracksuit that looked three sizes too big, but what was really alarming was the way she walked. You could barely describe it as a walk, to tell the truth. She swaggered like a willowy, blonde version of Mr T in *The A Team*.

I guess I had imagined Vicky would be just like the five other foster children who'd come to us on short-term placements over the past couple of years. Without exception they arrived for their few days or week or two of short-term care, or 'respite care' as it's known, looking rather timid, dressed inconspicuously in a pair of jeans or jogging bottoms, and nervously clutching a small bag.

Vicky did have a bag in her hand – a supermarket carrier bag – but she wasn't clinging to her possessions for dear life like most kids did. No, Vicky's carrier bag was swinging wildly from side to side, keeping time with her exaggerated swagger.

She and Tricia disappeared from view as they got closer to the house, as we had a high fence running the length of our garden, to give us privacy from people using the busy passageway leading to the parade of shops our florists was situated in.

'What have we done indeed!' Jonathan stuttered, his eyes filled with a look of impending doom. 'Is it too late to . . . ?'

The doorbell rang and I felt my stomach churn, but as I went to answer it I took a deep breath and told myself to smile. However she looked, Vicky was a thirteen-year-old girl who was in the unfortunate position of not being able to live with her own family for the time being. Whatever fears we had, hers were doubtless far greater. As I've said many times over the years, it is hard being a foster carer, but it is a lot harder being a foster child.

'Hello! You must be Vicky!' I said, smiling gamely and trying to look as welcoming as possible as I swung open the entrance door on the side of the house.

'I am!' she grinned back proudly. As she did so, Vicky lifted her hand to her forehead and gave me one of those American soldier-style salutes. 'Pleased to meet you, Mrs Hart!'

'You can call me Angela.'

'Please to meet you, Angela!' she said, repeating the salute.

I smiled genuinely now because, despite the fact she seemed over-confident and perhaps even a little cocky, there was something appealing about Vicky that I liked immediately. She was clearly full of life, and I couldn't help but admire her sunny disposition under what must have been such difficult circumstances for her.

I led Vicky and Tricia across the hall and into the kitchen, where Jonathan was boiling the kettle and grinning bravely.

'Hello!' he said. 'I'm Jonathan. It's very nice to meet you. Would you like a cup of tea, or perhaps a cold drink as it's such a warm evening?'

'I'd love to but I can't stop,' Tricia cut in, addressing me even though Jonathan had spoken to her and Vicky. 'I have a visit to make across town that I'm already late for. Thanks for taking Vicky in at such short notice, Angela. I'll leave you to it then. I'll be in touch.'

With that she handed me some paperwork that simply had her name and Vicky's written on it, and no contact numbers other than the general Social Services office number, which I already knew by heart. I swapped a look with Jonathan that said 'classic Tricia'. She was always in a hurry, and she rarely acknowledged that Jonathan had anything to do with the fostering that went on under his roof, which was far from the truth.

When I first spotted an advert for foster carers three years earlier, back in 1986, Jonathan had been very supportive despite the fact that, from his point of view, my interest came quite out of the blue.

'Foster Carers Wanted,' I read from the local paper, feeling a surge of excitement as I studied the advert. 'Do you fancy it, Jonathan?'

'Fostering? It's not something I've ever thought about before, Angela. I didn't think you had either.'

'Well I haven't really, but this just caught my eye, that was all. I think I'd like to find out more.'

We sat down that evening and had a proper chat about it, and Jonathan listened patiently as I discussed why fostering appealed to me. I hadn't fully realised myself where my interest came from, but as we talked I found myself reflecting on my past and exploring how experiences I'd had when I was a young girl had drawn me to the advert.

At infant school I had a friend called Belinda who was adopted, and her mother used to take in kids on short-term placements in the summer holidays. Their house would be filled with chatter and clutter, and I loved going there because it was never boring, and my friend had lots of interesting playmates.

By contrast, I was more or less raised as an only child. My older brother, Andrew, was fourteen when I was born, and he left home when I was just five years old. I missed him terribly, and every time he visited I spent the whole time dreading the moment when I'd have to say goodbye to him all over again.

'Can we foster like Belinda's family?' I asked my mum longingly one summer, imagining how wonderful it would be to have other children to play with all the time.

'Goodness me,' she replied. 'I don't think I'm cut out for that, Angela. Belinda's mum has the patience of a saint! I tell you what though, if you're looking for something to do in the holidays, Mr Roberts said he could use your help again; he said you were brilliant last time.'

Mr Roberts was one of our neighbours, and he took in wild animals from a local rescue centre, nursing them back to health. I'd helped him several times and absolutely loved it, and my mum cleverly distracted me with the promise I could do more of the same.

'Did he really say I was brilliant?' I smiled, delighted by the compliment.

'He did indeed.'

'Could I feed the hedgehogs again? I loved that! The baby ones were *so* cute!'

Looking back this was a wonderful result for my mother. It was difficult for her to take time off from the florists, but this would keep me occupied for days on end throughout the school holidays.

My parents worked incredibly hard in the shop, and in most of my childhood memories my mum and dad are either behind the counter, at the wholesalers, making deliveries or recovering from a hard day's work at home, too tired to do much else but have a meal and an early night. The downside of this was that neither of them were what you might call spontaneous, but on the plus side my parents were always around, which generally gave me great stability.

Unfortunately, when I was seven years old my mother suffered a serious back injury and had to have an operation. With my father left in sole charge of the shop I was dispatched to stay with my Aunt Hattie for twelve long weeks while my mother was in hospital. My aunt was very kind, filling her little freezer with the Mini Milk ice lollies she knew I loved, and taking me on the bus most days to visit my mum at the hospital across town. I had a fantastic new Etch A Sketch, bought by my parents to cheer me up when my mother went into hospital, but I'd have given it back in a flash to have my mother home, and our lives returned to normal. I pined for my mum. My heart ached when I thought about her, and I cried each and every time I had to say goodbye and go back to my aunt's house. 'Don't want to go there!' I'd sulk. 'I want to go home! I want Mummy!'

Aunt Hattie had dug out a box of children's books from her loft, belonging to her grown-up daughter, which she tried to distract me with whenever I cried and complained. I was familiar with some of the books, like *Noddy* and *The Famous Five*, but when I looked at them at my aunt's house they seemed so *unfamiliar*. Everything was odd and different and, well, just not like it was at home. The house even smelled different to ours, like a mixture between talcum powder and mothballs instead of the sweet, heady scent of flowers that had just 'gone over', as my mother said, which we always had in a big ceramic vase in the hallway.

I wanted to go back to my house so badly I felt sick; truly homesick. My constant questioning about how long Mum would be in hospital must have driven poor Aunt Hattie mad. Looking back she must have been quite frustrated by my behaviour, as she did everything in her power to try to make my stay as pleasing as possible, but she never lost her patience and was incredibly kind.

One day I was visiting my dad in the shop on my way home from school with Aunt Hattie when a customer came in and said, 'Ooh Trevor, you must be so pleased! I heard Thelma's home.'

My ears pricked up and I darted straight past my dad, through the back storeroom leading to the kitchen and hallway of the town house Jonathan and I live in today, and dashed up the stairs as quickly as I could. My dad couldn't abandon the shop and probably wouldn't have caught me even if he could; I'd never run so fast in all my life.

'Mummy!' I cried as I ran into her bedroom on the first floor, opposite the lounge. 'Mummy, Mummy, Mummy!'

'Angela!' she exclaimed. 'What a wonderful surprise!'

Mum was propped up in bed, encased in plaster, and I zoned in on her as if she were a magnetic force pulling me in. In hindsight I realise my mother was planning to recuperate in peace and quiet for a little while before I came back from Aunt Hattie's, but once I knew she was home I wasn't leaving, ever, ever again. I clung to my mum for dear life, and to this day I can remember how euphoric and grateful I felt to have my mummy back. Life was back to how it should be, and my happy, carefree childhood could resume at long last.

Jonathan listened patiently as I described all of these memories, and then he studied the newspaper advert I'd read out. It mentioned respite care for children whose parents were unable to look after them for short periods of time, giving the example of when a parent is in hospital. There was a phone number to call for more information, and Jonathan picked up a pen, circled it and handed it to me.

'I think you should ring them tomorrow,' he said. 'I can see this is something you feel strongly about. I also think you'd be good at fostering.'

'What about you? It's something we'd both have to want to do.'

'I'm not sure yet, but I think you should look into it. We'll never know unless we find out more. I guess the worst that could happen is that we find it's not for us, but at least you'll have followed your heart.'

'Thank you,' I said. 'And if it works out I guess it will be good practise for when we have kids of our own.'

'Exactly. Nothing ventured, nothing gained. And you don't need to thank me. As usual I should probably be thanking you.'

'Why?'

'You make things happen, Angela! There's never a dull moment, thanks to you.'

I was flattered and very pleased. Jonathan and I had always had a solid relationship and his reaction was typical. I knew he'd support me whatever the outcome, and I felt a surge of love for him.

Now, having just seen Tricia out and returned to the kitchen to find Jonathan chatting easily with Vicky, I felt a similar wave of emotion. Jonathan was a natural with the kids we fostered, and I imagined that when we had children together he'd make the most wonderful father.

Vicky had made herself comfortable at the kitchen table and was glugging a large glass of orange squash and talking enthusiastically about birds, of all things.

'Robins are my favourites,' she was telling Jonathan. 'But I love all birds, really. I'd like to work in a bird sanctuary when I'm older.'

She was studying a postcard that had been propped up on the table, and Jonathan explained that it was sent from a friend who had visited a tropical aviary in Australia. Vicky looked up when I crossed the kitchen.

'Thank you for having me, Angela,' she said, and then she accidentally let out a loud burp.

'Oops, pardon me! I always do that when I drink too quick.'

Vicky laughed raucously and showed no embarrassment, and Jonathan and I couldn't help but smile. Some of the kids we'd had to stay wouldn't say boo to a goose, and it was refreshing to see Vicky behaving in such a relaxed manner so soon after her arrival. Social graces were normally something we were very strict about, but clearly this was not the time to make an issue about manners.

'I'll show you up to your room, shall I? And did Tricia tell you about Michelle?'

'No,' she said. 'Who's that?'

Just then Michelle appeared in the doorway, smiling shyly and saying hello.

'I can show Vicky to her room if you like,' Michelle said, eager to please as ever.

'Cool!' Vicky said, getting to her feet and grabbing her carrier bag. 'Let's go! Are you fostered too?'

'Yes I am. I've been here for two years.'

'Two years? That's a long time! Are they nice?'

Vicky flicked me and Jonathan a glance over her shoulder and winked as Michelle led her out of the kitchen.

'Yes, they are really nice, you'll love them,' we heard Michelle reply as they headed up the stairs.

My heart swelled.

'I'll be up in a minute to show you where everything is!' I called after the girls, and then I collapsed in giggles.

'Well, what a character! It just goes to show you can't judge a book by its cover. I feel quite ashamed of how we reacted when we first saw her.'

'Me too,' Jonathan said. 'What on earth were we worried about?'

# 2

## *'I'm not staying long'*

When I followed the girls up the stairs on Vicky's first evening I was delighted to hear them talking about travelling to school together. It turned out they were in the same local mixed comprehensive, though Michelle was in the year above.

'You can catch the bus with me,' Michelle was saying as I arrived outside Vicky's bedroom and tapped on the door.

'Can I come in, girls?'

They both shouted yes and carried on their conversation.

'I prefer to walk,' Vicky said as she took her uniform and a pair of school shoes out of her carrier bag.

'Why?'

'Just do. It's more fun; I meet all my mates on the way, why not come with us?'

Michelle said she'd think about it before going off to her own room, offering to show Vicky her record collection once she'd unpacked. I then took over, showing Vicky where the bathroom was and how to turn on the shower.

'This bathroom is for you and Michelle, as Jonathan and I have our own on the floor below,' I explained. I was just about to add: 'So you can feel free to leave your toiletries in here,' when I realised Vicky had only brought the school uniform and shoes, a toothbrush and a few items of underwear, which she'd tipped onto her bed before throwing the empty carrier bag in the bin.

Incidentally, in years to come I learned to tell the children that they did not need to ask permission to use the bathroom and were free to do so at any time of the day or night, as some had come from such dysfunctional backgrounds and were so afraid of doing the wrong thing they didn't realise this. Vicky wasn't the type of girl who'd have been shy about speaking up though; in fact she was quite the opposite.

'Is that the only soap you've got?' she said, pulling a face and looking at the bar of Imperial Leather that was stuck on a magnet and attached to the soap dish inside the shower unit.

'Yes, I think so,' I said. 'Don't you like that one?'

'I normally have shower gel. I don't like sharing soap. At my sister's, her husband leaves greasy marks on it after his bath.'

'I see. Well, in that case I'll fetch some shower gel from my bathroom. I'm sure I've got some.'

I made a mental note of what Vicky had said; it was a good point. However much I wanted Vicky to feel at home she was a stranger at this stage, and I realised I wouldn't have wanted to share soap with people I didn't know.

'I imagine you'll need to get some more of your belongings from your sister's,' I said tentatively to Vicky, as I wasn't sure what the situation was or what arrangements had been made at this stage, if any. All I knew was that Vicky's sister was pregnant and needed a bit of a break before the baby arrived.

'Well I won't need much,' Vicky replied breezily. 'I'm not staying long. Anyway, I always wear my tracksuit when I'm not in school, so I'll be fine.'

Even though I had fostered children for two years, I had never been given any training, but I instinctively knew not to press Vicky for information. Of course, I wanted to ask so much, like why she was living with her sister and not her mother or father, and exactly what had prompted her sister to call Social Services, because being tired in pregnancy did not seem like a convincing reason to put your little sister in care.

'OK. I expect the social worker will help us sort things out on Monday,' I said. 'Now when you're ready, come down and have a look at the takeaway menu. We're treating ourselves to a Chinese tonight.'

'Awesome! Do they do chips and gravy?'

'Probably! I always have Chicken Maryland, but we can ask.'

When Vicky came down the stairs about twenty minutes later she looked noticeably subdued and was very quiet. Jonathan tried to engage her in a conversation about films, as he was going to pick up a video when he went to collect the Chinese, but she was monosyllabic.

'What kind of films do you like?' he asked.

'Don't mind,' she shrugged.

'We all like funny films best. Do you like comedies?'

'Not bothered, really.'

'Is there anything you really don't like then, or anything you've seen recently and don't want to see again, so I can avoid those?'

'No, I don't think so. Well, I don't like scary movies. I don't understand why people want to be frightened. That's just crazy.'

'When you put it like that, I suppose it is! Perhaps I'll just ask Michelle and Angela if they'd like to choose something, and we'll steer well clear of horror!'

'OK.'

Honestly, it was as if Vicky had left her personality and energy up in the bedroom and was now just a shell of the girl who'd swaggered so confidently up to the house less than an hour earlier.

'Are you feeling all right, love?' I asked.

'Yes, fine, thanks. I'm just tired.'

Vicky was like that for the entire weekend. Whatever we suggested, be it a walk to the corner shop, a snack or watching something on television, everything was met with a resigned shrug or an unenthusiastic 'fine'. It was frustrating, but I figured it was inevitable; Vicky had been through a major upheaval and she clearly needed time to settle in.

'Would you like me to wash your tracksuit when you're at school tomorrow?' I asked on Sunday evening, as she'd worn nothing else since she arrived.

'No, thanks, I don't think it needs washing.'

'I could put it in the tumble drier after I've washed it. That way it'll be ready when you get home from school.'

'Thanks but there's no need. It's fine, honestly. I'll do it when I'm back at my sister's.'

'OK. I'll phone Tricia as soon as the Social Services office opens tomorrow in any case, and see about getting some more of your things.'

'Thanks, but I really don't need much because I'm not staying long, am I?'

Vicky was now staring into space.

'I'm just letting my sister have a rest, aren't I? That's all. The baby's due soon.'

It sounded to me like Vicky was convincing herself of this, rather than stating a fact.

'That's what I was told,' I said reassuringly.

'Good. I'll be going back as soon as the baby is born. It's due any day.'

'Really?' I replied, because I hadn't expected the date to be so close. 'That soon?'

'Er, I think so.'

On Monday morning Vicky got her way and walked to school, convincing Michelle to walk with her, but they returned home separately, with Michelle travelling by bus and arriving home a little earlier.

Michelle came to see me in the shop as usual, on her way through to the house.

'Hello, love! How was Vicky this morning?' I asked.

'Er . . . fine,' she said pointedly.

I knew Michelle very well, and I could tell when she wanted to pass something on. Being a bit of a tittle-tattle was a weakness of hers, to be perfectly honest, and Michelle quite enjoyed sharing gossip or snitching on someone who'd got into trouble at school.

I braced myself, wondering what she was going to tell me about Vicky. After the way she had behaved all weekend, being so quiet and withdrawn immediately following her loud and confident arrival, I really didn't know what to expect.

'Are you sure everything was fine, Michelle?' I said, taking the bait.

'Well, except . . .'

'Except what?'

'Except I know why Vicky likes to walk to school. It's because she smokes! She smoked three cigarettes on the way to school!'

For someone who had supposedly been reluctant to spill the beans, Michelle blurted this out rather triumphantly.

'Oh did she?' I said, raising an eyebrow.

'Yes, she did. I had to tell you, didn't I, Angela? But don't tell her I did, will you?'

'I'm glad you told me, and thank you for letting me know, Michelle. Don't worry, I won't dob you in.'

Michelle smiled at my use of the word dob, as it was the word all the teenagers used and not one that normally tripped off my tongue.

'Thanks, Angela, and you're welcome!'

When Vicky came home soon afterwards I could smell the cigarette smoke on her clothes and in her hair, but I didn't mention anything at first. She seemed to have brightened up considerably that day and was in a chatty mood, asking me if she could go to the youth club on Friday night, and a teenage disco in town on Saturday afternoon.

'I'm sure that'll be fine,' I said. 'Are you normally allowed to go?'

'Yes, I go every week.'

'And your sister is happy for you to go?'

'Lorraine? Yes. I think she likes me out of the house!'

'I see. In that case I'll talk to Jonathan and we'll work out what time you need to be home and how you'll get there and back.'

'Thanks, Angela,' she smiled. 'That's if I'm still here, of course! Maybe Lorraine will have the baby before then. You never know the exact day, do you?'

'No, you don't,' I said.

'Do you want to have your own kids, Angela?'

It was rather bold of Vicky to ask such a direct question and I was a bit taken aback at first, but I didn't mind answering her.

'Yes I do,' I said. 'Jonathan and I have always wanted to have a family together.'

'So what are you waiting for?'

Jonathan and I were in our early thirties so it wasn't an unreasonable question, as it was more typical to have children in your twenties in those days. Nevertheless, I laughed at Vicky's directness.

'We're just very happy fostering for the time being, that's all! We're in no hurry.'

Despite being put on the spot, I was actually relieved that Vicky was chatting away easily, and was not asking me about her own situation. Unfortunately, I hadn't succeeded in getting hold of anyone at Social Services all day. I'd left an answerphone message for Tricia first thing in the morning and tried her office again after lunch but nobody had called me back. This was not unusual; I knew that Tricia was dealing with a lot more children than she should have been, as one of her colleagues was on long-term sick leave and nobody had been brought in to replace him. It had been this way for many months and Social Services' funding was decreasing, so there wasn't a lot anyone could do about it. This was no consolation for Vicky though, because even if she was only here for a very short time, in my opinion she still needed some more of her belongings, and she also had a right to know what was planned for her.

For dinner that first Monday evening I made a lasagne, garlic bread and salad, and at 6 p.m. Jonathan and I sat down at the table with Vicky and Michelle. The atmosphere was relaxed and the girls seemed to be getting along very well together, which was very good to see.

'Ooh I love lasagne!' Vicky exclaimed when I placed the steaming dish on the table and served everyone a portion.

'This is delicious,' Jonathan said, tucking in as soon as it was cool enough to eat. 'Oh dear, is everything all right,

Vicky?' he suddenly added, glancing across the table. 'You haven't burnt yourself, have you?'

Vicky's face had fallen as soon as she'd tasted the lasagne, and she was now wincing quite dramatically.

'No,' she stammered after struggling to swallow the contents of her mouth. 'It's just that I've never had lasagne like this before.'

'Really?' I said. 'It's just the traditional recipe; I haven't changed any ingredients.'

'It's home-made,' Michelle said, giving Vicky a knowing look. 'That's why it doesn't taste the same as the ready meals, or the one they do at school.'

Vicky forced a smile. 'I thought it would be like the one Lorraine gets from the supermarket. I've never tasted home-made lasagne before.'

'Oh well, why don't you try a bit more, love? You might find you like it better than the processed one, once you're used to it.'

Vicky nodded and tentatively ate a tiny morsel of pasta, swiftly followed by a large hunk of garlic bread. The salad was left untouched on her plate.

'I never used to eat salad either,' Michelle said, eying the sliced tomatoes and cucumber Vicky had tried to hide under a lettuce leaf. 'But I like it all now, especially the tomatoes. Angela's mum grows them, you know, I help her in the garden sometimes.'

Michelle was sounding like a bit of a goody two-shoes now and I could see Vicky had had enough of this conversation and was beginning to get irritated.

'Well good for you, Michelle!' she said rather impatiently.

When we'd finished eating, Michelle helped me clear the table as usual and Vicky pitched in too, though rather less willingly, and she had to be asked to do so.

'I hate clearing up,' she muttered, doing the bare minimum before disappearing to her room.

Later that evening I broached the subject of smoking with Vicky, after we'd watched some television together and she seemed in a fairly responsive mood. I didn't let on that Michelle had told me about it; instead I said I had smelled it on her uniform, which was true.

'Oh,' she said, not looking too bothered her secret was out. 'It's not a crime though, is it?'

'Well, it is actually against the law at your age,' I replied. 'For that reason alone I can't sit back and say nothing, but it's your health I'm most worried about. Smoking is extremely bad for you, especially at your age. Jonathan and I both smoked for many years before giving up in our twenties, and it was a horrendous struggle for us. I look back now and wonder why on earth I started in the first place, and I shudder to think about all the money we wasted too. Honestly, sweetheart, you should give it up before you get hooked like we did.'

Vicky looked at the floor and bit her bottom lip.

'I've been smoking since I was nine, Angela,' she said, looking ashamed of herself. 'I'm already addicted.'

With that she started to cry.

'Oh, love, I'm sorry to hear that. I really am. Here, can I give you a hug?'

Vicky sniffed and nodded, and I moved closer to her on the settee and gave her a gentle cuddle. As soon as she was in my arms the floodgates opened, and Vicky began sobbing uncontrollably.

'I thought Lorraine was joking when she said she'd had enough of me,' she blurted. 'Honestly I did.'

'I'm sorry to hear that, sweetheart.'

'She put me in the car and said she was taking me to Social Services, but I thought she would drive around the one-way system and then take me home. She'd done that before, you see, when I got on her nerves.'

Vicky paused to wipe her grey-blue eyes and blow her nose. 'I never thought she was serious this time. Honestly, I thought she was joking.'

'Oh Vicky, it must have been a shock, love. I'm sorry.'

Vicky was now trying her best to compose herself, and she was making a very good job of it.

'It was,' she said, drying her eyes and taking a deep breath. 'She's my sister, after all. Sorry, Angela, I'll be all right in a minute.'

'Take your time, love, take your time.'

Vicky blew her nose and pushed her shoulders back and, even though she was pale and her gangly body was so slight she appeared fragile, she had a strong, steely look in her eyes that seemed to be saying: 'I won't let this beat me.'

Watching Vicky pull a brave face on so quickly made me think back to her arrival. Her confidence was probably a coping mechanism; it was her way of dealing with the unthinkable by trying to pretend everything was fine.

I wished I could tell Vicky that I was sure she would be back with her sister in the blink of an eye, but of course I couldn't, and I didn't even know if that was the best place for her. I was still in the dark about what had gone so awry at Lorraine's, and about any plans for Vicky's immediate future.

This sort of uncertainly is not unusual at the start of a placement. Events leading to a child being placed in care can be chaotic and traumatic for all concerned. Finding the child a foster placement is the priority; dealing with the fallout and planning the next move naturally takes second place. Even if I'd spoken to Tricia that morning, the likelihood was that at this stage I would not have got much further than arranging for Vicky to have more of her belongings brought over.

'I don't think the baby is due this week,' she said after a minute or two, turning to look me square in the eyes.

'What made you think it was?' I asked.

'I was only guessing, because Lorraine is absolutely massive. And I wanted it to be this week.'

'Oh, I see. Do you have any idea how many months pregnant she is?'

'No. She's huge though.'

'Well some women are huge at six months, others at eight months. It's hard to guess, and I don't want you to get your hopes up.'

Vicky suddenly brightened up as a thought occurred to her.

'Do you think if she has a good rest now she'll have me back *before* the baby arrives? I mean, if she is only six months pregnant she's not going to need three whole months to have a rest, is she?'

I looked at Vicky and remembered myself as a child, nagging my dad about how long my mum was going to stay in hospital. Vicky had the same desperate look I must have had, longing for life to go back to normal, whatever 'normal' was for Vicky. The fact she had smoked since the age of nine had made me concerned about what her life had been like, and I wished I had more information about her background, to help her move forward.

'I'll try to get some information for you tomorrow,' I said, tugging at her sleeve playfully in an attempt to lighten the atmosphere. 'If only so we can get you out of this tracksuit!'

Vicky laughed, which was a relief. 'Thank you, Angela,' she said. 'I don't want you to think I'm ungrateful. It's very kind of you to have me here, but I'd just rather be at my sister's.'

# 3

## *'She was always there for me'*

It was late afternoon on Friday, a full week since Vicky's arrival, when a half-empty carrier bag of clothes arrived for her. Apparently Lorraine had dropped it at Social Services earlier in the week, and now Tricia had placed it on the counter in the shop, just as I was about to start cashing up.

'Sorry, it's been in my car since Tuesday but I've not had a minute,' Tricia apologised. 'How's Vicky doing?'

If I'm truthful I felt like saying, *Fine, no thanks to you!* but I managed a politer, 'Fine, thank you. I'm sure she'll be very grateful to have some more of her clothes.'

'That's good. Right then, I'll be in touch . . .'

'Hang on a minute, Tricia! Can you spare two minutes?'

During the course of Vicky's first week I'd ended up buying her some new underwear and toiletries, as well as a new school bag and a fully stocked pencil case. I didn't mind about the money. Jonathan and I were not wealthy, but we weren't poor either, and I could afford what I'd spent. Eventually I'd receive the £25 a week allowance that was provided for each foster child at that time, but this typically took a while to work its way through the system. I could deal with that, and I had certainly not gone into fostering for financial gain. What did bother me, however, was that Vicky had been placed in foster care for a full week with one school uniform, a tracksuit that didn't fit her properly, a toothbrush and a few items of underwear. She had no knick-knacks or school equipment, and absolutely no personal belongings to help her feel more at home in our unfamiliar house.

Vicky had told me that she loved reading and had been in the middle of *The Thorn Birds* by Colleen McCullough, which she'd borrowed from the local library. Presumably it was still sitting in her bedroom at Lorraine's, as I could see that the thin carrier bag Tricia had brought only contained a few items of clothing. I wished Lorraine had been a little more thoughtful with the packing, but then again I scarcely knew a thing about what was going on in her life, did I?

'I love family sagas,' Vicky had said to me one evening during the week, completely without irony considering she was in the middle of one herself. 'Do you like books like that, Angela?'

'As a matter of fact, I do,' I said. 'I love all the Catherine Cooksons. You can read one of those in the meantime if you like. I've got a shelf full.'

Her eyes widened and she said she would love to. 'I used to read a lot more, before.'

As soon as she said this, Vicky immediately went quiet and looked nervous, as if she was remembering something.

'Really?' I said, leaving a gap for her to fill, but she didn't. 'So you're a big reader?'

'I am! I love going to the library. I like the peace and quiet, d'you know what I mean?'

'Yes I do. Sometimes we all need a bit of quiet time on our own, don't we?'

Vicky nodded.

I didn't want to pry, but I wanted Vicky to know I was interested and that she could carry on talking if she wanted to. Now, after many years of training and experience, I know that what you should do is repeat back the last thing the child has said.

'You used to read a lot more, before?' is what I ought to have said. That way you are not in danger of putting words into a child's mouth or leading them to say something they don't mean. I didn't know any of this then, but at least I hadn't inadvertently put my foot in it, as Vicky had not said anything I'd coerced her into saying, or indeed anything I needed to act upon or report to Social Services.

Anyhow, when I asked Tricia if she had two minutes to spare when she dashed into the shop with the bag, she said that she did.

'Thanks, Tricia,' I replied. 'I'm very grateful. Do you have any more information for me about the length of Vicky's stay? And even if she is not staying long can she please have some personal items from Lorraine, like the book she is in the middle of reading?'

'I'll do my best, but I should know more next week,

Angela. I have established that Lorraine's baby is due at the end of August, so for the time being all I can say is that it's possible, but not definite, that Vicky will be with you for a month or so, until after the baby is born. It seems Lorraine is worn out and she just can't handle Vicky on top of the pregnancy, and with the school holidays about to start. We are, however, trying to track down other family members.'

'You mean Vicky's parents?' I said.

Tricia rolled her eyes and sniffed rather haughtily. After looking around to check there was nobody else in the shop, she told me quietly, 'We know where the mother lives because Lorraine has told us, but she's not answering the door, or returning phone calls.'

'Oh dear. And the father?'

'We don't know anything about her father. The family has never been involved with Social Services before, so we have no file on Vicky.'

'Can't Lorraine help you?'

'All she's said is that she's had enough of Vicky. She's given me short shrift to be truthful; she just wants shot of Vicky, that's all she's saying. Anyway, it's very early days, and as I say I should know more next week. I have to go now, but please rest assured I'm on the case and doing everything I can.'

As Tricia left the shop I felt quite hopeless. I wanted to be more involved in Vicky's case and help find the answers we needed, but that simply wasn't my place. I was in Tricia's hands, and I had to accept my role and just continue doing my job as best as I could, which was to look after Vicky and provide her with a safe and happy home, for an indefinite length of time.

I was on autopilot as I went through my nightly ritual of feeding and watering the flowers and lifting vases and tubs of stock into the back of the shop at closing time. My mind was focused on Vicky, and the little Tricia had told me about her family. I wanted to know why Vicky's mother was not answering the door, and what had become of her father. It was very frustrating being so much in the dark, and I also felt saddened. I imagined myself as a thirteen year old, and how I would have felt if I didn't live with my parents, and then my sibling threw me out. It was unfathomable, it really was. At thirteen I was carefree, and I was cherished. It was 1969 when I was the same age as Vicky – the year Neil Armstrong landed on the moon.

'Isn't life amazing!' my mother had marvelled as we watched the incredible moment unfold on our little black and white television. When Mum saw the fascinating images of the Earth taken from the moon I can remember how she looked at me and exclaimed excitedly, 'Angela, what a wonderful planet we live on! Aren't we lucky?'

'We are!' I replied joyfully, and I really felt that was true. I was loved and cared for, everything I needed was provided for me, and the amazing planet we lived on was out there, just waiting for me to grow up and explore it to my heart's content.

When Vicky returned home I gave her the carrier bag Tricia had delivered, saying, 'I bet you'll be glad of these,' but she just wrinkled her nose.

'I don't wear any of that stuff,' she said. 'It doesn't even fit me.'

'How do you know? You haven't even looked what's in there.'

'I just know,' she shrugged.

Later that evening Vicky got ready to go to the local youth club. She was quite a tomboy and she appeared in the tracksuit again, with her freshly washed fair hair pulled back into a tight ponytail.

'Do you normally wear that to the youth club?' I asked tentatively.

'Yes,' she said defensively. 'Lorraine bought it for me. I love it. Don't you like it?'

With that she hugged her arms around herself, rubbing the sleeves of the tracksuit protectively.

'Yes, sweetheart!' I smiled. 'I just thought you might have wanted a change.'

'Well, like I said, the other clothes don't fit me. They're not even mine.'

'How do you mean?'

'They're all second hand, and they were too small when I got them.'

'Oh, I see. Well, would you like to come shopping with me tomorrow lunchtime and we'll get you some clothes that do fit? The weather's getting warmer and you're not going to want to wear the tracksuit when it's hot.'

'Er, maybe,' Vicky said cautiously. 'Can I go now? What time do I have to be back? And please don't tell me to come in when it's getting dark, because how do I know when it's getting dark?'

'Well that's a very good point! Now then, if the youth club finishes at 9 p.m., let's say you need to be home by 9.30 p.m. at the latest.'

I'd already discussed this with Jonathan. We were not used to negotiating evening arrangements as Michelle rarely went out, but we both agreed this seemed fair and sensible.

'That's fine! Thanks, Angela! See you later then!'

We had offered Vicky a lift but she had arranged to meet her friend Izzy at a bus stop halfway between our house and hers. Then they were going to meet a couple of boys from school and all walk to the youth club together. I gave Vicky £3.50, the same amount of pocket money we gave to Michelle each week, and she swaggered out with a wide grin on her face.

'See you at half nine!' she beamed, giving me a thumbs up.

Sure enough, at 9.30 p.m. on the dot, Vicky returned home and Michelle raced down the stairs to let her in. Jonathan and I were watching television in the lounge and Vicky bounded up the stairs, sat between us on the settee and told us all about her evening.

'They've got a new pool table at the club,' she said. 'We had a competition and I got to the final after beating loads of boys!'

'Well done, love! Have you played much pool before?'

'Yes, loads. I've been going to the youth club for ages. I love it there.'

Vicky was certainly a sociable girl, and the next day she was looking forward to going to the teen disco, which was held from 2.30 p.m. to 4.30 p.m. in an upstairs room at one of the nightclubs in town. First, though, I took Vicky down the high street when I had a break from the shop for lunch, hoping to buy her a few new items of clothing. She wasn't very keen at all, and I assumed it was because she simply wasn't into clothes, or perhaps because our local shops weren't particularly exciting. I generally drove about an hour away to the big out-of-town shopping mall when I wanted to have a proper spree, although we did have several independent boutiques in town that I knew were popular with the youngsters, as well as a department store with a teenage section and modest-sized branches of Tammy Girl and C&A.

'You don't need to do this, you know,' Vicky said when she came into the shop to meet me on the stroke of midday, the time we'd agreed.

'I want to,' I said. 'We've only got an hour but I'm sure we'll be able to get a few things. Come on, let's get going!'

Vicky dragged her feet across town, and when we got to the first boutique she refused point blank to go inside.

'I can tell already I won't like anything in there.'

'Oh well, let's try the next one.'

This time she barely even stopped to look in the window.

'No, it's not for me,' she said, quickening her pace.

'Well you choose the next shop then,' I said. 'Tammy Girl or C&A?'

'Er, neither, really. Can we just leave it? Honestly, I'm fine.'

'Come on, love, just have a look, for me?'

Vicky very reluctantly followed me into C&A, and as we took the escalator to the first floor she looked around nervously.

'I've never been in here before,' she said.

'Really? They've got quite a good clothes section, for all ages. You're bound to see something you like.'

Vicky looked increasingly uncomfortable as I led her to the appropriate rails and pulled out a selection of T-shirts, shorts and jeans. I chose unfussy ones I thought would suit an 'ungirly' teenager like Vicky, but she claimed she didn't like any of them.

'Anyway, they might not fit,' she added, putting everything I had picked out back on the rails.

'Well you could try them on,' I said. 'The fitting room is just there.'

Vicky looked over at the cubicles I pointed to on the side of the shop floor and seemed bemused.

'What, in there?' she said suspiciously.

The cubicles had doors that started three-quarters of the way up the door frames, exposing your ankles to anyone who happened to look over.

'Are you serious? You have to go in there?'

'Well they're not the best changing rooms I've ever seen,

I grant you, but they're fine, honestly. I've used them many times myself.'

'I'd rather not. Can we just go?'

'But we haven't bought anything, Vicky! Shall I at least just buy a couple of T-shirts and you can try them on at home?'

'No, thanks, I won't wear them.'

'Why not? You're really short of clothes and these would be really handy.'

'I don't like them. They won't suit me.'

'Well why don't you choose something that will suit you?'

'I've looked. There's nothing I want.'

I told Jonathan about our futile shopping trip when Vicky was at the disco, in her tracksuit.

'I suppose when you think of it, the famous purple track-suit is the only thing she has to remind her of home,' he pondered. 'It's no wonder she's so attached to it. Can you imagine moving into a new house and having none of your belongings with you, nothing at all that's familiar?'

'I have thought about that,' I replied. 'And no, I can't imagine it, not at all.'

We'd agreed that Vicky could return home from the disco by 6 p.m. at the latest and that we'd go out and buy some fish and chips as soon as Michelle was back too, half an hour later. Michelle always visited her mother for three hours on a Saturday afternoon, returning at 6.30 p.m. By that time everybody was generally tired and hungry, and it had become a tradition for me, Jonathan and Michelle to indulge in a 'chippie tea'. This wasn't ideal for me as I wanted to drop a dress size in time for our holiday; we were going to Florida the following Easter. Each week I promised I'd only eat a small portion and leave the batter off the fish, though I didn't always stick to my good intentions!

Jonathan and I had been to Disney World not long after we got married, and ever since we started fostering we had talked about how great it would be to take Michelle there, or any other foster child for that matter. When we first broached the subject with Tricia a year or so into Michelle's placement we'd expected her to be fully in favour of such an opportunity, but the social worker's many years of experience made her cautious, and actually quite pessimistic.

'I have to warn you that sometimes the parents don't like it, and if the child is on a voluntary care order then the parents have every right to refuse to give permission,' Tricia explained.

A 'voluntary care order' means the parent or parents have agreed to put their child in care, rather than having him or her removed, and they retain full parental responsibility. I knew this, of course, but so far it had only really impacted on me on one occasion, when we had a ten-year-old boy staying with us for a fortnight and he needed his mother's permission to go on a farm visit with the school. By the time I'd got the necessary paperwork signed, all the places had been allocated and he missed out on the trip. It was very frustrating for all concerned, but in Michelle's case I really couldn't imagine we'd have a problem. We had started planning the Florida holiday twelve months in advance, plus Michelle's mother had already agreed to another request, albeit a rather different one. Michelle had a severe overbite and we had asked permission for her to have orthodontic treatment through the dental practice Jonathan and I had used for many years. Her mother agreed and signed the necessary paperwork swiftly and without a hitch, and I pointed this out to Tricia.

'I'm sure she's got her daughter's best interests at heart,' I said. 'I can't imagine for one minute that she would stand in the way of Michelle being taken on holiday to Disney World!'

'Angela, not everyone sees the world like you,' Tricia had said, rather patronisingly, I thought. 'The fact is, when parents see a foster carer providing something they can't, it doesn't always go down well. It highlights the fact you are succeeding where they have failed. I'll ask Michelle's mother, but please don't count your chickens, and certainly don't book anything just yet.'

Unfortunately, Tricia's gloomy advice did hold water, as Michelle's mother did not readily agree to the holiday. First she said she'd have to think about it, leaving us all waiting for an answer for nearly two months when we really wanted to make the booking. Then, once she'd reluctantly given her permission, she took another six weeks to sign Michelle's passport application. This meant we'd only been able to book the holiday very recently – just before Vicky arrived, in fact.

'How's the holiday diet going, Angela?' Michelle asked

when we sat down with our fish and chips that evening, and she saw me reluctantly picking the batter off my cod.

'Oh, you know, so-so!' I said. 'I think I'll join the slimming club when the holiday is nearer, that always helps me.'

'That's a good idea. By the way, my mum was asking about the accommodation. Can you tell her where we're staying and what the sleeping arrangements are?'

'Yes of course, love. That's all in hand.'

'You're so lucky!' Vicky marvelled, when I filled her in and explained what we had planned. 'I wish I could go to Disney World!'

'Can't Vicky come with us?' Michelle asked.

'Well, it's still only July and we're not going for another nine months, are we? Vicky's not expecting to be with us for that long.'

'No, I'm not,' Vicky confirmed.

'Oh, that's a shame,' Michelle said. 'I was hoping you'd be here for a while.'

Vicky looked pleased at the unexpected compliment from Michelle. The girls were like chalk and cheese in terms of their personalities, but they did seem to get along very well together, and I'd noticed they'd been spending time in each other's bedrooms in the evenings, listening to Whitney Houston and even doing their homework together sometimes. Vicky typically went out for an hour to visit a friend when she'd finished her school work and I'd heard her asking Michelle if she wanted to tag along, though she never did.

'I hate staying in!' Vicky had said. 'How can you stand it?'

Michelle shrugged. 'I just do. I'm used to it.'

'Well I'm not,' Vicky had replied.

After we'd finished eating our fish and chips the girls both helped me clear the table, and then Vicky asked if she could go out to see her friend Izzy. Michelle looked disappointed; I knew she'd been hoping we'd all sit down and play Cluedo together after dinner, as this was something of a Saturday night ritual. Cluedo was Michelle's favourite game and Vicky had recently asked her to teach her how to play.

'Well, I don't see why not, Vicky,' I said. 'Are you invited to Izzy's house?'

'No. It's the "Saturday club" up by her house tonight,' she said. 'Don't worry, I can catch the bus and I'll be home by 9.30 p.m. like last night.'

I didn't feel I could refuse, as it was simply another youth club and Vicky had been extremely punctual the previous evening.

'That's fine, love. Please just write down the name and address of the youth club for me, because I don't know exactly where it is.'

'It's just in the community centre behind the Co-op,' she said. 'I don't like it as much as the Friday night youth club, but Izzy does. She's nagged me to go!'

'Sounds like you're being a good friend then,' I said. 'Good for you!'

'She was always there for me.'

Vicky looked very thoughtful when she said that last sentence, and she went very quiet and looked at the floor.

'Are you all right, sweetheart?'

'Course!' she said, snapping a smile back on her face.

'Izzy is a good friend to you, by the sound of it?'

'Yes.'

With that Vicky did one of her US soldier salutes and drawled in an exaggerated American accent, 'Permission to leave the kitchen, Angela.'

'Permission granted!' I laughed. 'See you at 9.30 p.m.'

Jonathan and I played Cluedo with Michelle and, once again, at 9.30 p.m. on the dot, Vicky returned. She began babbling ten to the dozen about her friends and all the fun they'd had playing dodge ball in the grounds of the community centre, and making strawberry milkshakes in the kitchen with the youth workers. Vicky smelled strongly of smoke again, but I didn't want to mention it in front of Michelle, who was curled up on the settee in her dressing gown and Winnie the Pooh slippers. However, Vicky went up to bed a few minutes before Michelle, who then arched her eyebrows and whispered disapprovingly, 'I wonder what Vicky spent her pocket money on?'

I didn't rise to it, simply saying, 'Come on now, Michelle, it's time you went up to bed too.'

'It's funny how different the two girls are,' I said to Jonathan when we were alone. 'It's amazing they get along so well.'

'Well I suppose they understand each other's situation like nobody else can,' he said. 'It must be comforting to both of them to know they have someone there who's in the same boat as them.'

Jonathan has always been wise like that, having the ability to take a step back, weigh up a situation with clarity and see things from another person's point of view.

'I think you're right,' I said. 'I worry about them both though, in different ways. I wish Michelle was a bit more outgoing, and I wish Vicky didn't go out so much.'

'They can't win, can they, these teenagers?' Jonathan teased.

'No I suppose they can't! I guess we should just be grateful that Vicky has settled in so well.'

'Exactly,' Jonathan agreed. 'She's a pleasure to have around. I'll miss her when she's gone.'

# 4

### *'My mum frightened me'*

As her stay entered its third week Vicky continued to be a
pleasure to have around, despite the fact the placement had
clearly extended into a longer one than she first hoped for.
Her routine followed the pattern she'd established from the
beginning. She walked to school every day, did her homework without being reminded, and helped in the house
whenever I asked, albeit rather reluctantly. When she went
to one of the youth clubs or the Saturday disco she always
returned promptly, and she also started to invite friends
over to our house. I was pleased about this as some foster
children don't like their friends to know about their situation, but Vicky wasn't in the slightest bit concerned about
it. In fact, she always made a point of introducing me to her
friends, and I had the feeling she was enjoying being part of
our family.

'Can I meet your mum, Angela?' she asked one afternoon.

'Of course!' I replied. 'She's been looking forward to

meeting you. We're all invited to lunch on Sunday, as it happens.'

'Really? Is she cooking for us all?'

'Yes, and she does a lovely roast dinner. It's always a treat.'

'Wow! I'm looking forward to that! Are you sure it's OK? I mean, isn't she quite old?'

'Don't let her hear you saying anything like that! No, she's only in her sixties, and she's full of beans. Her name's Thelma, by the way.'

Mum had always been supportive of my fostering, telling me she admired my patience, just as she had complimented my friend Belinda's mum when I was a child. Mum loved meeting the children we had staying. She had been away on a cruise with an old friend when Vicky first arrived, and I was now very much looking forward to introducing them.

When Sunday came Mum spoilt us all rotten, roasting a delicious leg of lamb, asking Vicky and Michelle to help her pick some fresh strawberries from her garden and then settling down to play games with them in her sunny conservatory while Jonathan and I did the washing up.

Vicky thoroughly enjoyed herself.

'Angela, you should play next time!' she smiled afterwards. 'All the games are really good. Have you ever played them?'

'Yes, love, quite a few times!' I laughed, as all of Mum's games were old favourites like Kerplunk, Operation,

Mousetrap and Buckaroo, which I'd played hundreds of times over the years.

The following day a holdall containing more clothes and a few other belongings, including a hairbrush and a pair of sandals, arrived for Vicky, via Tricia. Thankfully Vicky actually wore some of the clothes this time; they were all a bit worn out but at least they seemed to fit better. Her pitiful wardrobe didn't seem to bother Vicky at all, but I resolved to get her into another clothes shop at the next opportunity.

'There's still no news, I'm afraid,' Tricia had told me when she called in to the shop with the holdall. 'Vicky's mother is still refusing to answer the door or reply to our letters or phone calls. We'll keep trying, of course, as we want to get her to a review meeting as quickly as possible.'

Nowadays a review meeting must take place within twenty-eight working days of the start of a placement, but in the past this deadline was often missed. All parties, including the child, parents or legal guardians, foster carers, the child's social worker and his or her manager, are invited to the meeting to discuss how the placement is progressing, and to decide on future plans. Unfortunately, as in Vicky's case, getting the parent to attend is not always straightforward and can cause delays.

'I know you might not be able to discuss it, but do you have any idea what the problem is with Vicky's mother?' I ventured diplomatically, although what I really felt like saying was, *This is so frustrating! Give me the address and I'll go round there myself! A child's future is at stake and we really need her mother to answer the door!* Of course I knew better than to directly ask Tricia for any information that might be sensitive, such as a person's address. I'd learned from experience that it wasn't the done thing to ask questions at all; foster carers are in the hands of their allotted support social worker, and you have to accept the status quo, respect their authority and wait to be given information. Thankfully, on this occasion, Tricia did expand a little.

'The neighbours have told us that Vicky's mother never leaves the house,' she said flatly.

There was a pause I didn't fill, and Tricia added, 'It's only hearsay at this stage, but alcohol would appear to be the problem.'

As Tricia had decided to share this information I pushed my luck a little.

'I see. I don't suppose you know how long ago Vicky left her mother's house, to move in with Lorraine?'

'No. Lorraine's husband, Carl, dropped the holdall off so I haven't actually spoken to her again. He told me that Lorraine has completely washed her hands of Vicky and doesn't want anything to do with her, so I'm afraid I'm not hopeful of getting any more information from Lorraine any time soon. However, from the little I know, I don't think Lorraine would have put up with Vicky for very long.'

I was quite perplexed by this.

'I just can't imagine Vicky being that difficult,' I said. 'In my experience she is a lovely, polite and friendly girl. She always comes home on time and she does her homework, and she helps out around the house when you ask her to.'

Tricia snorted. 'I'm glad to hear it, but I'm afraid you may be experiencing a bit of a honeymoon period, Angela. It's not uncommon with kids in care, as I'm sure you know. Didn't you experience anything like this with Michelle?'

'No, not at all. Michelle was as good as gold when she arrived, and she's as good as gold now.'

'Well from what Lorraine has said, you may not be so lucky with Vicky. According to her sister she was impossible to live with. A "nightmare", is how she described her, in fact.'

I was very surprised indeed to hear this.

'In what way was she a nightmare?'

'Extremely untidy, leaving mess everywhere and going out all the time. That's what Lorraine said when she brought Vicky to us. Right then, as soon as I hear anything concrete I'll let you know.'

When Tricia left I thought back over what she said. Clearly Lorraine had not wanted to take Vicky back to their mother's when she found she couldn't cope with her herself, and now it seemed we had found out why.

I felt very uneasy, wondering what life must have been like for Vicky, living with a mother with a drink problem. I knew by now that Lorraine was ten years older than Vicky, so it was possible she'd left home a good number of years earlier, and that Vicky had lived on her own with her mother for quite some time. I remembered what Vicky had said about her friend Izzy – 'She was always there for me' – and my mind went into overdrive.

'What sort of a life has Vicky had?' I said to Jonathan

later. 'It must have been terrible for her, growing up with an alcoholic mother.'

As usual, Jonathan was the voice of reason and made me focus on the facts, not the maybes.

'We don't know for sure that Vicky was alone with her mother, or what actually went on,' he said. 'And we don't know how long her mother has had a drink issue, or how serious it is. Tricia said the problem was alcohol, but she didn't describe Vicky's mother as an "alcoholic" as such, did she? We don't know enough to start jumping to any conclusions.'

'I suppose you're right but . . .'

'Look, Angela, don't get yourself all worked up. Vicky seems perfectly well adjusted, and she's even talked to you openly about the smoking, which is about the only thing she seems to do wrong. Also, there are no Social Services records for Vicky, are there? If she'd been at risk over the years there'd be a file on her, but Tricia said there is no past history at all, not a single note.'

'I guess you're right. I just hope that if the drinking has gone on for years and years, Lorraine didn't leave Vicky with their mother when she was small . . .'

Jonathan gave me a hug. He is a very intuitive man and he had immediately sensed that I had turned my thoughts to my own childhood; it would be impossible not to, in the light of the conversation we'd just had.

My father had been an alcoholic in his younger days. Apparently he made my mother's life hell at the start of their marriage, but I didn't know much about this until many years later, when I was grown up and about to get married myself. Then, my mother told me all about how she had given my father an ultimatum when I was five years old, telling him that if he didn't stop drinking she would throw him out. I recollected the argument, and the fact that after the row, my father checked himself into what Mum called a 'drying out clinic', and he never touched a drop of alcohol from the day he left there.

Thanks to my mother, besides the argument, practically the only memory I have relating to my father's drink problem is of when he was 'away in the countryside', which was how my mum described his stay at the clinic to me. He was gone for six weeks in total, and I can remember that when my mother visited him she had to stay overnight as it was so far away. I spent the night at Aunt Hattie's when Mum was visiting Dad, which of course I hated, as I missed my mum so much and had never spent a night away from her before. This experience no doubt laid the foundations for how I reacted when I was sent to Aunt Hattie's again for a much longer time, when Mum was in hospital the following year.

'I was lucky,' I said to Jonathan. 'I had my mother there to mend the problem. She was very capable and did a terrific job, but poor Vicky probably had nobody at all to make things better.'

I took Vicky to the doctor's for her Social Service medical appointment later that week, which is something required by law within the first few weeks of a child's placement. Dental and optical check-ups also have to be kept up to date, so I would book those if Vicky was still with us when her appointments were due. Our GP preferred it if I accompanied the children into the surgery, where they would be weighed and measured, asked to answer some basic health questions and given a few routine checks, such as having their chest listened to.

'Are you happy for me to come in with you?' I asked Vicky.

'Yes, no problem,' she said. 'Why wouldn't I be?'

The doctor seemed pleased with Vicky's general health but she was wheezing that day, and he picked up on the fact Vicky was a smoker.

'How many cigarettes do you smoke?' the doctor asked.

'Er, as many as I can get hold of,' Vicky said, looking a bit embarrassed. 'Sometimes four or five, sometimes twenty.'

'I see. And how long have you been smoking?'

The GP was matter-of-fact and didn't appear to judge Vicky, and this approach seemed to pay dividends, as she was very frank with him.

'Three or four years. I used to nick my mum's cigarettes when she was asleep on the settee.'

'I see. Well, Vicky, I think you'll be able to breathe better if you have an inhaler. I'll give you a prescription. You have mild asthma and if you don't stop smoking it could get considerably worse. I want you to try to stop as soon as you can.'

'Yes, of course,' Vicky said obediently. 'I will. I really want to.'

While we waited for her prescription at the chemist

across the street I praised Vicky for her honesty, and told her that I would discuss a reward with Jonathan, so she had something to aim for to help her quit.

'Thanks,' she said. 'I know it won't be easy. That's really kind of you.'

That night Jonathan and I put our heads together and decided to offer to buy Vicky a couple of tickets for a music concert she had mentioned she would like to go to later in the year.

'Awesome!' she said. 'I'm definitely going to quit now. I'll start next week.'

Jonathan and I gave each other a sideways look. We both wanted to say, *Why wait until next week?* but we held our tongues. If that's how it was going to work for Vicky, then all well and good.

School broke up the following week and Michelle went off to stay with her father for a few days, a visit she had been eagerly anticipating. Jonathan and I were ready for a little break too, and we shut the shop and took Vicky on a three-night stay at a caravan park near the coast, where we'd been several times before. Vicky had never stayed in a caravan and was really excited, and Jonathan and I were very much looking forward to the trip too. This was something we did two or three times a year, generally on a Bank Holiday weekend, or when we had no weddings or other functions booked in the diary, which made it possible to close the shop.

'I've only been to the seaside once,' Vicky said on the way there.

'Really?' I said. 'Did you like it?'

'I think so. I was very small and I can barely remember it. I don't know who drove us there but it was a man, and Mum wanted to stay in the car with him and so Lorraine took me to jump in the waves.'

Before we set off I'd established that Vicky could swim, having been taken for lessons by the school, and she had agreed that I could buy her a swimming costume as she didn't own one and predictably didn't want to go shopping. The break was terrific. The three of us had a wonderful time going to a local water park, eating pizzas in the evening, ten-pin bowling and having barbecues. Vicky seemed very relaxed and didn't have a cigarette for the first two days, which I praised her for.

'I smoke when I'm stressed and I'm not stressed here,' she said.

One evening Vicky went to play crazy golf with twin sisters she'd met on the campsite. Jonathan and I were sitting outside our caravan enjoying the last drops of evening sunshine when Vicky came back. Her skin was tanned and glowing and her hair, which was tied back in a ponytail as usual, looked blonder and shinier than I'd seen it before. She was in a pair of shorts and a vest top I'd bought her along with the swimsuit, and it was great to see her looking so happy and healthy.

'I love it here,' Vicky announced, before unfolding a camping chair and sitting down beside me.

'I think the outdoor life suits you, Vicky,' I said. 'You're looking really well. Perhaps we should get a caravan and put it in the back garden for you when we get home!'

Vicky looked suddenly shocked and blurted out, 'You wouldn't do that, would you?'

'Of course not, sweetheart! I was only joking.'

'Oh!' she said. 'Just checking!'

'Why would you think I was serious about that?'

'My mum would have been.'

'How do you mean?'

Vicky shrugged and said, 'I don't know, I'm going for a walk.'

I realised this had probably triggered a memory for Vicky, and not a happy one. She was gone for about twenty minutes, and when she came back I could smell cigarette smoke on her breath. I decided this was a battle for another day and kept quiet, though I really wanted to ask what was on her mind.

On our last morning Vicky and I walked along the beach together while Jonathan went to get petrol and check the tyre pressures on the car.

'I don't want to leave here,' Vicky said. 'I wish I could just stay on holiday.'

'I'm glad you've enjoyed it,' I replied. 'Jonathan and I have always loved caravanning. We're planning a longer holiday later in the year that Michelle will come on, to a different site that's a lot bigger than this one. Perhaps you can come too, if you're still with us? We like to have a week away before the schools go back.'

Vicky didn't challenge my suggestion, and I realised she'd stopped asking when she was going back to Lorraine's. I'd passed on to Vicky what Tricia had said about the baby being due at the end of August, and she'd simply said, 'Oh, that's longer than I thought.'

Now, as she looked out to sea, Vicky commented, 'One of those twins asked me if I had a sister and I said no.'

'Well that's not true, love. Why did you say that?'

'Because me and Lorraine aren't like them.'

'You mean because they are twins and there is a big age gap between you and Lorraine?'

'Yes, I suppose. Lorraine left home when I was about four or five, I think. It was around the time I started at infant school, anyhow. I can hardly remember her being there, so I was like an only child, really.'

'And so after Lorraine left, it was just you and your mum?'

'Me, her and her *best friend*,' Vicky said sarcastically.

'Best friend?' I ventured gently.

'Yes. He was called "bottle of vodka"!'

Vicky laughed bitterly after she threw out the last sentence. It had tripped off her tongue in a way that suggested it wasn't the first time she had said this, or that she was repeating a line she had heard somebody else use.

I felt a pang of sorrow for Vicky and instinctively pulled her towards me, giving her a gentle rub on her arm. I wanted to hug her but I'd been told by the social worker to be careful about such physical contact; you had to ask first if you felt it was appropriate to give a hug.

'Hugs can be misconstrued,' Tricia had said. 'Best to err on the side of caution, especially when you don't know the child's background. And if you feel it is appropriate to give a hug, for instance when it would look like you didn't care if you kept your distance, then you should always ask the child first if it's OK.'

I understood the advice, but in the heat of the moment, in a situation like this, it often seemed inappropriate to start asking permission to give a hug, so I opted for the safer rub on the arm.

'Sorry, I don't want to ruin our last few hours,' Vicky said, turning to face me and noticing my sad expression. 'I hate talking about my mum; I don't know why I mentioned her. She's the reason I went to live with Lorraine, but I suppose you know that already.'

'I thought that must be the case, but I wasn't sure. How long have you been living with Lorraine?'

As I asked the question I was praying the answer was going to be several years but Vicky replied, 'About two months. I, er, told my mum I was going out to buy some bread.'

'What do you mean?'

'I said I was going to the corner shop, but I didn't. I ran all the way to Lorraine's instead. Lorraine didn't want me there really, but I refused to go back to Mum's.'

'Because of her drinking, I assume?'

I was aware that I might be pushing my luck but I wanted to find out more, so I could help understand and care for Vicky.

'My mum frightened me.'

Vicky spoke in a whisper and had turned very pale.

'Can we stop talking about this now, Angela?'

'Of course, love. But you know you can talk to me any time?'

'I know. Thanks.'

I took a deep breath, not looking forward to what I had to say next.

'Just one other thing though, Vicky. Because I'm a foster carer, I'm obliged to tell your social worker anything I feel is important for her to know.'

Vicky looked very worried. 'Will you tell her what I said about my mum?'

'I will, next time I talk to Tricia. I have to, love, but you mustn't worry. The only reason we talk to each other like this is to make sure you are safe and looked after in the best way, not to cause any more problems for you. Besides, I don't really think you have said much that Tricia won't already know. You mustn't worry.'

Vicky didn't look convinced and barely spoke another word on our walk back to the caravan. All I could think about was the fact I'd established that Vicky had lived alone with her alcoholic mother from the age of four or five to thirteen. It must have been very difficult for her, and unfortunately it now seemed inevitable there were more disclosures to come, though I wasn't sure how inclined Vicky would be to confide in me again. Whether Vicky's mother would turn up for the review meeting Tricia was trying to arrange was now uppermost in my mind. The fact Vicky was so frightened of her mum bothered me a great deal, and I couldn't imagine it would be an easy meeting at all.

When I'd first seen the advert for foster carers a few years earlier I hadn't considered the fact that you have to meet the parents of the children you foster. Jonathan and I were both so naive about the role, we imagined we'd take in a couple of children, give them love and provide them with a comfortable home, and that it would all go really well. Then, when the children moved on, we thought we'd simply repeat the whole process with other kids who needed a temporary home. It sounds ridiculous now, but I had no idea about reviews or that foster carers were expected to sit around a table and discuss the foster child's care with the mother or father, or whoever had parental responsibility.

In addition, all of the children we'd looked after had wanted to go back to their family as soon as possible, no matter what had caused them to be removed from their care in the first place. For example, Michelle's mother, Maureen, had suffered with a drug problem in the past and was unable to cope with her daughter, and she had placed Michelle in the local children's home when she was ten years old. Michelle had been there for two years before she came to live with us. I'd learned from Social Services that Maureen had failed to feed her daughter properly, or send her to school regularly, and one of her former boyfriends had been jailed for assaulting a close member of the family.

Michelle refused to be put off by these facts. Even now, two years on, she still talked frequently about 'when I'm back home', doing so in the fond and dreamy way you might look forward to returning to a favourite holiday destination. This was in spite of the fact her mother showed no sign of wanting her back, even though she was now a recovering addict and Social Services would have allowed Michelle to return. After her weekend visits Michelle always seemed out of sorts. There was something I couldn't put my finger on; she was just not quite herself, but Michelle never discussed why this was the case, and whatever made her behave differently certainly didn't put her off wanting to move back in with her mother. She'd have done so in the blink of an eye if Maureen had allowed it.

'Are you all right?' I'd always ask. 'Did you have a good time? What did you get up to?'

'I'm fine!' Michelle would say breezily. 'It was great. We watched telly and had chips.'

'How's your mum?'

'Great! I might be able to move back soon!'

I felt a pang in my heart whenever I heard Michelle talk so bravely and optimistically. In the two years she'd been with us her mother had only attended one review meeting, at which she'd used bad language and become aggressive when discussing future plans for her daughter. Still, Michelle never said anything critical whatsoever about her mum, and she never wavered in wanting to return to live with her. Her loyalty towards her father was equally strong. He had remarried and had a new family to support, which he claimed made it impossible for him to have Michelle live with him. She accepted his position without question or criticism and always seemed very happy to see him, rarely going more than a few days between visits to his home, which was a short bus journey away from ours.

The children we had staying with us on short-term placements all very much looked forward to going home too. This made total sense when, for example, a parent was in hospital; I knew exactly how it felt to spend every waking minute longing for a return to normality. However, one little boy of eight had been physically abused by his mother and had suffered a broken skull, yet he still couldn't wait to be reunited with her. Shockingly, in time we would learn that blood ties can be so powerful that even children who have been sexually abused by a parent often want to leave foster care and return home to their abuser as quickly as possible.

Things were clearly very different with Vicky. She was the very first child I'd encountered who had actually run away from her mother, and was scared of her.

'I'm feeling very nervous about Vicky's review,' I said to Jonathan once we were back home after our little holiday.

The review could happen any time now, and though I was very keen for Vicky to know where she stood and what would happen next, I was beginning to dread the meeting.

'I'm worried too,' Jonathan nodded. 'It could be very difficult, and whatever we're feeling, Vicky is going to be experiencing ten times the nerves and fears.'

'You're right. Poor Vicky. It's really not fair. I'd be more than happy for her to stay with us longer term if it comes to it, would you?'

'Of course! I'd love her to stay with us, but as you well know, what we want isn't the issue. We'll have to see what happens.'

The next time I managed to get hold of Tricia on the phone I told her that Vicky had spoken about her mother's drinking, and I passed on the information I had gleaned, that Vicky had lived alone with her mother from the age of four or five and was so frightened of her that she had run away to Lorraine's a couple of months ago.

Tricia told me that Vicky's mother, who I learned was called Brenda, was still refusing to answer the door, but that she had managed to talk to the elderly lady next door who had passed on some information.

'Are you able to tell me what sort of information?' I asked boldly.

Tricia sighed, and I heard the sound of her tapping her pen or fingernail on the desk in front of her.

'I'm afraid the neighbour said she used to hear shouting and banging coming from the house when Vicky was living there.'

'I see. Was this when Vicky was very young, or more recently?'

'Throughout the time Vicky was there. The lady said she had reported this to Social Services on more than one occasion over the years, but unfortunately we have no record of her calls. We should have had something on file, as every call of this nature is logged and responded to as you know, but there is nothing at all.'

'So what do you think has happened?' I asked.

Tricia took a deep breath.

'I'm sorry to say it looks like Vicky's file has simply gone missing somewhere along the line. Before we had computerised records, files were mislaid from time to time. Also, I know some paperwork went astray when we started to upload files to computers.'

I asked Tricia if it might be possible that the neighbour's calls were investigated by Social Services and nothing untoward was found, so therefore no file was ever created. I knew I was clutching at straws, especially after Vicky's admission that she was frightened of her mother, but I asked anyway, as Tricia seemed to be in slightly less of a rush than usual and I was desperate for answers.

'Vicky's mother would appear to have been drinking heavily for many years, so if she were investigated I can't imagine it would have been left there, and we'd still have something on file, even if no action was taken. The neighbour also told me that she often saw Vicky outside in her nightdress, even in winter. Clearly, this put Vicky at risk and is something a social worker would not have dealt with lightly; indeed, it would have been tackled as a matter of urgency.'

Whatever the truth about Vicky's missing file, she had suffered goodness knows what inside the house with her drunken mother, not to mention being outside in the cold in a nightie.

Tricia wound up the conversation by reassuring me that she was trying to talk to the neighbour on the other side, a middle-aged man called Alf. According to the elderly lady he was a close friend of Brenda and regularly did her shopping, but for some reason he was also refusing to answer his door.

'I'll keep trying,' Tricia said. 'We really need to get this review meeting set up. Hopefully I'll have more news soon, and if all else fails we'll have to have the review without Vicky's mother present.'

'Thanks,' I said. 'We are more than happy to keep Vicky with us for as long as it takes. She's absolutely fine. We've just had a lovely weekend away in fact. We took her to . . .'

'That's good,' Tricia interrupted, sounding a little distracted. 'Sorry, I have to dash. I have another call waiting now. Hopefully speak soon.'

The line went dead and I felt my pulse quicken. Tricia was a hard-working woman, and I could tell she found it as frustrating as I did that she never seemed to have quite enough time to do her job as well as she wanted to. She sounded genuinely apologetic about cutting our conversation short like that, but there was nothing she could do to change the situation. As well as supporting more carers and children than she was meant to have on her books, Tricia had to do shifts on the 'duty desk', which involved taking all calls to the office, some of which needed urgent attention. For example, if a member of the public or a teacher raised child protection concerns, the duty social worker might have to find emergency placements for youngsters. Tricia and her colleagues were also involved in recruiting new foster carers, which meant manning stalls in shopping malls or at fetes and encouraging members of the public to think about taking on the responsibility. In addition, Tricia had to keep up to date with all her paperwork and write up every conversation she had on the phone and in person. It had now been confirmed that her colleague who was on long-term sick leave was not returning to work, and no replacement was being brought in. Unfortunately, because of the stress of the job many social workers went off sick, and as they were entitled to paid sick leave there were typically no funds available to pay extra staff to bridge the gap. I knew Tricia was doing a sterling job under these difficult circumstances, but I still couldn't help feeling agitated.

'Everything all right?' Jonathan asked, bringing me a cup of tea.

'Not really,' I said, relaying the conversation.

'Biscuit?'

'Yes please,' I said, taking three out of the tin Jonathan offered.

He looked surprised, as I normally only treated myself to one biscuit, typically saying 'I shouldn't really!' as I did so.

'You know what,' I said, dunking a custard cream into my tea and devouring it in one mouthful. 'I'm really cross. Tricia needs to sit outside Brenda's house until she *does* open the door. Even if she never goes out she must have to open the door to take her shopping in from this Alf character, so she has to appear at some point.'

'Yes, I agree. But Tricia is far too busy to sit there for hours on end, isn't she?' Jonathan said, reasonably.

'I know that, but that is exactly my point! Everyone is too busy! I really wish I had the address myself and I would go there right now and find out what on earth is going on!'

'Now hold on . . .' Jonathan started.

'You don't need to say anything. I'm not going to do anything silly, and I haven't got the foggiest idea where Vicky's mother lives. I'm just letting off a bit of steam. It looks like Vicky has been at risk for years and years. Look how long it's taken just to get to this point! At this rate she'll be an adult by the time things are sorted out.'

# 5

### *'I had to lie to keep myself safe'*

In the week following our caravan trip a regular customer came into the shop and asked if she could have a quiet word with me.

'Of course,' I said. 'What is it?'

'It's about the girl you've got staying with you. Vicky, is it?'

'Yes, that's right. What's wrong?'

'It's like this, Angela. I'm afraid young Vicky has been making a nuisance of herself in the evenings, hanging around in the gardens up the side of the old folks' home with a group of teenagers. My sister works there and she asked me to mention it, as she knows I come in here.'

'I see. Thanks for passing this on. What exactly has she been up to? Do you know?'

'Being noisy, smoking, kicking litter, that sort of thing. Last night they stuck a load of chewing gum on the wall. There's about seven or eight of them, boys and girls. I hope you don't mind me telling you.'

'Not at all. I'm glad you did; leave it with me.'

Later that day Vicky asked if she could go over to Izzy's house in the evening, which is where she had told me she was the night before. I'd never stopped her visiting her friends and I'd got to know several of them by now, when they'd been over to our house. They seemed like a good bunch of kids, always making polite conversation and thanking us for having them. I was happy Vicky had plenty of pals, but I would never have let her out to hang around the streets with them, making a nuisance of herself.

'Are you sure you were at Izzy's last night?' I said, raising an eyebrow.

'What d'you mean?' Vicky snapped back, flushing bright red.

'I've been told you've been hanging around the old folks' home, smoking and making a noise and a mess, when I thought you were at Izzy's house. Or should I say, when you *told* me you were at Izzy's house.'

Vicky looked furious.

'Who said that? Have you got spies out looking for me?'

'Don't be silly. I run a business and I'm well known in the town, Vicky. There's not much that passes me by. I don't want you hanging around there again, or anywhere else for that matter.'

'What am I supposed to do?' she shouted angrily. 'Stay in and be a hermit like Michelle?'

Vicky stomped up the stairs to her bedroom, huffing and puffing as she went, and I hoped she would cool down if she was left to her own devices for a while before dinner, which would be ready in about half an hour. Unfortunately, dinner that evening was a very frosty affair. Michelle had overheard what Vicky had said about her being a 'hermit', which had upset her, and Vicky looked like steam was about to explode from her ears and nostrils and was not speaking to anyone.

'Now then, girls, there's plenty more spaghetti if anybody wants more,' I said breezily. 'Tuck in!'

'Very tasty!' Jonathan chimed. 'Does anyone mind if I finish this last bit of grated cheese?'

Both girls sat there glowering and didn't say a word, and they couldn't throw their spaghetti bolognese down quick enough so they could return to their respective bedrooms.

'What do we do now?' I said to Jonathan.

'I suppose we'll just have to wait for an apology from Vicky. I don't think it'll take her long, because she's wanting to go out tonight.'

'Well we haven't told her she's not going out again, have we?'

'I don't suppose we have, but isn't it obvious? There's no way she's going out tonight now, not after this.'

With that Vicky appeared at the door, looking incredibly sheepish and hugging the oversized arms of her tracksuit around her.

'I'm very sorry,' she said. 'I've had to lie to keep myself safe. I don't think sometimes. I had to lie so much, I didn't think . . .'

Huge tears dropped down her cheeks and she turned to walk away.

'Wait a minute, love. Come here.'

Vicky came over and gave me a hug, and she sobbed into my shoulder.

'What d'you mean, sweetheart?'

'I had to lie to keep myself safe. I can't tell you . . .'

I took a deep breath as I tried to digest what Vicky had just said. Should I ask her why she had to lie, should I tell her off for lying to us about her whereabouts, or should I just be grateful she'd apologised so quickly, and in a way that I knew was heartfelt and must have been quite difficult for her? I went with my gut feeling.

'Oh, love! Thanks for saying sorry. Now remember what I told you. You *can* talk to me, about anything you want.'

'Thanks, Angela.'

Vicky sniffed loudly and asked Jonathan for a tissue, as he was standing next to the window ledge where they were kept.

'D'you want me to go and let you girls have a chat?' he asked as he handed Vicky the box.

'No,' she said quite firmly, looking up at Jonathan and then back to me. 'I feel better now. I'm really sorry. I won't lie to you again, I promise.'

'That's very good to hear,' Jonathan said. 'Apart from anything else, we need to know where you are for safety's sake. And, of course, we need to think about other people who live in the town. Imagine if a gang came and stood outside our house and made a nuisance of themselves? We wouldn't like it much, would we?'

Vicky shook her head. 'I didn't even think, I just did it.

Nobody cared where I was before, or what trouble I caused, as long as I was out of the house. I keep forgetting it's different here.'

'It must have been hard,' I said. 'Living like that.'

Vicky shrugged and then pulled a sunny smile onto her face. 'I survived, didn't I? Can I go to Izzy's now, and I promise that is really where I am going tonight!'

'Oh I don't know about that love . . .' I said.

'Nor do I,' Jonathan said.

'But we're making some posters for the youth club together,' she replied, looking crestfallen.

Vicky then put her hands together in mock prayer and said, 'Pretty please! I will even phone you when I get there if you like.'

After swapping a look and a nod with Jonathan I told Vicky she could go, as long as she went straight there and back and absolutely nowhere else, and came home on the dot. Plus she had to apologise to Michelle before she went out, for upsetting her earlier.

'Agreed! Thank you! I'll phone you as soon as I get there.'

'Thanks, I'd appreciate that. And can you give me Izzy's number? I won't phone to check up on you, but I'd like to have it, in case I need to get hold of you.'

'Fine,' Vicky said, reaching for a pen and paper from our telephone pad on the kitchen worktop, and writing out a number from memory.

'This is it. Only it's not in her house. It's the phone box outside. It's on a busy corner, and someone always gets it. If you need to ring, just ask whoever answers to knock at number thirty-six.

Jonathan and I swapped another glance.

'That's a funny set-up!' I said. 'Hasn't Izzy got a phone in the house?'

'Yes but it's been cut off. The phone box is the best way if you need to get hold of me. Don't worry, everyone uses it like that way.'

'Right. So I suppose that's how come you know the number off the top of your head?'

'Yes. I know all the phone boxes up there like the back of my hand. I'll just go up and see Michelle before I go. Thanks again, and I'll see you at 10 p.m. !'

With that Vicky turned on her heel and tore up the stairs.

We allowed her to be out until 10 p.m. as it was the summer holidays, and as always she returned punctually, having also phoned as promised.

'How did the poster making go?' I asked.

'Oh, we didn't get round to that,' she said thoughtfully.

'Why not? Is something wrong, love?'

'Well, yes, I suppose. Izzy's not having a good time at home. Her mum's left, run off with another bloke.'

'Oh! I'm very sorry to hear that. It must be an awful shock for Izzy.'

'Not really, her mum's done it before.'

'So who's at home with Izzy?'

'Her stepdad, and she can't stand him. Hates his guts. He's a horrible man.'

'Oh dear, that doesn't sound good at all.'

'It's not. Izzy says she's seen how much better off I am living with you, and she wants to go into care too.'

'Really?' I said, shocked at what I was hearing.

'Yes. Izzy says she always thought going into care would be the worst thing ever. So did I, but obviously it's not! I told her I'd have done it sooner if I'd known what it was like, but I didn't think anyone would care like you do. Anyway, I'm whacked. Night night!'

Vicky got herself a glass of water and went upstairs, leaving Jonathan and me feeling a mixture of emotions. We were obviously worried about Izzy, and we were also touched by what Vicky had said. Without realising it, she had just paid us a huge compliment. We would normally have felt terrific after receiving such praise. If a customer in the shop complimented us on a particular bouquet or order it made us feel great; it was as simple as that. But there was something a little unsettling about feeling proud of ourselves for providing for Vicky's basic needs and giving her what every child deserves. It was pitiful, really, that she was in the position of being so grateful for the normal things most children take for granted, and I felt sorrow more than any sense of triumph.

'She's a good kid really,' I said to Jonathan.

'She is,' he agreed. 'I suppose it would have been a bit too good to be true if she didn't cause us a few headaches. That's what teenagers do, isn't it?'

I nodded. 'It's funny, isn't it? We're learning how to parent teenagers without having even done the baby bit. It's all back to front!'

'I know,' Jonathan laughed. 'We'll be dab hands by the time we get to this stage with our own. Experts, in fact!'

Jonathan and I had always wanted to have a family. We met at a dance in a local ballroom when we were both seventeen, back in the early seventies. I had actually gone along with one of Jonathan's friends, Norman, but the moment I spotted Jonathan poor Norman didn't get a look in. Jonathan was incredibly dapper and had a wonderful smile, and when he asked me for a dance I was in heaven. After that he walked me home and gave me a kiss on the cheek. I thought I was floating on air, and we became inseparable from that day on.

As soon as we had both turned eighteen and finished our A levels I wanted to leave the local area and experience life in a big city. I'd grown up watching my mum and dad run the florists and I wanted to work away and enjoy some independence before I settled down. Jonathan completely supported me, and agreed to come with me. I didn't want to leave my home town forever; my plan was always to return when the time was right, most probably to run the shop. My brother, Andrew, being so much older, had long since built his own successful company at the other end of the country, and so if I didn't take over the family business there was nobody else to do it when my parents wanted to retire. The business was very well established and it would have been foolish to let it go, but nevertheless it was always presented to me as a safety net, rather than an obligation or a pressure.

'The florists will be here for you if you want it,' my mother and father often told me. 'The world's your oyster. You go and follow your dreams, Angela.'

They had raised me to be ambitious and have a 'can do' attitude, and I'm very grateful to them for that. Working the long hours they did, it would have helped them no end had I joined the business sooner rather than later, but they were selfless and would never have clipped my wings in any way.

Jonathan had a completely different upbringing to me. He was the youngest of four brothers who grew up on a farm and, because he was the smallest and thinnest of all the boys, his father always treated him like the runt of the family. When Jonathan wasn't strong enough to chop the wood his father hit him with a belt, and as soon as he was old enough to drive the tractor, from the age of about twelve or thirteen, Jonathan was regularly beaten for having crashes and damaging fences. It wasn't until several years later, when Jonathan was learning to drive a car, that he discovered the reason he had so many collisions was because he was very short-sighted. He couldn't read the registration plate of a vehicle ten yards in front of him, and Jonathan realised he probably should have been wearing glasses since childhood. When he told his father this, the comment he received back was, 'So you're half blind as well as feeble! No wonder you're so bloody useless!'

It's hardly surprising that Jonathan was more than happy to come to the city with me, leaving his three strapping brothers to run the farm with his father. Subsequently, for nearly a decade, Jonathan and I lived an exciting, fast-paced life in a vibrant city, two hours from our home town. I worked in administration for a bank and Jonathan had an interesting job in logistics. In the beginning we rented separate flats, though we still saw each other every day, and after we married at the age of twenty-three we bought a modern apartment near the river. My father passed away five years later, in 1985, and by that point I had finally got the city out of my system and my mother was ready to hand over the shop to me, should I be interested in taking it on. It seemed like fate was trying to tell Jonathan and I which path to take, and we were both very willing to listen. We wanted a bigger house, which we couldn't afford in the city, and we were both ready for a less hectic pace of life.

'It seems like the right time to move,' I said to Jonathan. 'What d'you think? Shall we sell the flat, go home and be florists?'

'I think we should,' he concluded after we'd talked it through at length. 'But I can't say I ever really saw myself as a florist! Seriously, though, I think we'll enjoy it. And once we've got settled we could think about starting a family.'

'I'd love that. It feels right. I can't believe we've been away for ten years!'

'I know. But as your mum would say, the world's still your oyster, Angela.'

'Yours too,' I replied. 'We're in this together.'

Of course, the business involved a lot more than arranging bouquets and we had to get ourselves up to speed to take it on. I did an evening floristry course at college while working out my notice at my office job, and Jonathan did bookkeeping and basic accountancy at night school. As well as running the shop there was a busy delivery service to maintain, and my mother had built up an excellent reputation for providing high-quality wedding flowers and all the trimmings. We were very fortunate to be able to take over such a thriving business, and the fact we were ready to start a family seemed to fit in perfectly. Jonathan and I had always agreed that it would be better to have children back in our home town, where we both had relatives around who the children could grow up knowing. In addition to the business, we would also take over the adjoining town house my mother lived in, as it was too big for her on her own, and she owned another smaller property nearby that she was going to move into.

As soon as we moved, Jonathan and I stopped taking precautions, hoping we'd start our family very soon, and it was several months after that when I saw the advert for fostering. Now here we were, almost three years on from when I answered the advert. Since starting fostering we'd looked after seven children in total, including Michelle and Vicky, and we enjoyed it so much the time had flown by.

Between us Jonathan and I could manage fostering alongside running the business, though we acknowledged things might have to change when we had a baby of our own.

Of course, I hadn't fallen pregnant though, not yet. In hindsight, three years seems like a very long time for nothing to happen, but the reality was that I was happily getting on with my life, I was still young and I can honestly say I wasn't worried in the slightest. I think that's partly because it was a different era back then. Infertility was not something people generally talked about, and I was very much of the mind that I would fall pregnant if and when it was meant to be. Jonathan and I had never discussed going for tests, but when he made his remark about us being 'dab hands' once any children of our own became teenagers, it triggered a discussion.

'Do you think we will actually have any?' I asked frankly.

Jonathan and I were so close we never had to tiptoe around conversations like this. It was typically me who asked bold questions, though; I'd much rather have everything out in the open. Jonathan is not a person to bury his head in the sand either, but nevertheless he prefers to take the lead from me when there is something of this magnitude on the agenda. He had been standing up when I asked the question, and he hesitated and sat down thoughtfully.

'I don't honestly know, Angela. I suppose we will just have to keep being patient. What do you think?'

'Well that's the problem, isn't it? I don't know either. I think I'd like to know what's going on. If there's a problem and we can't have children, I think I'd like to know now, rather than just waiting to see.'

Jonathan cleared his throat before he spoke again.

'I can understand that, Angela. But how do you think you would feel if there does turn out to be a problem?'

'I won't mind,' I said straight away. 'Honestly. If it's

78

meant to be it's meant to be. I've realised that I've reached the point where I'd just rather know, one way or the other.'

'Are you absolutely sure about that, Angela?'

'Positive. Honestly, I am. How would you feel, if we can't have children?'

'To tell the truth, it worries me. I think if it's bad news we'd both be more disappointed than you might imagine. Mind you, we've not exactly been feeling desperate, have we? It's taken us a long time to reach this point and even have this conversation.'

'Exactly! We've had so much on our hands with fostering. What I do know is, I'd like to carry on fostering, whatever the news is.'

'Are you sure?'

'One hundred per cent. What about you?'

'I'm not sure about that either. I'm enjoying fostering but I never really imagined it would be something we'd do long term. I think I thought we'd do it for a few years and maybe move on. Let's see what the doctor says, shall we?'

I made an appointment with my GP, and eventually Jonathan and I were given a hospital appointment several months hence, at the start of 1990, when we would have some tests.

Meanwhile, three days after my customer had reported seeing Vicky making a nuisance of herself outside the old folks' home, a neighbour from a few doors down popped in to the shop and also asked if she could have a 'quiet word' with me.

'Is it about Vicky?' I said, my throat tightening.

'Yes it is. I think you need to hear this.'

The neighbour explained that her son was a volunteer at the Saturday afternoon disco Vicky attended, and she said he had become concerned about Vicky's relationship with the DJ who worked there, Jason Brown.

'I see. What's been going on?'

'Jason's been taking Vicky for drives in his car after the disco.'

'Has he now? How old is he?'

'Late twenties, probably about twenty-six my son reckons.'

'Twenty-six? Good Lord! Surely he knows how inappropriately he's behaving? No wonder you wanted to tell me, thank you so much. Do you know any more about him?'

'Not about him, but about his family, I'm afraid. Apparently his younger brother, Jeremy, was questioned by the police recently.'

'What for?' I asked nervously.

My neighbour leaned closer to me.

'For having sex with an underage girl,' she whispered. 'He's a well-known drug dealer in the area, apparently. He is denying everything, claiming someone with a grudge against him has invented the whole thing.'

My blood ran cold. Whatever the truth about the brother, Vicky should not be driving around with a twenty-six-year-old man, and I hoped to goodness I'd got to know about this before anything untoward had happened. I thanked my neighbour profusely and assured her I would keep her name out of things when I sorted this out, which she was grateful for.

'What's up, Angela?' Vicky said when she breezed into the shop about an hour later. 'You look like you've seen a ghost!'

'I'm not surprised about that,' I said. 'Can I have a word with you?'

She rolled her eyes as if to say, 'what now?', as I signalled to Jonathan that we were going through to the back.

'I haven't been anywhere near the old folks' home, if that's what you're thinking,' she said. 'If anyone says I have, they're lying!'

'Vicky, love, it's more serious than that I'm afraid. It's about the DJ from the disco. You've been going for drives with him, haven't you?'

Vicky nodded uncertainly.

'Yes, but only up to the recreation ground. We listen to music, that's all. He's got loads of tapes and a really good stereo. We're into the same bands, you see.'

'Yes, but the problem is, Vicky, he really should not be driving you around and taking you anywhere in his car. You're a child and he's an adult, and it's not appropriate.'

'We're not doing anything like *that*!' Vicky said, looking horrified. 'I'm not like that, and nor is he!'

She huffed and folded her arms tightly across her chest.

'I am not for one minute accusing you of anything,' I said, and from her reaction I felt reassured she was telling the truth.

'It is he who is behaving inappropriately, and I don't want you to get in his car ever again, is that understood?'

'Whatever,' she replied, shrugging her shoulders and curling her lip.

'No, Vicky, not "whatever". There are some men who try to take advantage of young teenage girls. I have no idea if he is one of them, but I'm afraid I have not heard good things about his family, and I certainly don't want you to be in any danger.'

The last word seemed to get through to Vicky.

'Danger?' she repeated back to me.

'Yes, Vicky, you could be in danger, and it is my job to keep you safe.'

She looked at the floor.

'OK, Angela. I won't do it again, I promise.'

I was satisfied that Vicky had got the message, and later that day I had a word with the person who ran the disco, who was shocked and apologetic.

'I want you to know we made all the appropriate checks. Jason Brown certainly doesn't have a criminal record; I made the checks on him myself.'

'I'm not blaming you,' I said. 'Unfortunately, if a person has no criminal record it doesn't guarantee they are not a threat, or that they will not go on to commit an offence, does it?'

'No, it doesn't, which is why it's very important that members of the community are vigilant. I'm really sorry this has happened. I'll see to it that he won't be working at the disco again. You have my word on that, and thank you for letting me know.'

I never discovered what was said to the DJ, but he was removed from his post and Vicky never saw him again. She had no idea I'd had a word behind the scenes and, for reasons best known to herself, Vicky kept up a charade for several weeks, claiming to me that she told Jason each Saturday, 'No thank you, I don't want to come for a drive in your car. Please don't ask me again. I'm not allowed.'

Why she told such unnecessary lies I have no idea; I can only guess that, ironically, she was trying too hard to prove to me that she was being true to her word and keeping her promise. I couldn't tackle her on this as I didn't want her to know I'd got involved; the most important thing was that Vicky was no longer in contact with this person.

Incidentally, I don't remember the word 'grooming' being in common parlance back then, and of course this was years before the shocking scale of child sexual exploitation in places like Rochdale and Rotherham was exposed, but looking back I do believe Vicky was being groomed, and to this day I'm very grateful to the neighbour who tipped me off.

# 6

## *'STOP! I'M GETTING OUT . . . !'*

It was an overcast Saturday morning and I had a van full of flowers to drop off around town. Vicky had started doing a few hours in the shop when we were particularly busy, as we were on this day. We had a big wedding on, and when Michelle was out visiting her father, Vicky had helped me prepare the corsages and tie the bouquets with peach and white ribbons.

'Fancy helping me with the deliveries?' I asked, as Jonathan could manage the shop on his own.

Delivering the finished goods was always something I found very satisfying, and I thought Vicky might like it too, especially after having worked so hard on the wedding flowers. I always liked to involve any children staying with us as much as possible in our daily lives, and Vicky was very pleased to have the chance to earn some extra pocket money.

'Er, OK,' she said. 'Will I still get paid for that?'

'Course you will, cheeky! It's all work, whether you're in the shop or on the road.'

'Oh good! Count me in then!'

Vicky was in a chirpy mood that morning and she began chattering non-stop as we set off.

'What was your wedding like?' she asked. 'Bet you had loads of flowers!'

'Oh it was in the seventies,' I laughed. 'The decade that style forgot. I'll show you some pictures later. Jonathan was in brown flares and I had a frizzy perm and wore a dress coat with great big collars that were probably six inches wide.'

'No way! Can't wait to have a good laugh at those!'

'Well they are funny, looking back. My mum arranged all the flowers for us and she did us proud, as you'd imagine. I think the flowers stole the show, actually. We must have had hundreds of white roses in the church, I had a posy of mixed roses for my bouquet and all the men, including Jonathan, had a red carnation in their button hole.'

Vicky laughed and said she'd remind me to get the wedding album out when we got home, and then she turned her attention to my slow and cautious driving. I was taking it very steady, as I had plenty of time and didn't want to risk disturbing any of the carefully packed flowers in the back of the van.

'Come on, Angela, can't you put your foot down? Just as well you're not driving the bride to church. Her bloke would think he'd been dumped at the altar!'

'Hey! I've told you once today not to be cheeky! I know what I'm doing. I have done this before you know, Vicky!'

She rolled her eyes playfully and I smiled. I didn't mind

the ribbing at all; I loved to see Vicky in such a light-hearted mood, and I was really enjoying her company. The chatter went on as I took the turning for the north end of town and then the slip road that would lead me to the large housing estate where the bride lived.

'You're going so slow you're holding up the traffic!' Vicky mocked, looking in the wing mirror on her side of the van. 'Ha ha! Did you say the wedding was today or next week? Hang on! Angela! Where are we going? This is . . . What . . . ? NO! STOP!'

Vicky was looking straight ahead now, and she suddenly shouted in panic and grabbed onto my arm. I felt her nails dig frantically through the sleeve of my top as she yelled: 'STOP! CAN YOU STOP, PLEASE!'

'Just a minute!' I gasped, completely taken aback. 'Just wait a minute, Vicky, while I find a safe place to pull over.'

My heart was racing as I tried to keep my focus on the road.

'JUST STOP THERE!' Vicky implored, pointing desperately to a bus stop. Her voice was quaking with fear and I wanted to do as she asked, but there was a queue of people waiting at the stop and the bus was right behind us.

'I can't just pull in here, love. I'll have to stop a little bit further along because . . .'

'Oh my God. STOP! I'M GETTING OUT . . . !'

Vicky's hand shot towards the door handle but I managed to pull over and jam on the handbrake before she pulled the door open. As I did so I heard trays slipping and sliding in the back of the van. Vicky froze, still with her fingers on the handle, and then everything went eerily quiet. I looked across and Vicky was statue-like, just as if a switch had been flicked in her brain, instantly immobilising her. It was extremely unnerving, and she was so silent and motionless that I could scarcely tell if she was breathing or not.

'Are you all right, love?' I asked, but I got no response whatsoever.

It was chilly in the van and I shivered and felt goose-bumps prickle my arms. Vicky's behaviour was so un-expected, and very alarming. Her eyes were glazed and she looked absolutely terrified. I wanted to hug her and shake her to her senses, all at the same time.

'Vicky? Can you hear me? There's no need to be afraid. I've stopped the van now. We're not going anywhere.'

Vicky stared through the windscreen, her eyeballs glazed like marbles, and she continued to sit rigid in her seat with her hand reaching for the door handle. Looking back, it was like a scene from a cartoon where a character is struck with an ice gun and is instantly stopped in their tracks. Poor Vicky was frozen with fear. I took a deep breath and mentally counted to ten, and then I asked Vicky again, as gently as possible, if she was all right, and if there was anything I could do to help her.

'I'm here, right beside you, Vicky. Can you hear me? I'm here and I can help you. Do you think you can move your arm away from the door?'

She still didn't move or respond in any way at all. Her normally rosy cheeks had turned ivory white and she looked as cold and still as stone. The expression of terror on her face was like nothing I'd seen before: I had never seen a child look so scared in all my life. Instinctively, I didn't touch Vicky. With no training to call on I was acting on my wits and drawing on common sense to help me deal with the situation. I felt that if I made a sudden movement or took hold of her it might startle her, or provoke some other negative reaction. As it happens, I did the right thing; talking calmly is nearly always the first thing you should do, unless a child is in physical danger.

'Take a deep breath, love. That's what I've just done. Just breathe and try to calm yourself down. You're with me, Angela, and you're safe.'

The words hung in the cold air between us. The smell of the lilies and freesias, usually something I couldn't get enough of, was suddenly sickeningly overpowering, and I felt ripples of nausea in my stomach.

'Vicky, love, we don't need to go onto the estate if you don't want to. Shall I turn back?'

Ever so slowly, Vicky turned to face me, looking for all the world like a mechanical puppet as she moved a fraction of an inch at a time, in tiny jerking movements. Finally, when she was staring me straight in the eye, I heard her release a breath, and then she gave a loud, snotty sniff that seemed to snap her out of her paralysis.

'Have you got a tissue?' she asked quietly, barely moving her lips.

I had never been so relieved to hear such simple words,

and I leaned across the van and grabbed a fistful of tissues out of the glove compartment and thrust them at her.

'Thanks,' she said shakily, taking hold of them with a trembling hand. 'Can you take me back? Just turn around here?'

'Of course, love. But what happened? Do you want to tell me what the matter is?'

Vicky said nothing at all. I did a clumsy three-point turn, clipping the kerb on both sides of the road, which provoked another clatter of trays in the back of the van.

'Oh dear! Silly me!'

'It's not your fault,' Vicky said, deadpan, while gazing through the windscreen and absent-mindedly wiping her nose.

It was only once the estate was behind us that I sensed Vicky's tension starting to ease a little more. It didn't take a genius to work out that something, or someone, had frightened her there.

'You know you can talk to me about anything you like, don't you?'

'I know,' she replied quietly.

'What is it about the estate you don't like?'

'Everything,' she said. 'My mum lives there. You can just let me out by the library if you like, and I'll walk the rest of the way. I don't want to make you late. I hope the flowers are all right.'

Vicky's voice had returned to its normal level, and by the time we'd reached the library a few minutes later she even had the colour back in her cheeks.

'Are you sure you want to get out here? I can take you home if you like?'

'Nah! I'm fine now. Don't worry. I'll see you later! I want a book, anyhow. I fancy another Colleen McCullough.'

As she stepped away from the van I recognised the cocky swagger Vicky had on the day she arrived to stay with us, and I was very glad to see it.

'Thanks, Angela,' she said, waving at me through the van window. 'Hope the flowers are OK! Hope the bride's happy!'

Much to my surprise, she then pulled up both corners of her lips with her index fingers, creating an exaggerated smile, before giving me a slow-motion thumbs up and a diva-like wink. I laughed out loud; it was such a relief to see her back to her normal self. The warm and funny Vicky I knew had returned, just as quickly as she'd slipped away and turned to ice.

'I'm sure the bride will be very happy,' I called back, but in my head I was only thinking about Vicky.

All I wanted was for Vicky to be happy, without whatever happened in the past spoiling her present, and possibly her future. She had been scared stiff back there, and clearly she didn't want to be anywhere near her mum's house. What on earth could have happened in the past to bring on such an extreme reaction? I knew Social Services were doing all they could to find out about Vicky's history but it seemed to be taking forever, which was becoming increasingly frustrating. It now seemed very naive that I had ever dared hope the reason Vicky had no case file was because she had not needed one. She had a mother with a long-term drink problem who clearly terrified her. I wanted to know why, so I could help Vicky move forward in her life, but would she ever tell?

When I finally got back to the shop, just before lunchtime, Jonathan was behind the counter, looking ashen-faced.

'What's wrong?' I asked, immediately thinking of Vicky.

'Oh, Angela,' he said, walking to the door and turning the 'open' sign around to 'closed'. 'You aren't going to believe the news. It's just appalling.'

'Is it Vicky?' I asked, panic-stricken.

'No,' Jonathan said. 'She's in her room, reading a library book. It's Aiden. He's got . . . leukaemia.'

Jonathan began to cry.

'No! Oh my God! The poor little mite. When did all this happen?'

Jonathan could barely speak. Aiden was our six-year-old nephew, the son of one of Jonathan's older brothers. Of all our seven nephews and nieces, Jonathan was probably closest to little Aiden. He and Jonathan seemed to understand each other, perhaps because Aiden was also the youngest of four boys, just like Jonathan.

'You tell me if they give you any trouble!' Jonathan would say, nodding at Aiden's three big brothers conspiratorially, 'and I'll beat them up!'

'You couldn't!' Aiden would laugh. 'You're too nice, Uncle Jonathan!'

This was absolutely devastating news, and very shocking indeed; in the coming weeks we would find out that Aiden's chances of survival were just fifty per cent. We were both utterly heartbroken and cried in each other's arms when we heard the prognosis. However, Jonathan was absolutely marvellous once he's got over the initial shock, rallying around his brother and making Aiden laugh whenever he visited him at home or in hospital.

'It makes you question life,' Jonathan said after one visit. 'I mean, you can make all the plans you like for the future and then something like this happens.'

'I know. You just have to make the most of what you have each day, don't you? You have to enjoy life and live for today.'

'You do. I'm so glad we're fostering, Angela. You were right to follow your heart. If we can help a few kids out and make their lives better, why not? It's what life is all about.'

Having Michelle and Vicky in the house undoubtedly helped us carry on through this incredibly difficult time, because life was busy and there were always plenty of distractions. In fact, immediately after hearing Aiden's news I'd gone upstairs to check Vicky was all right after the upset she'd had near her mother's home, and found more than I bargained for.

'Are you all right in there, love?' I called through her bedroom door. 'Do you think you could give me your washing? I'd like to get the machine on. The forecast's good all day.'

I'd introduced a rule whereby Vicky was only allowed to go to the Saturday disco, as she no doubt planned to do later that day, if her bedroom was tidy. So far she'd done a reasonably good job of keeping to the deal, though she always grumbled about it.

'Haven't got any,' she answered.

'Well you must have some. Can I come in, love?'

'Yes, hang on a minute.'

I heard a rustling sound and then Vicky opened her door, thrusting her laundry bin towards me.

'Actually there is some washing in here.'

'Oh your room's nice and tidy!' I exclaimed, glancing at the empty floor, but just as I spoke a nasty smell caught in my nose.

'What's that?' I said.

'What's what?'

'Can't you smell it? It's like something's gone off.'

Vicky sniffed the air and said she didn't know what I was talking about, but as I stepped closer to her the smell got worse, and I realised it must be coming from underneath the bed.

'D'you mind if I have a look under here?' I said, lifting the edge of the quilt.

'If you like,' Vicky shrugged.

I got down on all fours and the smell made me heave as I peered under the bed frame. There, right under my nose, were the remains of an old chicken leg, lying on a greasy plate alongside a hardened dollop of tomato ketchup. Next to the dirty plate was an old mug with an inch of mouldy-looking brown liquid in the bottom, and a rotten apple core, discarded on the carpet.

'Oops!' Vicky said. 'Sorry! Forgot about those!'

'Vicky!' I coughed. 'I thought I told you we don't allow food upstairs!'

'You did, sorry, Angela.'

'For goodness' sake, this is a health hazard!'

'Oh my God! I think that's a bit of an exaggeration!'

'Less of your lip, Vicky, please. This is not acceptable at all.'

At that moment I glanced into the laundry bin and realised that the clothes she'd put in there were all ironed and folded

'And what on earth is going on here? These things haven't been worn, Vicky.'

'Well, no. But they were on the floor so . . .'

'So you just thought you'd put them in the laundry bin to make your room look tidy? Do you know the trouble I go to, washing and drying and ironing your clothes? The least you can do is put them back in the wardrobe if you take them out and decide not to wear them!'

'So-rreee!' she said quite rudely.

'I think what you're trying to say is: "I'm sorry Angela. I do appreciate what you do for me and I won't take food into my room or put clean washing back in the wash ever again."'

'Well that's what I mean, *obviously*!'

'Vicky, love, I know you had a nasty experience earlier on this morning but that doesn't mean you can give me cheek like this. We all have difficult things to deal with in our lives, Jonathan and I included, but that doesn't mean we can go around treating each other disrespectfully.'

'Sorry, Angela,' she said, sounding genuinely apologetic this time. 'It won't happen again. I promise.'

I decided to tell Vicky about Aiden, as I realised I was stressed and was probably being harder on her than usual as a result. I thought she ought to know, but in reality Vicky was too young to comprehend what a tragedy it was for the family, or to support me in any way.

'That's sad. I hope he gets better,' was all she said. 'By the way, am I still allowed to go to the disco?'

Like most teens she was focused on herself and her own issues, which I understood. When there is something as dreadful as Aiden's diagnosis on your mind, I think it makes you more accepting of others, because life really is too short to waste time arguing.

'Yes, love,' I sighed. 'Of course you can go to the disco, and we'll get fish and chips later, shall we?'

'Yes, please!' Vicky said, eyes lighting up. 'Can I get a battered sausage?'

'Why not? I might have one myself.'

'Angela! What about your diet?'

'Oh I know, I'll get back on track next week. You only live once.'

# 7

## *'She made me watch'*

Tricia phoned me the following Wednesday to tell me that Lorraine had had the baby, a little boy, and that Vicky could go round and visit.

'That's great news!' I said. 'When did she have him?'

'Last week, actually. Her husband said Lorraine didn't want any visitors at first, but she's prepared to let Vicky meet the baby now. She suggested Friday lunchtime.'

'Vicky will be delighted, I know. Thanks Tricia. That's wonderful. I don't suppose there's any other news?'

It was the middle of August and Vicky had been with us now for over a month.

'No, clearly we'll need to let the dust settle and see how Lorraine feels when she's established a routine with the baby. I do have a review date though, it's the first week in September, a few days before the schools go back.'

'Oh! Have you finally made contact with Vicky's mother?'

'Yes, sort of.'

'Well, what did she say?'

'Nothing. Her neighbour Alf left a message to say Brenda had read our letter and she would attend the review, and so we didn't need to keep knocking on her door or phoning her.'

'I see. Well, it's good news all round I guess. I'll talk to Vicky as soon as I can. She's at my mum's at the moment, helping her with a bit of gardening.'

Vicky returned home triumphant from my mother's, clutching a bunch of sweet smelling freesias that she'd picked from the garden, and a basket containing onions, lettuce, a few tomatoes and several radishes.

'I'm going to make a salad!' she declared. 'And these are for you, Angela!'

'Well, that's very kind of you,' I said, taking the flowers from her and smiling to myself as I glanced at the buckets of freesias I had in the shop.

'And I've got something for you!'

'What?'

'Good news.'

'What? Go on, Angela, tell me!'

'Lorraine has had the baby. A little boy!'

'Oh my God! That is amazing! What's his name?'

'I don't know, but you can find out on Friday. She says you can visit at lunchtime.'

'Wooooooh!' Vicky shouted, punching her fist in the air. 'That's just so awesome! I'll have to get Lorraine some flowers from your mum's.'

'I could make you up a nice bunch, if you like?'

'Nah! You might charge me! Ha ha! This is the best news!'

When Friday came Vicky was adamant that she wanted to catch the bus to her sister's flat and didn't want a lift. I was fine with this, as Vicky had told me where Lorraine lived and it wasn't far away. Normally, within seventy-two hours of a placement starting there should be a meeting at which you are given background information and contact details of appropriate relatives, and instructions on who to ring in case of emergency. I had none of that with Vicky: Tricia was my only port of call and I think this had slipped her mind, but thankfully Vicky had willingly volunteered Lorraine's address without me having to ask.

'I'll be fine on the bus!' Vicky said as she set off. 'Don't worry about me! I'm going to meet my new nephew! Woohoo!'

Vicky looked really well. She inevitably had the purple tracksuit on, and she'd washed her hair and tied it in a neat ponytail. My mother had helped her pick a small, mixed bunch of purple and white flowers from her garden, and she'd helped Vicky wrap the stems in foil to make a neat bouquet.

'Have a wonderful time, love!' I said as I waved her off. 'Enjoy the visit!'

Vicky returned about an hour and a half later and was grinning from ear to ear and couldn't stop talking about baby James.

'Oh Angela!' she said. 'He's absolutely gorgeous! He's the most beautiful little thing I've ever seen in my life.'

'You'll have to get a photo of him next time. I'd love to see the little chap. James! What a lovely name.'

Michelle was all ears, lapping up every detail.

'What colour are his eyes?'

'Blue!'

'Has he got any hair?'

'Loads! It's thick and black like his dad's and it looks like he needs a haircut already!'

'Oh he sounds adorable!' Michelle said. 'I want a baby!'

'Well there's plenty of time for that!' I remarked, feeling a little alarmed by this statement.

'I know there is,' Michelle replied. 'But I want my babies young. I don't want to be an old mum.'

'Not too young, I hope! You need to be able to support yourself before you start having babies.'

'Yes, I know, but if I couldn't manage I could always put them in care.'

'Michelle!' I said, horrified at what I'd just heard. 'That's absolutely not the way to think.'

'Why not? That's what my mum did.'

'Yes but you wouldn't want to do that, would you?'

'Well it's all right, isn't it? It's working out OK for me and my mum.'

I was so shocked at Michelle's attitude I really didn't know what to say next, and I found myself thinking I was very glad she didn't have a boyfriend. Even Vicky was looking a bit gobsmacked.

'I'd like to be married like Lorraine when I have a baby,' Vicky said. 'I want everything to be better than I had.'

'You've got the right idea, Vicky.' I said. 'Michelle, you should listen to Vicky. And when you are old enough to have a sexual relationship you really must take precautions until you are sure you are ready to have a baby. I've heard of two young teenagers recently who are pregnant and it is a very difficult position to be in, let me tell you.'

'I know who you're talking about,' Vicky said, flicking me a very serious look. 'They're both in my year at school. I feel really sorry for them both.'

Vicky was not embarrassed to discuss this but Michelle had turned scarlet and changed the subject. 'When are you going to see little James again?' she asked Vicky.

'On Sunday afternoon. I said I'll go after lunch at Angela's mum's. I don't want to miss that, do I? Thelma's doing roast beef this week and I'm learning how to make Yorkshire pudding. Can't wait!'

Our summer caravan holiday to the coast was planned for the following week and I wondered whether the baby's arrival would dent Vicky's enthusiasm for going away. I'd briefly mentioned to her that we had the review in early September, and that therefore she would be staying with us at least until then. She didn't ask me anything at all about the meeting and was far more interested in the fact this meant she was staying put for the time being, and was therefore able to come on holiday with us.

'I can't wait to go away again!' she said. 'It'll be great to have a holiday all together, with Michelle included. Did you say it's a bigger caravan site than last time, Angela?'

'Yes, it's huge! There are two outdoor pools, a disco and theatre, a big leisure complex with a fun pool and hot tubs and water rapids.'

'Oh my God, no way! It'll be really good. This is turning into the best summer ever!'

As it happened, the fact she would miss out on seeing baby James for a week was not an issue at all, as when Vicky went to visit her sister on the Sunday afternoon as planned, her brother-in-law, Carl, wouldn't let her into the flat.

'Whatever's the matter, sweetheart?' I asked when Vicky returned home much earlier than expected, looking very upset.

'Lorraine's had trouble feeding the baby and she needs peace and quiet. Carl says I'm not allowed to see her or James for a while.'

'I'm very sorry to hear that, love, but it does happen. Feeding a new baby is not easy and a lot of new mums find it difficult and need some peace and quiet to adjust and get the hang of it. I expect your sister will be as right as rain once we get back from our holiday.'

'I hope so. I'm just so disappointed! I saved up and bought James a toy and everything. I can't see why I couldn't have just gone in for five minutes! What harm would that do?'

I had to admit that it did seem a little extreme not to have let Vicky over the doorstep. The poor girl had taken a bus across town, carrying her present for the baby, and it seemed such a shame. However, I knew not to judge; I did not know enough about Lorraine and Carl's life, and it would only make matters worse if I were critical of them in any way.

'At least you've met the little chap once,' I said cheerfully. 'And you can look forward to seeing him again when we get back from our holiday.'

'Yes, I suppose. How long does it take to grow teeth?'

'Why do you ask?'

'I've got James a teething ring with a rattle in it.'

'Oh, I see! Teething goes on for years and years! Don't worry, he won't have grown all his teeth while we're on holiday!'

'That's all right then. I'll give it to him when we get back.'

The holiday proved a great distraction and we all had a wonderful break, going on trips to several local attractions, using the pool and leisure complex and enjoying the campsite entertainment in the evening, which both girls loved.

One day we went into the local town to pick up some food for a barbecue, and Michelle spotted a clothes shop she wanted to go in.

'Come on, Vicky, let's have a look in here,' she said. 'I'd like to get a new top.'

Social Services had given me an additional allowance as I was taking the girls on holiday, and I had told them both that they could have some extra spending money to buy new clothes if they wanted to. This had been music to Michelle's ears, but Vicky had predictably baulked at the prospect of clothes shopping, claiming she was fine in the few well-worn items she owned that she somehow made do with.

'Well you might be fine but I'm not,' I joked, trying to chivvy Vicky along. 'At home I can wash your clothes and have them back in your wardrobe – or even your laundry bin – the same day.'

'Very funny, Angela,' Vicky snorted sarcastically, acknowledging my dig at the way she'd put ironed clothes straight back in the wash.

'I can't do the washing that quickly in a caravan though, can I?' I replied. 'And I don't think you've got enough clothes to last you a whole week!'

'I'll just try to keep them clean,' she said, giving me a cheeky grin. 'Or I'll wash them myself, in the sea!'

'You can't do that!' Michelle said, not realising Vicky was only joking. 'Come on, you're coming with me!'

With that Michelle linked arms with Vicky and led her into the clothes shop, with me following behind. Just like in C&A back home, Vicky looked extremely uncomfortable and started to protest that this wasn't her sort of shop.

'What about these?' Michelle said, picking a pair of black jeans in Vicky's size off a rail. 'I think you'd like these. They're nicer than your other jeans. Try them on!'

Michelle chose several tops for herself and then Vicky very reluctantly followed her into the changing rooms. While Vicky was a captive audience I seized the moment and grabbed a jacket and five or six T-shirts and tops that I thought would also suit her, and I waited outside the cubicle.

'How are the jeans?' I called.

'Er, quite nice actually,' Vicky replied.

'Oh good. Can I see?'

Vicky tentatively opened the cubicle door and showed me the jeans, at which point I shoved the other clothes at her and told her to try those too.

'Awwww! Angela. Do I have to?'

'Yes! The jeans look great. Leave them on to try on the T-shirts and tops. You're not coming out until you have!'

In the end we spent almost an hour in the shop, with me passing various different items of clothing through to Vicky in the cubicle. She pulled a face every time I gave her something new, but when she finally emerged she'd agreed to buy the jeans, two tops, a jacket and two T-shirts. Combined with Michelle's purchases the total bill inevitably exceeded the allowance I'd been given, but I really didn't mind; I considered it a triumph to have finally got Vicky the clothes she badly needed.

It was cloudy that day and rain was forecast for the afternoon, so we decided to go ice-skating in the next town.

'I've never done it before,' Vicky said. 'Is it difficult?'

'No!' Jonathan said. 'It's very easy to pick up.'

Michelle and I shared a knowing look when he said this, because we'd seen Jonathon in action on the ice several times and he was very uncoordinated. However, Vicky actually did find it very easy to pick up and was soon looping the ice rink with ease, leaving Jonathan in her wake. He fell over so many times you could have wrung out his trousers by the end of the session.

'Come on, Jonathan!' Vicky cried whenever she saw him fall. 'What's the matter? It's very easy to pick up, you know!'

'I'm getting better,' he called. 'It's just practice I need!'

Both Vicky and Michelle ribbed Jonathan relentlessly all the way back to the campsite, and then they proceeded to tell all the friends we'd made in the neighbouring caravans how hopeless he was. It was all done in good spirit and Vicky, being by far the cheekier of the two girls, led the teasing.

'Let's hope it doesn't rain all night,' she said. 'Or how will Jonathan dry his wet clothes! Hey, Jonathan, would you like ice with your Coke or have you had enough today?!'

Jonathan jokingly waved his fist and chased a squealing Vicky around our caravan. It was great to see her looking so happy and carefree, and it was also a relief to see Jonathan letting his hair down: his nephew's illness had hit us both very badly, and the holiday could not have come at a better time.

One of the teenagers from the caravan next door who had heard about our ice-skating trip suddenly started telling a story about a friend of hers who had had a 'wipe-out' at an ice rink.

'I think he was like Jonathan,' she giggled, 'a little bit accident-prone! He fell over by the exit, landing on his hands, and you won't believe what happened!'

'What?' everybody chorused, including Vicky.

'Another skater ran over his hand and his little finger was nearly sliced right off.'

This was a very unexpected ending to the story. The way

the teenager had set it up I was expecting there to be a funny twist in the tale, not a nasty accident.

'Did he lose it?' someone gasped.

'Nearly. There was blood all over the ice and apparently it was touch and go, but in the end the doctors managed to sew his finger back on.'

'Is he all right now?'

'He's fine! Amazing! Just has scars on his fingertip. Urgh! Imagine all that blood on the ice? That would properly freak you out, wouldn't it?'

I noticed that Vicky had gone very quiet and turned a bit pale, and then she disappeared inside our caravan without saying a word to anyone. Jonathan and I gave each other a sideways glance, and when Vicky hadn't emerged after several minutes I went to see if she was all right. She was standing very still in the middle of the caravan, not moving a muscle and staring blankly into space.

'Are you OK, sweetheart?' I asked tentatively, speaking in a soft voice so as not to startle her.

Vicky blinked repeatedly several times without looking at me.

'I'm fine,' she whispered eventually, but I could see that she wasn't.

The colour had completely drained from her face and she was holding both her wrists with the opposite hand.

'Are you squeamish, Vicky?' I asked gently. 'It was quite a gory story. I didn't like it much myself.'

Vicky sunk onto the bench that pulled out to make her bed and then she sat there incredibly still, without speaking or looking at me. I slowly crossed the caravan and sat myself down beside her.

'Not everybody likes to hear stories like that, Vicky. Some people find it difficult to listen and it makes them feel sick. Is that what happened to you?'

Vicky gazed forlornly ahead, not moving a muscle and not even acknowledging I was there, just as she had when we'd been out making the deliveries and she froze near her mum's estate. What felt like several minutes went by and Vicky continued to sit statue-like. Eventually she took a slow, deep breath, and as she did so she bit her bottom lip.

'My mum,' she said flatly, still staring straight ahead. 'She used to smash glass and then cut . . .'

'It's OK, sweetheart, you can tell me.'

'Cut her fingers, the ends of her fingers.'

'Did you see her?'

'Yes. She only did it when I was watching. She made me watch.'

'I'm so sorry to hear that, love. It must have been awful.'

'It was. I didn't want to watch but she made me. I would ask her to stop, over and over again.'

'And did she listen to you?'

'Sometimes. But other times she carried on, and it got worse.'

'Worse?'

'Yes.'

Vicky had tears dripping down her cheeks but she didn't wipe them away; she still had hold of both her wrists. After a few minutes she stood up and washed her hands in the sink, splashing water all the way up to her elbows.

'Sorry, Angela.'

'You don't need to say sorry at all. I am here to listen and to help if I can. Do you want to tell me any more?'

Vicky smudged her tears away and shook her head. The two of us then sat in silence for quite some time before she added, 'I'm really sorry about being a nuisance with the clothes.'

'Goodness me! That's all right, love! It's not that important, is it?'

'I suppose not, but I'd like to explain. It must have been annoying to you, but the thing is, Angela, I've never had new clothes before.'

'Oh, I see,' I said, silently berating myself, because I *had* been irritated by Vicky's awkward attitude to clothes shopping. Now it all seemed so obvious, but how many thirteen-year-old girls had never had new clothes before? It wasn't a thought that had crossed my mind.

'I had no idea,' I stammered. 'I'm sorry, I should have realised there was more to it . . .'

'It's OK, how would you know? That time you took me to C&A, it was the first time I'd ever been in a clothes shop. I didn't really know what to do. It kind of spooked me!'

'Well I can imagine it did! So, where did your clothes come from?'

'Alf – he's the man who lives next door to my mum – he used to bring bags for me, from the charity shops. That's why nothing fitted and all my stuff was old and horrible.'

'I see. That's such a shame. I'm sorry.'

Vicky suddenly looked me straight in the eye, inhaling deeply as she did so, her eyes locked on mine intently. She appeared more angry than upset now, and then her eyes suddenly narrowed and blazed.

'The only time my mum bought me a new outfit was when I was six, and my nan was visiting. I was so pleased with it! I couldn't believe how beautiful it was!'

'What was it like?'

'It was a dress with buttercups all around the hem, a pair of white tights, a yellow hairband and some shiny shoes.'

'That must have been lovely . . .'

'It was. But . . .'

I noticed that as she was talking Vicky was squeezing her hands into tight fists, and she was using so much force her knuckles had turned white.

'I put it on and stared at myself in the mirror in the hall. It didn't look like me! I'd never had such a pretty dress, and I'd never had new shoes, or even ones that fitted properly. Everything smelled nice and new too. I never wanted to take it off, ever, but . . .'

Vicky caught her breath and stopped speaking. I waited, expecting her to say some calamity had befallen the new dress, like she'd torn it or spilt something on it, but what she said was far worse than that.

'I wore the outfit for about an hour, that's all. As soon as Nan left my mum made me take it off and put on the smelly old stuff Alf gave me. And then. Well . . .'

'Go on, love. Tell me what happened next.'

'Then my mum put everything back in the packet it came in, and returned the whole lot to the catalogue company. I even had to be the one who handed it back to the delivery driver, because Mum was asleep on the settee when he came to make his rounds on the estate.'

I could feel tears pricking my eyes as Vicky spoke.

'Can I give you a hug?' I asked, but she shook her head.

'It's OK. I also want to explain about the tracksuit, because I know you think I'm some kind of weirdo wearing it all the time!'

Vicky laughed bravely, but that just made me want to cry even more, and I couldn't help letting a few tears escape from my eyes.

'What happened is that Lorraine bought the tracksuit for me when I went to live with her. It was the first thing that had been bought for me that I could keep, and that's why I like it so much. Lorraine couldn't afford to get me anything else but she did get me some second-hand stuff that actually fitted, and they're the other things I wear. I'm really sorry I've been a pain.'

'Vicky, love, you really don't need to apologise.'

'Thanks,' she said, sniffing and giving me a little smile, which seemed to signal the end of the conversation. 'Now,' she declared decisively, standing to her feet, 'is there still time to take the mickey out of Jonathan?'

'Yes!' I grinned. 'Of course there is! There's always time for that!'

'Great! OK. I'll be out in a minute.'

I took my cue and stepped out of the caravan, leaving

Vicky to compose herself – or so I thought. Two minutes later she appeared with a jug full of water and ice cubes, clearly having emptied the contents of the ice cube tray from the little freezer in the van.

'Jonathan, would you like *more* ice?' she said, before very unexpectedly tipping the full jug-load over his head.

There were gasps and squeals all around. I could tell that Jonathan was not actually very amused. It had given him a real shock and he was on his feet now, shivering, gasping for air and saying, 'What on earth?'

Vicky was laughing her head off and so was Michelle, and soon everybody sitting in the vicinity of our caravan had joined in.

'Don't tell her off,' I whispered as I handed Jonathan a towel. 'I'll explain later.'

'OK,' he said through gritted teeth, before saying jovially, 'I'll get you back for this, Vicky!' and chasing her all around the van once more.

The next morning Vicky was up early and offered to walk to the convenience store in the centre of the campsite, as we needed bread and milk for breakfast.

'You're very willing today!' I teased, as Michelle had gone to the shop most mornings before Vicky was even awake.

'Just fancied a walk!' Vicky chirped.

Unfortunately, when she returned I realised why she'd wanted to go to the shop; Vicky now smelled of smoke and had clearly had a cigarette or two on her travels. I was disappointed by this on two levels, and I decided to talk frankly to her.

'Vicky, I'm not daft and I know you've had a cigarette this morning,' I said as she put the milk in the fridge. 'I thought you were trying to stop. I'm disappointed that you're still smoking, but I'm also very upset that you've lied to me again.'

'I haven't! If you'd asked me if I'd had a cigarette I would have admitted it! The whole reason I did it behind your back and told a stupid little fib about the shop was because I didn't want to upset you!'

'But you did lie, Vicky. You said you volunteered to go to the shop because you wanted a walk, but the truth was you wanted a cigarette. I know things aren't easy for you, but you're not making it any easier by sneaking around behind my back. I'm on your side, you know!'

Vicky huffed and puffed, in a kind of 'I can't be bothered with all this' way.

'Well if you really are on my side, get off my case. I'm doing my best, OK?'

'Vicky! I won't have you talking to me like that. That was rude! I know you've been through a lot and I care about you a great deal. I want to help improve things, but I can't if you're lying to me. You said yourself that you want to stop smoking, so let's talk about how we can keep you on track, hey?'

'I just don't think I can do it, Angela!' she blurted out. 'I can't stop because I'm too stressed! Having a fag calms me down.'

It was an awful thing for a thirteen-year-old girl to admit and I had a lot of sympathy for her, and not just because of the way she had started to smoke, stealing cigarettes from her sleeping mother as she did. I had been through the pain of quitting myself, and I knew exactly how tough it was, even with the full support of Jonathan and with virtually no other stress in my life.

'I know it's very, very difficult, but you have to try harder, Vicky. I'm worried about your health. I don't want you making yourself poorly or doing any long-term damage.'

'I know all that, Angela. I'm so stressed though! It's so hard!'

'OK, let's talk about the stress then. What is it that's stressing you out the most? Is it the fact Carl wouldn't let you see James?'

'Er, that's part of it, but I know it will all be fine once Lorraine has had a rest and I'm back living with her and can help her and stuff.'

By now I had serious doubts that Vicky would be moving back in with her sister any time soon, but I kept any such thoughts to myself.

'OK, and so is it stressing you out living with me and Jonathan?'

'No!' She smiled. 'I love living with you! It's not that at all.'

'What then?'

'Seeing my mum,' she said nervously. 'I really don't want to see her, Angela. I'm so stressed about that meeting thing that Tricia has organised. Honestly, I can't see her, I really can't! I don't have to go if she's there, do I?'

'Well, Tricia would prefer it if we all sat around a table together. That's you, me, Jonathan, Tricia and your mother. Tricia's manager would probably be there too, to oversee the meeting. You'd be perfectly safe.'

'I hate her though! I'm terrified of her! I haven't seen her for months so why should I have to now?'

'Nobody will force you to be there, don't worry. But the thing is, Vicky, the meeting is all about you. It really would be best for you to be there. You need to tell the people in charge where you want to live, and why; that is what the meeting is all about.'

'So they'll listen to me, to what I want?'

'Of course they will; your view is the most important one.'

'So if I say I don't want to live with my mum, I don't have to?'

'If you would be at risk there, then no, you won't have to return to live with her.'

'Well I would be at risk, wouldn't I? So that's it. I'll be allowed to go back to Lorraine's.'

Vicky seemed to be overlooking the fact Lorraine had put her in care in the first place. It was not a question of Social Services allowing her to go back to her sister's house, but more a case of Lorraine and Carl accepting and inviting her back, if it was deemed appropriate. With a new baby to cope with and in the light of what had happened on Vicky's cancelled second visit, it seemed unlikely that Lorraine was going to take Vicky back as quickly as she hoped.

Having a sometimes messy and occasionally unruly teenager to contend with is tough for any family at the best of times, and Lorraine had clearly hit breaking point when she put Vicky in care. The fact she did this when she, more than anybody, knew what life had been like for Vicky in the past, made me think things must have been really very tough for Lorraine.

'Do you mind me asking, Vicky, is Lorraine your only other family? Only you mentioned your nan earlier?'

'Her!' she huffed. 'She died a couple of years ago, and she was horrible anyway. She never wanted to know me.'

'I'm sorry to hear that. What makes you say that?'

'She fell out with my mum ages ago. The last time I saw her was about five years ago, when she had a big argument with my mum and said she was washing her hands of the lot of us. My nan was a very selfish woman, and my mum didn't even go to her funeral. As for my dad, he was worse. He was horrible – a very nasty man indeed.'

This was the first mention Vicky had made of her father and my ears pricked up. It is routine practice to make every effort to contact both parents and any other close relatives in cases like Vicky's, but I'd heard nothing from Tricia about how she was getting on with her enquiries. In those days, before we had the internet and social media to hand, tracking people down was often a long-winded and frustrating process, and I was therefore not surprised this was taking some time.

'Your dad was a very nasty man, was he?' I said, trying to sound as calm and collected as possible, though I had all kinds of questions racing through my head. I still hadn't been taught to mirror what a child says when they are making a disclosure, but this instinctively felt like the right thing to do.

'Yes he was. He and my mum split up when I was just a few months old, and then he disappeared. He's probably dead. He had something wrong with him, some kind of disease.'

'Oh, I see. I'm so sorry to hear all this. Did your mum tell you this, or Lorraine, by the way?'

'My mum. Lorraine never knew him, as far as I know. She's got a different dad, you see, and she was living with him when I was born. If Social Services are looking for my dad you should tell them not to waste their time. Even if he's alive he's a lost cause, a total loser.'

My heart sank. Poor Vicky had been dealt a terrible hand in life and it was so sad to think she had never known her father, and that she had no idea if he was alive or dead. I did have an alarm bell ringing in my head though, because Vicky's very negative description of her father was purely based on what her mother had told her.

'We only have Brenda's word for it that he was a nasty character,' I found myself saying when I relayed the conversation to Jonathan later.

'Yes indeed,' he said. 'I see what you're saying. We don't know how reliable this information is, do we?'

'Exactly. It could be clutching at straws, but I sincerely hope Social Services will do everything in their power to find out what became of him. Even if Vicky's father has passed away as she suspects, she ought to know, and at least she might find out more about him, something that hasn't come from her mother.'

I jotted down some notes in my diary so as not to forget any details, and I passed all the information I had gleaned to Tricia at the next available opportunity. I wasn't officially required to keep a diary but I liked to do so. I wanted to ensure I gave accurate information to Social Services and it also helped me remember key dates and events, as I also took plenty of photographs of Vicky that I eventually put into albums for her, along with dates and captions. I did the same for Michelle, and other children we had staying.

Nowadays social workers put together 'life story' books for kids in foster care, which are like a biography, dating back to the child's birth. The books include information about the child's place of birth, pictures and details of their former homes and schools, names of relatives and so on. Social workers need to be specially trained to compile life stories, as they can bring to the forefront issues that can cause stress or behavioural difficulties, while foster carers are now asked to keep what are known as 'memory books' for the children, which include photos and keepsakes like concert tickets, party invitations and school certificates, to help the child remember their time with you. Such records were unheard of back in the late eighties though, but I felt it was only natural to take photos and keep some kind of scrapbook for the children, just as I kept souvenirs and photographs of my own life.

Whatever happened next, I wanted Vicky to remember her time with us. It was part of her childhood and, no matter how short her stay, it should not be forgotten.

# 8

## *'Vicky can go to hell!'*

'I saw James today!' Vicky beamed. 'He's grown loads already! He's so cute, Angela! You should see his tiny fingernails.'

'Oh that's great! I didn't know Lorraine was up to seeing you yet?'

'If you ask Carl then apparently she's not, but I called round when he was at work, just on the off chance, when I was on my way to meet my friends.'

'Oh! And Lorraine was OK with that?'

'Totally! She was pleased to see me.'

'Well that's lovely. I'm glad that worked out. And so Lorraine's doing well now?'

'She's great! I think Carl's a bit overprotective. Lorraine even asked me if I wanted to babysit, so of course I said yes! I'm going back tomorrow, so she can get to the shops and that.'

I was very pleased for Vicky, although I was slightly concerned about her being left in charge of such a new baby.

She was about to turn fourteen in a few weeks' time, but nevertheless Vicky was a very young girl with no experience of looking after a newborn.

'Are you sure you're happy to be left alone with your nephew?' I asked. 'You've never done it before and it could be harder than you think.'

'I'm completely fine! Lorraine said she won't be long, not even an hour, and she'll feed and change him before she goes out.'

'Right, then. Promise you'll phone me if you're worried about anything, won't you? You have the shop number and the house number in your purse, don't you?'

'Yes, Angela!' Vicky said, turning on her fake American accent. 'Interrogation over? Permission to visit my nephew granted?'

I mimicked the American solider salute Vicky often made.

'Permission granted, officer Vicky!'

She set off to Lorraine's with a spring in her step the next day, but unfortunately she returned in a terrible mood and with a face like thunder about an hour later.

'Vicky, love! Whatever is the matter?'

She had barged through the shop door with such force the open/closed sign on the back of it was swinging precariously and the bell hanging overhead had rung out like a warning siren instead of making its usual gentle tinkle.

'Nothing. Leave me alone!' she shouted.

I was behind the counter, serving a middle-aged gentleman who was buying some red roses for his wife's birthday.

'I'm terribly sorry,' I said to the customer, as he'd nearly jumped out of his skin when Vicky stormed in.

'It's quite all right,' he said stony-faced as he shot a look at Vicky and then began fumbling for his wallet, no doubt hoping to pay as quickly as possible so he could make his exit.

'What are you looking at?' Vicky suddenly snapped, very rudely indeed. She had her hands on her hips and was scowling aggressively at the gentleman. 'Well? I *said*, what are you gawping at?'

'Vicky! That's very rude! Goodness me! Go straight up to your room, right now!'

Turning to my customer I said, 'I'm terribly sorry. I can't apologise enough.'

'Well I'm not sorry!' Vicky shouted as she made her way to the back of the shop. 'I hate people who poke their noses into other people's business! Nosy parker!'

The poor gentleman was speechless.

'That is enough, Vicky. Go to your room immediately!'

'Don't worry, I'm going! I'll just GO TO HELL, shall I? AND YOU CAN TOO!'

'Vicky!'

I heard the door between the shop and the house slam, leaving me shocked and red-faced as I dealt with my dumbfounded customer. I told him to have the bunch of flowers on the shop and offered my humblest apologies.

The man took the flowers and shuffled out without saying a word, leaving me fuming and deeply embarrassed.

The minute Jonathan arrived back I dashed through to the house and found Vicky in her bedroom, blasting out extremely loud 'acid house' music.

'Vicky! What on earth is the matter? What's going on?'

I hammered on her door, because I would never go into a child's bedroom without their permission, and after a minute or so she begrudgingly shouted, 'Come in then, if you really have to!'

'Right, Vicky!' I shouted. 'Turn that music down and let's talk. You were extremely rude back there and I'm grounding you for a month! I don't care what has happened, you cannot speak to me or to our customers like that. It is completely out of order!'

'A month?' she said, jaw dropping as she turned down the volume on her stereo. 'Are you *serious*?'

'Totally serious, Vicky. You are not going out for a month, unless it's something I want you to do, of course.'

'But I'm back at school soon! It's nearly the end of the school holidays! I'll miss out on loads!'

'I don't care what is going on! You should have thought of that before you were so disrespectful. My customer didn't know where to put himself. I never want to see that kind of behaviour from you again.'

'Yes, but a MONTH?'

'Yes a MONTH! What has happened, anyhow? What made you behave that way?'

'Nothing, it doesn't matter. All you care about is GROUNDING me!'

'That's unfair and untrue. Now what is going on? Did

something happen at Lorraine's, or on the way home? Have you fallen out with Carl? Did he stop you seeing the baby again?'

Vicky thought long and hard before steeling herself to answer.

'If you must know, Lorraine told me she went to visit our mother.'

Vicky looked very uneasy at the mention of her mother.

'I see,' I said softly, leaving Vicky space to carry on.

'Lorraine thought she ought to show her the baby. I won't be going anywhere near her if I have babies! Lorraine must need her head testing!'

'Is that why you're so cross and upset?'

'No, not just that. It was all fine for them, apparently, but not for me! Lorraine said that my mum was really pleased to see her. It had been a long time. But my mum had a message for me.'

'Did she?'

'Yes she did. The message from my mum was: "Vicky can go to hell. As far as I'm concerned I only have one daughter, and that's you, Lorraine."'

A mass of emotions swamped me. I immediately felt guilty for grounding Vicky, I was appalled and angry at Lorraine's insensitivity in passing this dreadful message on, but most of all I was utterly horrified that the words had been spoken in the first place.

'Vicky! That's absolutely terrible.'

'I know,' she shuddered. 'I hate my mum. She's a witch.

D'you know what? When I was living with her I was so scared I thought she was going to murder me.'

'Murder you?'

'Yes, I'm deadly serious. I don't know what I've done to her, but she hates me. She used to say, "It's all your fault." She's gunning for me, I tell you, Angela. This is why I don't want to go to that review thing. I know she can't harm me there, but I'm terrified of even being in the same room as her.'

I had the date and time of the review in my diary now and I was starting to get a bit stressed about it myself. I certainly sympathised with Vicky, though of course I couldn't imagine what it must be like to be in her shoes. It was a very upsetting and unusual situation indeed.

'Look, you said it yourself, sweetheart. Your mum can't harm you there, can she? I'll sit beside you the whole time, and . . .'

'Can't you just say I'm grounded?' Vicky blurted. 'So I can't go!'

'You know that's a silly thing to say.'

'Well you grounded me! Oh my God! I hate my life! Can you just leave me alone now please, Angela?!'

She stood up and turned her music back on, but thankfully not as loud as earlier.

'We'll talk again, Vicky,' I said. 'But until I say so, you are grounded. I'm very sorry about what you heard today, but you have to learn not to take things out on other people.'

As I was walking down the stairs Michelle was making her way up them, looking downhearted.

'Hello, love!' I said as brightly as I could muster. 'How are you?'

'Very, very fed up!' she grumbled.

'Oh dear, I'm sorry to hear that. What's the matter?'

'My mum's changed her mind about Florida.'

'Oh no! But she's already agreed to everything!'

'She says she doesn't like the set-up in the hotel.'

'What d'you mean?'

'I showed her the brochure you gave me. We are all sharing one room, aren't we?'

'Sort of. It's a family room with an interconnecting door. You'll have your privacy without being on your own.'

'Well she doesn't like it. She's told me to tell you to cancel it.'

'It's too late for that! Honestly, I'm sure we'll be able to sort this out. Leave it with me, Michelle. Don't worry about it; she can't just cancel like this.'

'Well she can, and she has. She's told Tricia and everything. I suppose I'd be worried if my child was going to the other side of the world with people I hardly knew.'

'Is that what she said? Jonathan and I are not exactly strangers, Michelle, are we? We're your foster carers and you'd lived with us for two years! As I say, leave it with me.'

At that moment Vicky appeared on the landing above us and invited Michelle into her bedroom to listen to some music.

'OK,' Michelle said, 'what are you listening to?'

'Acid house. Do you like it?'

'Ooh I'm not sure. I'll come up.'

By the time I'd reached the ground floor of the house the music was blasting out so loudly I could feel it thudding in my chest, so I darted back upstairs and banged on Vicky's door again.

'Vicky! What did I say! Turn it down!'

'Well what am I supposed to do, being stuck in?' she retorted.

'I don't know, but turn it down!'

'You're so boring!'

I didn't argue back as the volume did go down and I'd had enough for the time being. All I wanted to do was sit down, have a cup of tea and a biscuit and gather my thoughts, but the phone rang just as I was going into the kitchen.

'What now!' I said out loud, grabbing the receiver and barking 'Hello?' impatiently.

'Hello, is that Mrs Hart?'

'Yes it is.'

'Hello! I just wanted to introduce myself. My name's Hayley Jenkins. I've taken over from Tricia as your social worker.'

'Oh! Thank you for phoning. I didn't know Tricia was leaving.'

'No, another foster carer just said the same thing. I don't know why she didn't tell you. Tricia's moved to another post outside the county.'

I found myself feeling upset about this. Though I didn't always appreciate Tricia's abrupt manner I'd got to know her quite well over the past two years, and I understood that she behaved so brusquely at times because of the pressure she was under, and not because she was impatient or didn't care.

'Well that's come as quite a surprise,' I said. 'If you speak to her again please send her all my best. I'm sorry I didn't have the chance to say goodbye.'

Hayley wanted to arrange to come over and visit us, and I explained that we ran the shop and Jonathan and I would prefer to see her after hours if at all possible.

'That's fine!' she said brightly. 'I know you have the florists and I suffer from terrible hay fever, so I'd rather keep well away from the shop in any case.'

I had a good feeling about Hayley. She sounded younger and more enthusiastic than Tricia, and when I met her in person a few days later I discovered she was only in her early twenties and was newly qualified. She also happened to be the physical opposite to Tricia too, with slick blonde hair and a tall, slender figure, and she was dressed in a smart suit as opposed to the slacks and baggy jumpers Tricia favoured.

'It's so nice to meet you, Angela!' Hayley beamed, shaking my hand enthusiastically.

'And you. This is Jonathan, my husband.'

'Lovely to meet you. It's great that you are both foster carers, I have to say. There are a lot fewer men than women prepared to put themselves forward. I think you have a great arrangement, what with running the business together too.'

Jonathan was used to being overlooked by Tricia and he

warmed to Hayley immediately. Once the pleasantries were over, however, we were disappointed to discover there was nothing further to report in terms of tracking down Vicky's father, or about Lorraine's situation. All Hayley had wanted to do at this stage was make our acquaintance, see how Vicky was getting on and make sure we were happy to carry on fostering her for the time being.

'Can I meet Vicky now?' Hayley asked.

'Yes of course! I wasn't sure if you'd want to see her but she's upstairs in her room. She's grounded, as it happens. Can you go and fetch her, Jonathan?'

'Thanks. Didn't Tricia normally see Vicky when she visited you then? I would have thought that was to be expected?'

As Jonathan climbed the stairs I explained that in the six weeks Vicky had been with us Tricia had never made an appointment at the house like this. Instead, we'd spoken on the phone or she'd dropped into the shop if she happened to be passing, where she had seen Vicky briefly on one or two occasions.

'How are you, Vicky?' Tricia had asked at one such chance encounter. 'Happy here?'

'Er, yes. I like Angela and Jonathan.'

'Great! Any problems, Angela?'

'No, not that I can think of right now . . .'

'Good. I'll put this down as a visit . . .'

Hayley kept her counsel as I described Tricia's methods, but I could tell from the look on her face she wasn't very impressed by this set-up. She then inevitably asked me why Vicky was grounded, and so I explained the full story.

'To tell the truth, I know I've made a mistake in grounding her for a month. It's only been a few days and she's already been making a terrible nuisance of herself in the house. I've reached the point where I think I'm going to have to un-ground her for everybody's sanity!'

I made light of it but this was no joke. Vicky had got so bored being in the house all day long that she'd caused all kinds of havoc. First she'd decided to use some rhubarb from my mother's garden to make a crumble, but she'd tried to 'bake' it in a metal tray in the microwave instead of the main oven, and our microwave was now broken and waiting to be taken to the tip. Next she'd used a tea tray instead of a baking tray to grill some cheese on toast, and the tray had melted and filled the kitchen with choking smoke.

'Do you like having me around so much?' Vicky had said sarcastically one evening, and then she proceeded to follow Jonathan everywhere he went, just like a little shadow, as she could think of nothing better to do.

'What are you doing, Jonathan?' she babbled incessantly. 'Can I help? Do you want to play a game?'

She was so irritating that even Michelle had snapped, 'Go and read your book!' at one point.

'Finished it!' she chimed. 'But I can't go to the library for another one because *I'm grounded*!!!'

When Jonathan brought Vicky into the lounge to meet Hayley I couldn't help but admire her nerve. Vicky was wearing a bright red oversized sweatshirt with the slogan 'Let Me Out!' emblazoned in yellow lettering on the front.

'Where on earth did you get that, Vicky?' I asked.

'It's one of Lorraine's old maternity tops. Do you like it? I think the slogan is very appropriate for someone who's *grounded*!'

Hayley laughed, and while the atmosphere was light and warm the social worker impressed me by slipping the review into the conversation, and making it sound very safe and manageable to Vicky.

'So we'll see each other next Tuesday. It'll be a chance to get out the house for a while, Vicky!'

'I don't want to go, actually.'

'I can understand that. Nobody likes those things. I'd rather be painting my toenails, believe me, but I've got to be there. We'll all support each other, won't we? It's for your benefit, Vicky, just remember that and it will help you get through it. You won't come to any harm, we can promise you that, and afterwards you'll be glad you've done it.'

'OK,' Vicky nodded. 'I won't wear the sweatshirt though. I don't want anybody thinking I want to get out of *here*.'

'So you'd like to stay here, with Angela and Jonathan?'

'I'd be happy to stay, if I can't go back to Lorraine's. I love Angela and Jonathan.'

'Now look how easy that was!' Hayley beamed. 'That's really all you have to say next week. Think you can manage it?'

Vicky smiled.

'Yep.'

*

Unfortunately, in the days leading up to the review Vicky became very anxious and moody. I'd bought her a few school shirts plus a new pencil case as she'd lost her old one on the last day of term, but Vicky was rude and ungrateful.

'I don't like that style,' she said, turning her nose up at the shirts.

'What do you mean? There's no choice, they are the ones recommended by the school.'

'Exactly! I won't wear them. You might as well get your money back. I'll choose my own.'

'But where else will you get them? These are pale blue, Marks & Spencer. What can possibly be wrong with them?'

'Everything! Look at the collars! They're massive! My other ones aren't like that!'

This was true, but the shirts Vicky had arrived with last term were practically worn out and were a brand I didn't recognise, with tiny collars you could barely fit the school tie underneath. My guess was they were originally sold on the market; they were poor quality and certainly didn't match the regulation uniform.

'I think you'll find lots of girls have the same shirts as these this year, Vicky. They're the latest stock and the cut is lovely. Look!'

'Well the rest of them can wear them but I'm not!' she moaned. 'And I don't want that pencil case either.'

'For heaven's sake! What's wrong with that? It's just a plain pencil case, and I've stocked it up.'

'It's disgusting!'

'Disgusting? How can you describe a pencil case as disgusting?'

'When it *is* disgusting! I don't want it. You've wasted your money!'

The next day she upset Michelle after she cooked everyone a cottage pie and Vicky said she's didn't fancy it and wasn't hungry, as she'd just eaten some toast and jam.

'Never mind, love,' I said to Michelle, who looked crestfallen. 'It smells delicious. Jonathan and I have been looking forward to it. All the more for us!'

'Aren't you going to tell Vicky off?' Michelle asked.

'I will have a word, but I think she's out of sorts, as it's her review tomorrow.'

'Oh!' Michelle said. 'I had no idea. Wish her luck from me.'

'I will, love. None of us are looking forward to it.'

'I'm not surprised. You just never know what's going to happen, do you? It's like being in *Coronation Street* or *EastEnders*!'

Michelle laughed as she said this but there was a bittersweet look on her face and I felt a pang of sadness. Her quip was a little too close for comfort. Rather like the characters in a soap whose destinies are decided by script writers, I really did have a sense that Vicky's life was in the hands of others, who would determine which path her life would follow next. Myself and Jonathan were not central to the storyline, and as such we were extremely easy to write out. However much we cared about Vicky, and we really did care very much about her, we could be taken out of the picture at any time. That's probably the most difficult part of being a foster carer, and I had a sleepless night before Vicky's review, worrying about what was going to happen to her next.

# 9

### *'You're the biggest mistake I ever made'*

'I feel sick,' Vicky said solemnly when she came down to breakfast on the morning of the review. 'I don't think I can go.'

'I don't feel so good myself, Vicky. We have to go though, perhaps it won't be as bad as you imagine.'

'It will. You don't know what she's like, Angela. She hates me so much. Even when she just looks at me she makes me feel terrified. Just one look, the look she always gave me, I'm so frightened of her doing that.'

Vicky was wrestling with a new packet of Rice Krispies and she suddenly pulled it so tight it burst open, sprinkling the cereal all over the kitchen floor.

'God! I'm so useless!' she muttered.

'Don't say that, Vicky,' I soothed. 'It's just an accident, and I know you're stressed.'

'D'you know what she used to tell me? She used to say I was the biggest mistake she ever made. Even when I did all the jobs she wanted and delivered all her notes and letters, she still said it: "*You're the biggest mistake I ever made.*"

'Notes and letters?' I repeated back.

'Oh, God! I don't want to even think about that now. I'm going to have to have a cigarette. Sorry, see you in a minute.'

By the time she'd got herself ready and Jonathan and I had steered her into the car, Vicky was very quiet; too quiet. She sat rigid, strapped in the back seat and staring like a zombie at the headrest behind Jonathan throughout the journey to the office where the meeting was taking place. It was only a fifteen-minute car ride away but it felt like much longer, because the atmosphere in the car was so tense and heavy.

'Take some deep breaths,' I said to Vicky, twisting round in the passenger seat to look at her. 'It might help you release a bit of tension.'

Vicky totally ignored me, and I noticed she'd balled her hands into tight fists as she had done in the caravan that time, when she told me how her mother used to cut her fingers.

'By the way, I've decided to un-ground you,' I said. I'd discussed this with Jonathan and we decided we'd made a rod for our own backs in grounding Vicky for a month, and that she had already learned her lesson from the punishment. I hoped the good news might evoke a response, but there wasn't a flicker.

After a few minutes of silence I turned to Jonathan.

'How are you?' I asked him, more as a way of trying to break the ice in the car than because I wanted to know the answer; I could already see he was feeling under pressure too.

'Not bad,' he said loudly, so Vicky could hear. 'At least after today we should have a plan, hey, Vicky? We'll all know what's happening next, and that's a good thing, isn't it?'

Vicky said nothing at all, and when I glanced back at her I saw that she had a very noticeable twitch below her right eye, though the rest of her face and her body were completely frozen. It upset me a great deal to see her like that.

'We're here now!' Jonathan said a few minutes later as he drove into the car park.

'Marvellous!' I said, though it clearly wasn't and I wondered why on earth I said that; I was not myself at all.

We'd never been to this Social Services building before, but apparently it was the only one available to accommodate the meeting on this particular day. The car park was extremely uninviting. The cracked tarmac was sprouting weeds and dandelions, the bins were overflowing with old lager cans and chip wrappers and the sign warning motorists that spaces were for 'staff and visitors only' had been sprayed with offensive white graffiti. To add to the gloomy atmosphere the weather was cold and dull, with splinters of rain falling from the grey sky.

'Well then, ladies, let's get going,' Jonathan said breezily, stepping out of the car.

Vicky didn't move, and so Jonathan opened her door and did a little charade, pretending to be her chauffeur.

'Miss Vicky, allow me to help you out of the car!' he said, bowing towards her and proffering his hand.

Still Vicky sat motionless, totally ignoring Jonathan. I was at his side now, and I leaned in the car, put my hand on Vicky's shoulder and gave her a gentle squeeze.

'Vicky, love, we're here now. Shall we get inside? We don't want to be late.'

Vicky appeared to wake up when I said the word late, and then she stumbled out of the car apologising and looking nervously around her.

'I wonder if everyone else is here,' I said, looking around and inevitably thinking about her mother, though I had no idea what Brenda looked like.

'I doubt *she's* here yet. There's no way *she'll* be on time.'

After giving our names at reception the three of us were shown to a small, hot waiting room adjacent to the car park. There was a low table underneath the window with a pile of old magazines on it, and in the corner behind the door there was a water fountain with a handwritten 'out of order' sign stuck to the side with yellow, crispy-edged sticking tape.

Vicky sat down next to the table and I sat beside her, with Jonathan alongside me.

'Do you think perhaps everyone else is here and we'll just get called when they're ready?' Jonathan asked quietly after a few minutes had passed.

'It's possible I suppose,' I said, glancing at the clock hanging above the door.

'It's gone ten to.'

All the reviews we'd attended in the past with Michelle had been in our local Social Services office in town, which we were very familiar with. The routine was the same each time. After signing in at reception, Michelle would usually be taken to one side by her social worker for a brief chat, and then all three of us would be shown upstairs and asked to wait outside the glass-walled meeting room where the review would take place. You could see who had already arrived and was in the room, and therefore you knew who was missing and who to expect. We were very much in the dark sitting here though, and of course the thought on all our minds was that Vicky's mother might walk in unannounced at any given moment.

'Do you want to look at a magazine?' I said to Vicky. 'There's plenty there.'

'No, thanks.'

I stood up and shuffled through the magazines.

'I don't think you're missing much!' I commented, trying to raise a smile. '*Auto Trader* from 1987 doesn't appeal to me much either!'

Vicky looked at the floor and started biting her nails.

'Who else is coming, did you say?' she asked.

'As far as I know it's just Hayley, the new social worker you met, and Stuart Williams, who's the head social worker, and Hayley's manager.'

'What's *he* like?'

Jonathan and I swapped glances. Stuart was an extremely laidback character who in our experience rarely contributed anything to the meetings. He typically sat looking at his notes the whole time, giving very little eye contact and saying virtually nothing. Privately, Jonathan and I had nicknamed him Stuart 'will that be all?' Williams, as that was usually one of his few contributions to the proceedings.

'He's fine, you don't need to worry about Mr Williams,' Jonathan said, adding diplomatically, 'He's there to preside over the meeting more than anything. He'll maybe take a few notes and he might ask you how you are, but I expect Hayley will do most of the talking.'

At that moment Hayley entered the room. She was wearing a pretty white dress and orange cardigan and had a big smile on her face.

'Vicky!' she said. 'Lovely to see you again. Hi Jonathan! Hi Angela! How is everybody doing this morning?'

Vicky shrugged.

'I'm a bit nervous,' I said, glancing at Vicky. 'We all are.'

'Well don't be. Vicky, is there anything you want me to say at the meeting that I don't already know?'

'Like what?'

'Well, I know you'd like to go back to Lorraine's if that's an option, and you also told me you'd be happy to stay with Jonathan and Angela if not.'

'Yes, that's right. I'm happy with either of those, but I don't want to go back to my mother's. There is no way I'm going back there.'

'Right. I've got that. Mr Williams isn't here yet. He'll fetch you when he comes in and bring you to the meeting room, which is just at the end of this corridor. I'll see you down there shortly.'

'Is *she* here?' Vicky asked pointedly, searching Hayley's face for the answer before she had chance to reply.

'No, not yet.'

'Typical,' Vicky said, looking down. 'Told you she'd be late.'

It was very stuffy in the waiting room. I'd put on a smart skirt, blouse and jacket, plus tights and court shoes. I was used to being dressed in the loose-fitting trousers and cotton tops I wore for work, and as the minutes ticked past I felt increasingly hot and uncomfortable. Looking across at Jonathan I could see he was feeling the same; he was wearing suit trousers and a formal shirt, and I noticed small beads of sweat had formed on his forehead. Seeing him like that reminded me of the day a panel of officials decided whether to pass us as foster carers or not, more than two years earlier, and I found myself thinking back over the process we had been through.

After I'd answered the advert in the local paper I attended a meeting at the local Social Services office in town, on my own, leaving Jonathan in the shop. I expected the meeting to focus on the qualities required to be a foster carer, but to my surprise and dismay the male social worker who greeted me proceeded to tell me a series of horror stories that seemed designed to completely put me off.

'Some of these children have been through a lot of trauma in their lives,' he said. 'And I mean serious trauma. You have to be prepared to deal with all kinds of issues.'

'What do you mean?'

'We're talking kids who smear excrement down the walls, kids who might attack you, kids with mental health and behavioural problems, kids who've been sexually abused who display sexualised behaviour . . . the list goes on.'

I was incredibly naive, and I was shocked to hear this. In my youth the majority of kids who were in children's homes or put up for adoption or fostering were given up by their mothers because they were born out of wedlock, or were sadly orphaned. The children were not mentally ill, out of control or survivors of abuse as this social worker was describing. The meeting had made me realise how much society had changed over the previous few decades. By the mid-eighties it was gradually becoming more socially acceptable for a woman to raise a child alone, and so unfortunately the kids who were ending up in care typically had problems a lot worse than being illegitimate or orphaned. They were much more likely to be the ones parents couldn't cope with for one reason or another, whether it was because they had mental or physical problems, had come from broken, dysfunctional families or had been victims of abuse or neglect.

'You need to think long and hard about this,' the social worker had cautioned. 'Are you sure you want to do this, Mrs Hart?'

'I wasn't expecting to hear this at all, but you haven't put me off,' I replied straight away. 'I'm shocked but, if anything, it makes me want to help kids more.'

It was the social worker's turn to look surprised, and I asked him to tell me more about the process, which I relayed to Jonathan when I got home, along with all the other information I had gathered.

Then it was Jonathan's turn to look shocked.

'I honestly had no idea,' he said, 'I was exactly like you. I thought the only problem these kids had was that they didn't have a mum or dad who could look after them.'

'I know, it's an eye-opener. I still want to do it though. What about you? Has it put you off?'

'It's certainly a bit frightening. I need time to think about it. What would happen next, if we wanted to go ahead?'

'We'd have to do what's called a "form F",' I said, as this is what I'd been told by the social worker. 'It's an incredibly long and detailed form, which the social workers fill in on our behalf. You basically have to go back to the year dot, providing them with every address you ever lived at, every job you've ever had, listing any health issues or convictions you've had and describing the support network you have.'

'Support network?'

'That means which relatives we have near us, and what our relationships are like with other family members. You have to draw this sort of family map, putting yourself in the middle and all your relatives around the outside. The closer your relationship is with them, the nearer you place them to yourself, in the centre of the map.'

'And so obviously if you're not close you still include the relative but put them on the edges of the map?'

'Exactly. And then you draw a line from yourself to each person. A solid line indicates a good relationship, a dotted line means you get on all right with that person, and a zigzag line means you have a love-hate or on-off relationship.'

Jonathan laughed. 'I can think of a few zigzags,' he

smiled, no doubt picturing a couple of his brothers who he didn't always see eye to eye with. 'Seriously, though, it sounds intense, Angela. I didn't imagine it would be so detailed. How do you feel about doing all this?'

'I definitely want to do it,' I replied without hesitation. 'I'm excited by it, actually. I know it's going to be hard but I want to give it a go; I want to help some children. None of this has put me off at all. What do you think?'

There was a pause.

'Look, Angela, if you feel this strongly I'll support you; you know I will. I'd never hold you back from something you feel this passionately about.'

'Really?' I grinned.

'Yes, really. Come on, Angela. Don't act surprised. When have you ever not got your own way?'

I laughed and gave him a kiss.

'Thank you,' I said. 'I don't think we'll regret it.'

'Like I've said before, Angela, we won't know until we try. What happens once the form has been completed?'

'We would then be thoroughly interviewed, separately and together, answering questions about what kind of a childhood we had and what made you happy as a child. You're right about it being intense, and it's potentially very intrusive too, but I honestly think it'll be worth it. I have a very good feeling about it.'

Jonathan was slightly nervous when I mentioned the questions about our own childhoods, as he finds it upsetting to talk about how he was treated by his father, growing up on the farm. Similarly, I was not relishing the prospect of having to tell strangers my father had been an alcoholic, but after talking through these concerns at length we both agreed that we had nothing to hide, we were strong enough to cope and we were ultimately prepared to give it a go.

'How long does this whole process take?' Jonathan asked next.

'About six months, maybe a bit longer. It depends how busy the social workers are at the time.'

'Six months? That's some vetting process!'

'I know, but that's a good thing, isn't it? Social Services have to be incredibly careful, and we're not in a rush, are we?'

'No, and at least that will give us time to change our minds, if that's what we want to do. I think I might need that length of time to get my head around all of this, to be quite honest.'

I gave Jonathan a big hug and thanked him again for being so open-minded and big-hearted. Even then, knowing precious little about fostering, I was aware it was a huge ask for anybody, and I was very grateful to him for supporting me so generously, despite his own misgivings.

Inevitably, we did find the process gruelling. Even providing basic facts was harder than we anticipated. For a start, it turned out that between us we'd lived in seven different rented flats in the city, and some of them were very short term and we had trouble remembering the addresses. However, far more difficult was dealing with an obstacle we hadn't anticipated. On his stag night, Jonathan's friends had thought it would be a laugh to do a runner from the Chinese restaurant they took him to. He was quite drunk and, in his inebriated state, Jonathan went along with the ill-advised plan. Unfortunately, the restaurant owner swiftly called the police, and Jonathan and his five friends were caught running down the high street, arrested and eventually fined £30 each for their misdemeanour. The upshot of it was that Jonathan had a criminal record, which had to be declared on our form F.

'I hope I haven't messed this up for us,' he said. 'I feel absolutely terrible about this.'

'Look,' I said. 'It's a one-off mistake on your stag night, over a decade ago, and you didn't even instigate it. I really don't think that will go against us.'

'Well we don't know, do we? We'll have to cross our fingers and hope for the best.'

'I'm sure it will be fine. I'm really sorry this has been dragged up though, Jonathan. I didn't for one minute think it would be.'

'It's not your fault. Actually, it's made me realise I don't want to fail. I'll be upset now, if things fall through before we've had the chance to try.'

Unfortunately, as if to test our nerve even more, the interviews were much more intense and intrusive than we'd imagined they might be. Jonathan was in tears describing to the Social Services official who came to our home how his father beat him, and how he suffered from low self-esteem for many years as a result. Similarly, I became surprisingly upset when I relived how I had to stay with Aunt Hattie when my mother went to visit my father at the drying out clinic. I cried too, when I remembered how I'd overheard the row between my parents about my father's drinking, the one when my mother threatened to throw him out if he didn't stop.

'It's me and Angela or the bottle,' my mother had shrieked. 'It's a straight choice. You decide, Trevor!'

I was five years old, lying in bed and pushing my little palms as tightly together as possible, silently praying.

'Please choose us, Daddy,' I said in my head. 'Pleeeease, Daddy. Choose us! Choose us!'

It was very upsetting indeed to bring this memory to the forefront of my mind, as it was one I had buried deep and not revisited for many, many years.

'Would you describe your childhood as unhappy?' I was asked after telling my story.

'No,' I said truthfully. 'This was one of very few occasions when I was aware my father had a problem. My mother did a phenomenal job of protecting me from his drinking, and of helping him give up alcohol.'

'Would you say you had a happy childhood then?'

'Yes,' I replied. 'Without question. I was well cared for and never wanted for anything. I didn't know how bad my father's drinking had been until I was grown up and about to marry. My mother was extremely hard working and capable, and I have spoken to her about our fostering application and she is very supportive to this day, and would give us any help she could in our role as carers.'

Jonathan and I also had to describe exactly how we met and what our lives were like when we first got together, after we moved to the city and when we eventually married. Next we were interviewed together and separately about our friends and associates, our mental and physical health, our plans to have children, our financial situation and the strength of our commitment to each other.

I have heard other foster carers describe how their previous partners have been grilled too as part of the process, but as neither of us had been in a serious relationship before we got together this was irrelevant. Incidentally, over the years I have also heard tales of potential foster carers being put off because of negative comments and feedback from their previous partners. Social workers are careful to take into account the fact break-ups may have been acrimonious, but it still strikes me as harsh that the input from a disgruntled ex could scupper a person's ambitions to foster.

Anyhow, the process was incredibly gruelling and exhausting for Jonathan and I, and when it came to the question of his criminal record my optimism about how it would be handled unfortunately turned out to be misplaced. To my dismay, Jonathan's arrest and fine were taken incredibly seriously, with Jonathan being grilled at length. He was left feeling embarrassed, remorseful and extremely concerned about whether the incident had jeopardised our application. We were on tenterhooks when a social worker representing us finally had to go in front of a panel of Social Services officials to find out if we'd been passed or not. It had actually taken twelve months to get that far, rather than the suggested six, as the social worker dealing with our form F was overloaded with work. Just like for this review meeting today, Jonathan and I were kept waiting in a small, stuffy room in a hot, airless council building, trussed up in our smart clothes, and feeling incredibly nervous about what the outcome would be. I can clearly remember the moment when the social worker came out of the meeting and walked along the corridor towards us, to deliver the verdict. My pulse quickened and I could see Jonathan's jaw tense as she approached.

'Congratulations! You have been passed for two children!' is about the only phrase I can remember hearing, though I'm sure she also filled us in on how the meeting had gone.

'Really? That is just fantastic!' I exclaimed. 'I honestly can't believe it.'

I was euphoric and incredibly relieved.

Jonathan was grinning like the Cheshire Cat. 'I feel like I've won the Pools!' he said. 'I'm absolutely delighted.'

Back then, of course, we were focused on all the positives we had in store: what a pleasure it would be to look after lots of different children and give them a comfortable, happy home, if only for a little while. We knew the kids might have issues and problems, but we innocently believed that there was nothing that couldn't be put right with love, and the provision of a safe, comfortable home.

Sitting here today, waiting anxiously for a review with a teenager like Vicky, whom we'd grown very attached to but might lose at any moment, was not something we had anticipated. Her future was hanging in the balance and we cared very deeply about her indeed. If the social workers decided she was moving out we'd be very sorry to see her go, but we would simply have to accept the ruling and hope it was for the best.

I looked at Vicky and felt my stomach turn. What it must have been like for her I could only guess; I felt nauseous with nerves. I was not only dreading the meeting, but I was fretting about what would happen next week, next month and next year in this young girl's life.

The black plastic minute hand of the clock above the door clicked around to quarter past the hour, making the same slightly louder tick it had done on the hour. Jonathan stood up and paced around the ten metre square room I was now beginning to feel encased in, and Vicky put her head in her hands.

'This is horrible,' she muttered. 'Why is it taking so long?'

'Mr Williams must be running late,' I said. 'We will just have to be patient.'

'What about *her*?'

'I'm sorry, Vicky. I know as much as you, sweetheart. I don't know what's going on with your mother.'

I'd heard several cars in the car park while we'd been sitting and waiting but I didn't look out the window, and nor did Vicky. The room fell silent again, apart from the ticking of the clock, and it felt to me as if the temperature was rising with every second that passed. My clothes were sticking to me and my hands felt clammy. I desperately wanted to say or do something – anything – that would make the waiting easier or the situation better, but I felt helpless. In my head I was imagining myself saying to Vicky, 'So what does your mother look like?' because I really wanted to know, but of course I didn't want to ask that question. I could see that Vicky was struggling more and more as the waiting went on, and I certainly didn't want to make matters worse. She was pale and looked scared to death, poor girl.

'Are none of the magazines any good?' Jonathan asked, nodding towards the table Vicky was seated beside.

Vicky completely ignored him, her eyes now focused on the grey carpet squares at her feet. She was sitting incredibly still and was now staring down at the floor in an almost trance-like state.

'You might like *Auto Trader*,' I said to Jonathan.

'Let's see,' he said, picking up one of the dog-eared copies, which had a circular coffee stain on the front. 'Well I never, there's an article in this one about towing. That could be interesting.'

'Why's that?' I asked.

'Well I was thinking next time we changed the car we should get one with a tow bar, because then we could get a touring caravan.'

'A touring caravan! I didn't know we were going down that route, Jonathan.'

'I'm not sure really, but we've loved all of our caravan holidays, haven't we? Maybe getting one of our own is the next step. What do you think of that idea, Vicky?'

We both looked at Vicky but she seemed oblivious to the

conversation we'd just had. I imagined her blurting, *What do I care, Jonathan! I don't even know if I'll be living with you, do I?*, which would have been a fairly reasonable response given the circumstances.

I felt like shouting something similar myself, if the truth be told. It was unacceptable to be kept waiting like this. This meeting was about Vicky's future, and it seemed cruel to add to her distress in this way. She continued to gaze anxiously at the floor and her hands were now wedged beneath her thighs, which was a tactic I'd seen her employ before when she was trying not to bite her nails. Her shoulders were sunken and her chin was on her chest, and Vicky looked incredibly frail and vulnerable. The sudden shriek of tyres skidding onto the tarmac of the car park cut through the silence, drowning out the sound of the ticking clock and our collective breathing. Vicky sprang to her feet and then immediately froze, as if she'd been shot with a stun gun.

'It's all right, love,' I said, getting up and glancing out of the window behind our row of chairs.

'Don't panic. It's all going to be all right. It's only Mr Williams arriving.'

Vicky didn't appear to register the fact I'd just spoken to her.

'Are you all right, sweetheart? Can you hear me? Vicky, love, why don't you sit down again?'

She said nothing, but she did allow me to guide her gently back into her seat, and then she sat rigid on the edge of it. Moments later Mr Williams blustered into the room, attempting to tame his combed-over hair, which had been

151

dislodged from his bald patch and was now sticking to his sweaty brow.

'Sorry to keep you waiting,' he said. 'Dreadful traffic. Right then, please follow me.'

Jonathan and I stood up and I rubbed the top of Vicky's arm.

'Come on, love.'

Her eyes were bulging in her head and she appeared to be staring straight through me. I felt her shudder, and then she blinked several times.

'Is she . . . ?'

'Mr Williams!' I called. 'Can I just ask you . . . ?'

He had already turned and left the room, so I darted to the door and stuck my head out.

'Mr Williams!'

He was several paces away from me, charging along the corridor, so I dashed after him, leaving Vicky and Jonathan in the meeting room.

'Can you hang on a moment?' I called, at which point Mr Williams stopped and turned, allowing me to catch him up. 'Vicky is very anxious about seeing her mother. Is she here?'

'No, she's not here yet. She must have got caught in the traffic too.'

'I see. Right, I'll go and fetch Vicky.'

Once I'd explained that her mother was not in the building some of Vicky's tension seemed to leave her body, and she got to her feet and followed me, Jonathan and Mr Williams quietly to the meeting room along the corridor. Hayley gave a relieved smile when we all entered, and she indicated that we could sit wherever we liked around the large oval table. Vicky placed herself between myself and Jonathan and Mr Williams sat facing us, next to Hayley, who handed each of us a sheet of paper headed with the date and time of the review. Also on the paper was an explanation that the meeting was primarily to discuss the possibility of Vicky going back to live with Lorraine.

'I'm afraid we'll have to get started without your mother,' Hayley said to Vicky once we were all seated. 'The meeting is already running half an hour late and we can't wait any longer.'

Vicky nodded. 'I'm glad about that. I never want to see her again.'

Mr Williams didn't seem to acknowledge the gravity of this remark; he was reading some paperwork which may or may not have been related to Vicky's case. Hayley then explained to Mr Williams that Vicky would like to return to live with her sister but was happy to stay with us until Lorraine was ready and willing to have her back. Then she asked Vicky, myself and Jonathan some brief questions about whether or not we had any issues we wanted to discuss, and how comfortable we all were with the placement.

'I'm happy to stay with Angela and Jonathan while Lorraine sorts herself out,' Vicky reiterated. 'Nothing has changed since last time I spoke to you. I just don't want to live with my mum.'

Jonathan and I confirmed that we were very happy to continue the placement, and we also answered some standard questions about how Vicky was getting on, such as any behaviour issues we'd faced and how we'd dealt with them. We gave the dates of appointments we had made for the opticians and dentist, and we confirmed we'd taken Vicky to the doctors and explained that she had been given an inhaler and told to stop smoking by the GP.

'And have you stopped smoking?' Mr Williams asked.

'Not completely, but I'm smoking a lot less. It's hard.'

'Well done,' Hayley interjected. 'I think it would be a good idea if you drew up a contract with Angela and Jonathan. In it you should agree to continue the good work towards stopping smoking completely; agree to work hard on controlling your cheekiness, particularly in front of customers in the shop, and to keep your room tidier and stick to the house rule of no food upstairs.'

Vicky's face lit up.

'That's a deal. Does that mean I'm staying with Jonathan and Angela, and I don't have to go to my mum's?'

'For the time being, yes. I've spoken to Lorraine and she is not ready to have you back with her. She needs more time to settle in with the baby. As your mother is not here we can't discuss a return to her care, so you will be staying with Angela and Jonathan.'

'OK,' Vicky said, breathing out deeply. 'I'm happy with that. Does it mean I never have to go back to my mum's?'

'I'm afraid I can't say that, Vicky. I need to hear what your mother has to say. I will have to find out why she isn't here, and I will need to arrange another meeting.'

Mr Williams lifted up his paperwork, tapped it into a neat pile on the table and asked Hayley, 'Will that be all?'

which of course prompted Jonathan and I to share a knowing look.

'Yes,' she replied. 'We will carry on with this placement and I will arrange further meetings with Vicky's mother and sister in due course. Are you happy if we conclude there for today?'

Jonathan and I swapped another quick glance, giving each other a discreet smile. 'We're happy,' I said to Hayley. 'Thank you for your time, Mr Williams.'

'Thank you,' he said, checking his watch. 'I'll just sign the paperwork and we can all go,' he added, reaching across and placing a squiggle on the form Hayley had filled in during the meeting.

Once he'd left the room Hayley got to her feet and declared, 'There! It wasn't that bad, was it?' to which Vicky replied, 'It was a waste of time really, wasn't it?'

'Vicky!' I scolded. 'You can't say that.'

'Well it's true. Nothing changed. I'm not complaining, I'm just saying.'

Hayley smiled. 'Remember your contract!' she teased gently. 'Less cheek, please, young lady!'

Vicky smiled. 'OK!' she said, saluting Hayley. 'Message received and understood!'

As we left the building Vicky turned to me excitedly. I expected her to say something about the meeting and its outcome, but instead she asked if she could go out with her friends that evening.

'Of course,' I said. 'As long as you're back by 10 p.m. that is fine.'

'Thanks, Angela!' she said brightly. 'I'll be home on time, I promise.'

It was the first time Vicky had referred to our house as her home. She didn't appear to register this, but it certainly didn't escape my attention and I was very pleased that she saw it that way. We still had no idea how long she would be staying with us, but right now that didn't matter. Vicky was happy and her fear had subsided, for today at least.

# 10

## *'I don't want to know about Vicky'*

When Vicky and Michelle went back to school they slotted easily into the routine they'd established before the end of term in July. The only difference was that after a couple of days Vicky started taking the bus with Michelle, as she said it would help in her continuing battle to stop smoking. In the evenings they both did their homework and spent some time in each other's rooms before coming down for dinner together, and Michelle had somehow managed to get Vicky to wear the new shirts and use the pencil case I'd bought her: to this day I've no idea how.

'Do you know, they've become as thick as thieves,' I found myself saying to Jonathan one evening, as the girls had been so engrossed in whatever they were doing they had to be called three times to come downstairs to eat.

'I've noticed that too. I never would have thought they'd get on so well. It's great to see.'

Unfortunately, one evening I noticed Michelle wasn't

quite herself around the table, and I took her to one side as soon as we'd cleared the dishes away.

'What's the matter?' I asked. 'Has something happened at school?'

'No, it's not that, Angela. I've been dreading telling you this, but it's about Florida. My mum really has put her foot down and it's as I thought. I can't go, there's no way.'

By now Hayley had also taken over as Michelle's social worker. She had picked up where Tricia left off and had been talking to Maureen about the holiday, hoping to nudge her in our direction despite her reservations about the hotel accommodation. I'd been so focused on Vicky's review that I hadn't chased Hayley up on this for a week or so, but the last I'd heard was that Hayley was hopeful she could talk Maureen round.

'Really? Are you absolutely sure, Michelle?'

'Certain. She said that is her final word and she really means it.'

'OK. Let me talk to Hayley again,' I said. 'I'm sure there must be a way of fixing this for you.'

It took me three days to get hold of Hayley, and when I did so she said she'd call round and see me straight after work the following evening.

'Great,' I said. 'I'd like to sort this out as soon as possible. Apart from anything else I need to pay the next instalment on the holiday shortly.'

'I understand. Actually, I also have several other things to discuss, some involving Vicky. It's been a busy week. Can you make sure both girls are in?'

'Yes, of course.'

'Great. See you tomorrow. By the way, would it be all right for me to come to the front door rather than through the shop?'

'Yes, no problem. I've remembered about your hay fever. I'll also make sure we don't have flowers in the house.'

'Brilliant! Thanks so much. I know summer's over but I don't want to take any chances.'

Jonathan was out making a delivery when Hayley arrived. She was looking uncharacteristically sombre, and I was hoping Jonathan would hurry home, as I instinctively felt this was going to be a difficult meeting.

'Both girls are in their bedrooms,' I said, showing her up to the lounge. 'Please make yourself comfortable. Shall I make us some tea?'

'No, thanks, I've not long had one,' Hayley said, perching herself on the edge of the settee.

'I have quite a lot to say about both Michelle and Vicky,' she went on, taking out her files. 'It's been an incredibly hectic week in the office, and there are several issues and developments to discuss. Can I have a word with Michelle privately, before we begin?'

'Of course. I'll fetch her.'

Michelle looked sheepish when I brought her down to the lounge, and I left her and Hayley together while I went to the kitchen to get myself a glass of water.

'Just give me a shout when you want me back,' I said.

'I will do,' Hayley said.

Ten minutes went by before I heard the lounge door open and Michelle climb the stairs back up to her bedroom.

'Are you there, Angela?' Hayley called down to me.

'Coming!' I said as cheerfully as I could manage, though I was trying to swallow the lump in my throat.

Hayley didn't beat around the bush.

'Right,' she announced as soon as I was back in the lounge. 'Michelle has been telling her mother that you and Jonathan are too strict, and Maureen has put in a complaint.'

'Oh!' I said, extremely taken aback. 'In what way?'

'Michelle claims that you force her to scrub the floors, clean the toilets, do all the washing and ironing and peel sack loads of potatoes.'

I laughed indignantly.

'That's simply not true!' I said. 'Has she honestly said all that?'

'Yes, and her mother is hopping mad. She has asked if Michelle could be moved to another foster home. Needless to say, she has also refused permission for Florida.'

'OK,' I said, taking a deep breath, my mind going into overdrive. 'And I take it you've checked this with Michelle, and you aren't just taking Maureen's word for it?'

'Yes, I have spoken to Michelle about it just now, and she says it is all completely true.'

I was shocked to the core and it took me a moment or two to try to digest this information.

'Well!' I finally exclaimed, feeling myself getting very annoyed indeed. 'I think this is Maureen's way of derailing the holiday once and for all. She has been awkward about it all along. I think she regrets giving her permission in the first place.'

'OK,' Hayley said, jotting down some notes. 'What Maureen has said is that she has lost trust in you as foster carers, and she doesn't want you taking her daughter out of the country.'

'That is just so unfair and unbelievable! And the most outrageous thing is that Michelle is the loser in all this!'

Jonathan walked into the room to hear my outburst, and once the details had been explained to him he was equally cross and indignant.

'I'm actually really bloody offended,' he said, which was a shock as he very rarely uses bad language. 'After all we've done for Michelle, I really can't believe it. I'm stunned.'

'So am I!' I added. 'I'd like to fetch Michelle back, to speak to her myself, if you don't mind, Hayley.'

'That's fine by me, if she's willing,' the social worker replied.

Minutes later, Michelle was installed on the settee beside me. She had looked embarrassed when I'd knocked on her bedroom door and asked her to come back down, and she hadn't said a word or given me any eye contact whatsoever as we returned to the lounge together.

Hayley spoke first.

'I have just explained to Angela and Jonathan that, ultimately, the reason your mother has refused to give permission for the holiday is because you have told her you are unhappy living here, as you are forced to do too many chores.'

Michelle blushed and remained tight-lipped.

'They are shocked by this and say it isn't true.'

'That's right,' I said, looking at Michelle. 'Because it's not true, is it?'

'Er, it is true, actually,' she said, looking intently at her Winnie the Pooh slippers.

'Michelle!' I gasped.

'Just a moment, Angela,' Hayley said. 'Can you repeat what you told me earlier, when you described the chores you say you have to do?'

'Er, all the cooking and cleaning and washing and stuff,' Michelle muttered.

'Michelle! I ask you to do the bare minimum of chores that any fourteen-year-old would be expected to help with around the home!'

'It's too much!' she shouted. 'I want to go home! I want to go back to my mum!'

With that she ran out of the lounge and back up to her bedroom, and then she refused to come out or even speak to anybody.

'I'm afraid parents can sometimes cause the breakdown of a placement, even when this does not put their child's best interests first,' Hayley consoled. 'But I'm sure you know that already.'

Jonathan and I looked at each other in despair.

'We know that in theory,' I said. 'But we've never experienced the breakdown of a placement before. And of all the children, Michelle is the person we would have least expected this to happen with.'

'I do sympathise,' Hayley said. 'I'll need to discuss the case with my manager, but I'm very glad you are in the picture. Is there anything you would like me to report back?'

'Yes, there certainly is. I want it to be stated very clearly that Jonathan and I have never, and would never, place unreasonable demands on any child in our care. We have nothing but Michelle's best interests at heart. She has willingly helped with chores like clearing the table and keeping her bedroom tidy, and she has regularly volunteered to peel vegetables and help with the cooking, but she has never been forced to do so.'

I spoke firmly and confidently. I wanted to set the record straight, and I was very keen that this breakdown would not affect the way Social Services viewed us as foster carers.

Hayley scribbled some notes in her pad, reassured us she would prioritise discussing Michelle's case with her manager, and then swiftly moved the conversation on to Vicky.

'There is good and bad news to report regarding Vicky,' she stated, which made me catch my breath.

'Go on,' I said, afraid of what Hayley might say next.

'I'm sorry to tell you that her sister, Lorraine, is in hospital. She took an overdose a few days ago.'

'No! Oh my God, is she going to be all right?'

'As far as we know it appears to have been a cry for help. She's been struggling with the baby, and her husband has reported that she has a history of depression. It's not the first time she has done this, apparently.'

'That's terrible! What does this mean for Vicky?'

'It certainly rules out a return to her sister's home, in the foreseeable future, at least.'

'So she'll continue staying with us?'

Hayley hesitated and I had a dreadful feeling she was going to talk about Vicky's mother.

'You've spoken to her, haven't you? Brenda?'

'Yes. I knocked on her door last week and she actually answered it long enough to tell me she does not want to know about Vicky.'

I gasped, feeling a mixture of shock, upset and relief. Brenda had been so elusive that in my mind's eye I'd started to view her as an almost fictional, ghost-like figure, shut away from our reality. Now she was suddenly catapulted into my conscience as a living, breathing human being, and I felt a wave of fear that she could somehow cause further heartache for Vicky now she was back in the picture. My mind was reeling. I was horrified that any mother could be so cruel and dismissive towards her own daughter, but I took some comfort from the fact that at least Vicky would not be returning to her mother.

'Can I ask . . . what exactly did Vicky's mother say?'

'Just as I said,' Hayley replied. 'I think her exact words were: "I don't want to know about Vicky." She opened her front door for all of the ten seconds it took to deliver the sentence, and then she slammed it shut, telling me not to bother coming back.'

'You mentioned good news,' I ventured.

'Yes, we've made some progress in finding out more about Vicky's father.'

'Oh. That sounds promising.'

'Let's hope so. Lorraine went round to Brenda's with the baby a few days before she took the overdose, and she managed to obtain Vicky's birth certificate, along with a little bit of information.'

I was on tenterhooks, desperately wanting to know more about Vicky's dad. I was also concerned about what may have happened to Lorraine during the visit to her mother, and whether it contributed to her taking the pills.

'So Vicky's father is still alive?' I asked, probably quite impatiently.

'We don't know. What we do know is that he was in the Armed Forces and, though Vicky had always used the same name as her mother, she was actually given her father's surname, Taylor, at birth. We're very hopeful we'll know more soon. The Ministry of Defence is being very helpful.'

'Should we tell Vicky this?'

'I would like to tell her about Lorraine, as it's something I've been trained to deal with. Perhaps I could talk to her now, if she's here? I'm happy for you to stay in the room, if she has no objection.'

Jonathan and I both nodded.

'It's fine,' I said. 'I'll go and get her. Will you mention the progress with her dad?'

'Yes, if I think it's appropriate after telling her about

Lorraine. Let's see how she is. Needless to say, I will not tell her exactly what her mother said.'

Vicky was quietly doing her homework when I went up to her room, and when she came to answer my knock on her door she looked very pleased to see me.

'Look, Angela! I got an A for my home economics,' she said, showing me a marked test paper. 'I want to show your mum, because do you know what got me lots of marks? It was remembering the rhubarb crumble recipe by heart.'

'Really?' I said, recalling how she broke the microwave the first time she made it.

'Yes! I even remembered to bake it in the oven at gas mark 6 for half an hour. Mind you, I won't forget that in a hurry, will I?'

'No, I don't expect you will! Listen, Vicky, Hayley's downstairs and she has some news for you. Can you come and talk to her?'

'What news?' she asked, a flash of fear flickering in her eyes

'I'll let her tell you, but don't worry, you don't have to go back to your mum's house.'

Her frightened expression softened.

'That's all right then. As long as it's not that, I don't care.'

Of course, when Hayley explained what had happened to Lorraine she did care, very deeply. As soon as she heard the word 'overdose' she went into a frozen trance, staring through us and appearing not to hear any of our voices, no matter what we said.

'Lorraine is going to be fine,' Hayley reassured. 'The doctors and nurses are looking after her, and the baby is perfectly safe and happy too, being cared for by your brother-in-law. You don't need to worry, Vicky. Your sister is in good hands and the doctors say she will make a full recovery. She'll be out of hospital in a day or two.'

When Vicky failed to respond to Hayley, I tried to bring her round by reiterating the fact she would not have to return to her mother's and could stay with us.

'That's good news, isn't it, sweetheart?' I said. 'You can stay here, with me and Jonathan. We'll keep looking after you while Lorraine gets better.'

After about a minute of total silence Hayley broached the subject of Vicky's father.

'We've found out something about your dad, Vicky,' Hayley said softly.

There was no response, and Vicky's glazed eyes didn't flicker.

'Your dad was a soldier. He served in Northern Ireland before you were born.'

Vicky turned to look at Hayley, her head clicking slowly round in the mechanical, puppet-like way it had done when she had panicked in the delivery van with me. Once she was looking straight at Hayley, Vicky released a long, slow breath and blinked rapidly several times.

'Is he . . . still alive?' she asked quietly, barely moving her lips.

'We don't know yet, but we will find out shortly. The Army has agreed to help us find out more about him.'

'Wow,' she said. 'Maybe that's why he was nasty, being in Northern Ireland. That's got to be hard.'

I caught Hayley's eye.

'I have been trying to explain that Vicky's father might not have been nasty,' I said. 'Her mother said he was nasty, but that might just be her opinion.'

'Angela has a very good point, Vicky. As soon as I hear any more I'll be in touch, and hopefully you can judge for yourself, when we know more about him.'

'What if he's dead?' she said flatly.

'Well, you will still get to know more about him. His name is Vincent Taylor, by the way. The Army will be able to tell us more, very shortly, I hope.'

'OK,' she shrugged, looking thoughtful and giving the tiniest flicker of a smile. 'Can I go back to my room now?'

Hayley nodded. 'Thanks, Vicky. It's a lot to take in. Are you feeling all right?'

'Yes, I think so.'

After we saw Hayley out, Jonathan and I asked each other the same question.

'I feel like I've been hit over the head,' I said. 'My nerves are jangling.'

'I feel the same,' he replied, squeezing my hand. 'I'm so shocked by Michelle, it's unbelievable, isn't it?'

'Totally. I never expected that in a million years. As for Lorraine, I suppose it explains a lot. It's hardly surprising she put Vicky in care if she was so vulnerable herself. And I guess it's no wonder she was so unreliable about sending

Vicky's belongings, or that she wasn't up to having visitors after she had the baby.'

We sat in silence for quite some time, trying to digest all we'd heard in the last hour, and then Jonathan went out to pick up a takeaway. Michelle refused to come down and eat with us, but Vicky ate heartily before getting ready to go to the youth club with her friends.

'Can I come home at 10.30 p.m. tonight?' she asked.

'No!' I said. 'The nights are drawing in and it's term time. I want you back by 9.30 p.m., please.'

'Will it be dark then?'

'Yes, it will be. Do you want a lift?'

'No, thanks. I can get myself home. No need to send a search party!'

'No need to be cheeky, Vicky!' I smiled, glad to see her in such good spirits, considering all she had heard that evening.

She winked at me and swaggered out of the house with her 'gangster gait' as I'd jokingly started to call it.

'Thanks, Angela!' she called. 'You're a diamond!'

'All right, love. Have a good time!'


The next morning everybody was up early. Jonathan was manning the shop, Vicky was coming with me on my deliveries and Michelle was going to spend the weekend with her dad. She could barely look me in the eye when we met in the kitchen.

'Morning, Michelle!' I said brightly. I wanted her to

know I was not holding a grudge, although clearly the matter of her lies and allegations was far from resolved.

'Morning,' she just about muttered as she helped herself to a glass of milk, drank it down quickly and then headed back upstairs.

'What time are you back tomorrow, love?' I called after her.

'Dunno.'

'Will you let me know? We'll be at my mum's for Sunday lunch. I expect you won't be back for that?'

There was no reply, and so I finished my breakfast and went to work, taking Vicky with me and leaving a note for Michelle on the kitchen worktop.

'Michelle,' I wrote hastily. 'Please ring me when you get to your dad's and let me know what time you are home tomorrow. If you need a lift back, no problem. Remember it's a school night so home for 9.30 p.m. at the latest please. I hope you have a good time, Angela xxx'

Vicky was in a bubbly mood as she helped me make the deliveries that morning. Her birthday was coming up soon, and I asked her if there was anything she particularly wanted, or something special she might like to do.

'I don't know,' she said. 'I've never had a birthday present or a party. I'll be happy with anything, really!'

As she spoke I was holding a huge bouquet of pink and white flowers that had been ordered for an eighteenth birthday party. On the tag it said: 'To our wonderful daughter. We are very proud of you and hope you enjoy your special day. Lots of love, Mum and Dad xx'. I'd written the message out myself after taking the order over the phone, and as I did so I'd thought how lucky the teenager was who would be in receipt of such a lovely gift. Now that feeling overwhelmed me, and I was heartbroken that Vicky had never received a single present, let alone one as beautiful and heartfelt as this.

'We'll have to put that right!' I smiled. 'Have a think if there is anything you might like, perhaps a piece of jewellery or something to keep? And what about going out for a meal?'

'I'd love that!' she said. 'That would be great! Can we go to that new pizza place?'

'Why not! I'll break my diet especially for the occasion.'

'What, again?!'

'Cheeky!'

The mention of dieting turned my mind to the holiday. I had to accept that whatever happened next with Michelle, Maureen had finally scuppered our chances of taking her daughter to Disney World. It had dawned on me that we might be able to change the name on the booking and take Vicky instead of Michelle, but I kept my thoughts to myself at this stage, resolving to discuss this with Hayley when the time was right. The holiday was still six months off, and I supposed we'd have to wait and see what happened next in the search for Vicky's father before we made any plans that far into the future.

Michelle did not phone as I'd asked her to, but she was in her bedroom on Sunday afternoon when Jonathan, Vicky and I returned from lunch at my mother's house.

'Do you want a cup of tea, love?' I called through Michelle's door. 'I'm just putting the kettle on.'

'No, thanks.'

'Can I come in?'

'No, I'm just getting changed.'

'All right. Are you sure you're OK?'

'What?'

I heard her music go on and decided to leave her to it for a while, but when I went back upstairs later she was equally monosyllabic.

'Michelle, love, are you feeling all right?' I called.

'Yes, just tired,' she said. 'I'm going to have an early night.'

'All right, can I come in to say goodnight?'

'Oh God! Do you have to?'

'I'd like to. I haven't seen you for two days.'

'All right then.'

Her light was off and I tripped over a bag in the middle of the floor as I crossed the room.

'Sleep well, love. I'll see you in the morning. Night night.'

'Night,' she said half-heartedly.

In hindsight I can see that Michelle knew something I didn't, but at the time I didn't suspect a thing. On Monday morning, Michelle told Vicky she was walking to school and not taking the bus as she usually did.

'That's a turnaround,' I said when I caught her heading out the door much earlier than usual. 'I thought you didn't like walking to school.'

'I'm entitled to change my mind,' Michelle replied

rudely before slamming out of the front door with a scowl on her face.

I was glad to be at work that day. There were lots of orders to make up, and I always found it quite therapeutic to arrange bouquets and create fancy bows and trimmings with my floristry ribbons. I liked chatting to customers too, and I found it a pleasure helping them to select the right blooms for whatever occasion they had in mind.

When there were no customers in the shop there was always a wonderful calmness in the air, and I'd often take a deep breath, appreciate the wonderful scents of the flowers and count my blessings while I had a little bit of peace and quiet. Taking over the shop had proved to be a great move for me and Jonathan. We worked extremely well together, and fostering had fitted into our lifestyle as we'd hoped it would. Of course, it was stressful dealing with teenage strops and finding ourselves embroiled in the complications we had on our plate right now, but we could manage it, and we were well aware that our lives were very easy compared to so many others.

Very sadly, our young nephew had received more bad news, and we had learned that Aiden's chances of recovering from leukaemia had declined rapidly, to less than twenty per cent. It was unbelievably tragic, and whenever I felt any sort of discontentment with my lot in life I reminded myself how very fortunate I was to have my health. I was also lucky to have a strong and supportive husband, a good business and the means to follow my heart and work as a foster carer. We could not cure my nephew, but Jonathan and I could be there for him and his family, and at least we could help other children, if not him.

I don't know how long I'd been lost in my thoughts, but when the shop's bell rang out very loudly, late on that Monday morning, I nearly jumped out of my skin. It gave the emergency clatter it had done on the day Vicky had barged through the shop in a bad temper. When I looked up at the person standing before me I was even more alarmed.

'Hayley!' I said, immediately thinking about her hay fever and aversion to coming into the shop. 'Whatever is it?'

She looked very flustered indeed.

'I've got some bad news I'm afraid, Angela.'

'Vicky's father?' I instinctively said. 'Is he . . . not alive?'

'It's not that. It's Vicky's mum.'

'What about her?' I stammered, feeling a shockwave pass through me.

'She's dead, Angela. Vicky's mum died yesterday.'

# 11

## *'It's too much to take'*

On Hayley's advice, I decided to wait until Vicky got home from school before telling her about her mum's death. I was in full agreement that it would be better for her to hear it at home, rather than in the school environment, and Hayley gave me some advice on how to handle it, as she had to travel to a social-worker conference that afternoon and so couldn't come over to help.

'Just stick to the few facts we know, and don't be drawn in to any speculation or attempt to answer questions you aren't sure of the answer to,' Hayley said. 'Make sure Vicky's sitting down and tell her you are there to support her, and that you will do everything you can to help her deal with it. As for her father, let's leave that until another day.'

It turned out that just a few days before Brenda's death, Hayley had discovered Vicky's father was alive and living in the UK, albeit many miles away from us. The Army had an address for him, and Hayley was planning to write an initial letter to Vincent to ask if he was happy to make contact with Vicky.

'In the circumstances, I think it's best to wait for his response until informing Vicky that he is alive,' Hayley said. 'Let's deal with her mother's death first.'

It was nearly 5 p.m. when Vicky returned home, as she had netball practice after school. Michelle wasn't home yet either as she also had an after-school club on Mondays this term, but I expected her back shortly.

'I'm starving!' Vicky declared when she walked in the shop. 'What's for tea?'

'Oh, hi, love. Er, chops. Listen, I need to talk to you. I'll come through to the house with you now.'

Vicky looked at me suspiciously as I turned the shop sign to display 'closed' and led her up to the lounge; my thinking was that when Michelle returned and found the shop shut she would walk straight into the kitchen, so it was better if Vicky and I went upstairs, where we could talk in private.

'What is it?' Vicky asked, sounding agitated. 'Please don't tell me they've made a mistake and I have to go back to *her*!'

'No, Vicky, it's not that,' I said as we entered the lounge. 'Sit yourself down on the settee, and I'll tell you, love.'

Vicky obliged, though worry was now filling her face and I wanted to get on with this as quickly as possible.

'There is no easy way of saying this, but I'm afraid . . .'

'Is Lorraine all right?' she interrupted. 'Oh my God has she done it again?'

'It's not Lorraine, she's fine. It's your mum, Vicky. I'm very sorry to tell you this, but she passed away, last night.'

'Passed away? You mean died? My mum's . . . *dead*?'

Vicky's mouth fell open and then she immediately froze, a look of sheer terror etched on her face. For a split second I thought she was going to say something else as she appeared to move her lips ever so slightly, but no sound came out. Then her whole face turned a chalky white, as if she were numb with shock. From past experience I knew that this was Vicky's standard response when she was very upset or frightened. I also knew it would pass, and so I didn't panic as I had done the first time she'd reacted this way; I just kept talking. Taking hold of her right hand, which felt cold and stiff, I began to tell Vicky the few scant details we knew, as Hayley had advised me to do.

'We don't yet know how your mum died, love,' I said. 'Alf, her friend next door, found her, in the house, last night.'

When I mentioned Alf's name Vicky started to breathe more rapidly, though her face remained inanimate and only her chest moved, very quickly, in time with her breathing.

'It's all right, love, just try to slow down and take some long, deep breaths.'

For a second or two Vicky appeared to hold her breath. Her eyes were fixed in a faraway stare, but thankfully she did eventually start to breathe normally again. Her face and body stayed rigid and lifeless though, apart from the now tiny movement of her lungs in her chest.

'We'll know more later in the week, hopefully. Lorraine has been told, and Carl is looking after her and the baby at the flat.'

Vicky didn't respond in any way at all.

'Would you like to see Lorraine?'

Again there was no response at all; not even a flicker or the slightest sign that Vicky was even aware I had spoken.

I sat quietly beside her for five or maybe ten minutes, simply holding her hand, saying soothing words and offering her support and kindness.

'I'm here for you, Vicky,' I said softly. 'If there is anything I can do to help, just say. I'll help you through this as best I can, you know that, love, don't you? Jonathan and I will look after you. I'm very sorry, love. It must be such an awful shock.'

As we sat in silence together I heard the shop's van pull up outside the house. Jonathan had been out for most of the day, seeing our accountant and visiting suppliers. I'd managed to tell him the news when he phoned me in the afternoon, and he had naturally been very shocked and concerned about how Vicky would take it. Minutes after the van's engine cut out I heard voices downstairs; Michelle must be home too, I thought. I didn't want to leave Vicky alone and I knew I could rely on Jonathan to say the right things to Michelle, so I stayed in the lounge, holding Vicky's hand. I expected Jonathan to appear at any moment, but another ten or fifteen minutes passed. I heard Michelle clatter up and down the stairs once, twice and then three times, and after that I heard another vehicle pull up outside. I rubbed the back of Vicky's hand with my free hand, telling her I was just going to let go of her for a minute.

'I just want to look out the window,' I said. 'I want to see who's outside.'

For a moment I wondered if Lorraine or her husband had turned up. I wasn't expecting anybody else to call at the house so I was curious to see who was there, but Vicky suddenly clutched at my hand really tightly, as if she were afraid to let me go.

'It's all right, sweetheart,' I said, responding by giving her hand a reassuring squeeze. 'I don't need to move. I'm not going anywhere.'

Vicky's grasp relaxed slightly when I said this, but she continued to look scared, and her lips were now very pale and set in an oval shape, as if she were halfway through giving a gasp. Time seemed to stand still as I sat there, listening and waiting, wondering what on earth was going on downstairs. Finally, a full half hour after he had returned home, Jonathan appeared at the lounge door, looking extremely agitated and upset.

'How are you, Vicky?' he asked, crossing the room and crouching down in front of her, so he could look up into her downcast face. She didn't blink or move or speak, and Jonathan looked at me.

'She's very shocked, of course. I've told her we're here for her. She needs to just take her time.'

'I'm very sorry to hear about your mum,' Jonathan said,

trying to catch Vicky's gaze once more. 'It's very sad news. It must be a terrible shock, I really am very, very sorry.'

Vicky didn't react in any way whatsoever. Next, Jonathan inhaled and scratched the back of his head, as he has a habit of doing when he is gearing up to say something he'd rather not have to.

'Er, Angela,' he said hesitantly. 'I'm afraid I need to just borrow you for a moment. Do you think I can have a word, in private?'

I looked at Vicky.

'I can't really leave her,' I said anxiously.

'Angela, it's very important. Please?'

'Vicky, love,' I said. 'Will you be all right for just a minute? I'll just pop outside the room. I'll not be far away, I promise. I'll be right back.'

This time Vicky let me take my hand from hers and gave the faintest nod of the head, and Jonathan and I slipped outside. I knew he had something very serious to tell me, because Jonathan would not have taken me away from Vicky in such circumstances unless he really needed to.

'What is it?' I whispered, my stomach turning over.

'Michelle,' he said quietly. His voice started to falter as he continued. 'She's left, Angela. She wasn't even going to tell us, but I saw her.'

'Left? What do you mean? Where has she gone?'

'Her mother's.'

'Maureen's?'

'Yes, Maureen's. She's moved back in with her.'

'But her mother hasn't wanted her for years and years!

Oh my God, what's changed? What's happened? I don't like the sound of this at all.'

'I don't know,' Jonathan said. He was choking back tears now. 'I just don't know, Angela. I can't get over the fact she was just going to disappear. Maureen's boyfriend collected her; Michelle had all her bags packed, ready to go. She's left her key.'

I shook my head in disbelief and Jonathan and I locked eyes for a moment, sharing a look of incredulity.

'Does Hayley know?' I asked.

'I don't know. It's all happened so fast. I think Michelle was hoping to do a bunk while we were still in the shop. Look, you go back to Vicky. I'll phone the out-of-hours emergency number.'

Vicky didn't appear to have moved a muscle while I was out of the room. She was sitting upright on the edge of the settee and looked extremely tense and uncomfortable, so I suggested she should sit back a little. Vicky just stared at the carpet, but thankfully she did allow me to guide her backwards on the settee so she could at least support her rigid spine on the cushions. I sat back too, feelings of exhaustion and anger and sorrow enveloping me as the settee took my weight. My nerves felt pulled like elastic bands, ready to snap all around my body. Vicky's mother was dead, her father was alive and Michelle had gone back to Maureen. I just could not take it in. And how on earth had all this come crashing in on the same day? It felt like I was in some kind of badly staged tragedy, because the events felt so unreal and unexpected.

As Vicky and I sat in silence once again, my mind wandered back over the last few days, and my head started to ache. I thought about how Michelle had behaved, and what she had said a while back about the holiday, replaying her words in my head several times.

'I'd be worried if my child was going to the other side of the world with people I hardly knew.'

That was what Michelle had said, but the more I repeated the words the more I was certain they must have originated from her mother. Michelle knew us very well indeed. She'd lived with us for more than two years. By contrast, she had not lived with her mother since she was ten years old, when she was placed in the children's home. Michelle would turn fifteen in February next year, which meant Maureen had not had her daughter at home for the best part of five years. During her time with us Michelle had always been on a voluntary care order, so this was Maureen's choice. I understood she'd had a tough battle with her drug addiction, but in the past year or so her problems had been largely resolved and they didn't prohibit her from taking Michelle back. In my opinion she had left her daughter in care because it suited her.

Now I feared that Maureen was only taking Michelle back because she had the power to do so, and not necessarily because she had her daughter's best interests at heart. How long it would suit her for I shuddered to think, and I was extremely concerned – worried sick, in fact –

about the impact all this would have on Michelle. She clearly trusted her mum implicitly and would be shocked and traumatised if Maureen changed her mind and put her back in care, which from what I knew of Maureen's past behaviour, seemed a distinct possibility.

As for poor Vicky, whatever would happen next? However much she claimed to hate her mum, and despite the fact her mother terrified her, this sudden loss would obviously affect Vicky very deeply indeed. She hadn't seen her mother since May, when she ran away to Lorraine's. That was four whole months with no contact whatsoever, but how could Vicky have possibly known they would be the last four months of her mother's life? And what about her father? What if he did turn out to be the nasty character he'd been described as? God love her, Vicky didn't deserve all this, and of course she would also be upset about Michelle's sudden departure. Everything was a mess, and a very complicated mess.

I felt completely shattered as I pushed all these thoughts around my head, worrying about everybody. I wanted to make things better but I felt stymied by my status as a foster carer. I had absolutely no rights over Michelle now her mother had taken her back. That was the truth of the matter and it hurt, because I loved Michelle and wanted to remain a part of her life, to look out for her and make sure she was all right.

Jonathan eventually returned from making his phone call to Social Services, and I reluctantly left Vicky once more and went outside the lounge to talk to him. Vicky remained in an almost trance-like state, and I explained I would return as quickly as possible, which she again acknowledged with a vague nod.

'Hayley has spoken to Maureen,' Jonathan whispered urgently. 'Michelle is with her now, they both say they are happy with the arrangement and there is basically nothing we can do. That's it, the end. We've been dropped; our services are no longer required. Even if Michelle ends up back in care it won't be with us. Her placement here has "irretrievably broken down", to use Hayley's words.'

'Jonathan! I just can't believe it.'

'Nor can I. Do you know what, if Vicky didn't need us so much right now I would resign as a foster carer. I'm absolutely gutted. I feel like I've been kicked in the stomach.'

I'd never seen my husband looking and sounding so dejected and disillusioned in all the years I'd known him.

'Don't say that,' I comforted. 'It's very hard, but we're doing a good job. This isn't a judgement on us.'

'I know you're right in theory, Angela, but I'm just so incredibly hurt. It's too much to take, it really is.'

With Vicky still in shock in the lounge, this clearly wasn't the time to continue this discussion. I was also utterly devastated about Michelle, of course. She's been like a daughter to me for more than two years now. We'd bonded and shared so many good times, and losing her like this was a terrible blow that affected me deeply. My heart was aching, but I didn't for one moment feel defeated to the point where I was ready to give up fostering, as Jonathan seemed to be suggesting he might be. In fact, the situation made me want to carry on fostering more than ever. Even from this very dark place we found ourselves in, I felt this very strongly. I knew I could deal with this and eventually come to terms with it, and I felt duty bound to do so. This wasn't about me; it was about the kids. It was about helping another Michelle one day, and getting Vicky through this very rough patch in her young life. Some children have such terribly complicated and difficult lives, and that is exactly why foster carers like us are needed. Like so many others, Michelle was a very vulnerable teenager. God only knows what would happen to her from here on in. What if her mother got fed up with her again, as I feared she would? What if she needed another foster home? I couldn't give up this job, not in a million years; there were so many other Michelles and so many other Vickys out there, needing a decent home and some loving support. Fostering was so much harder than I'd ever expected it would be, but it was such a crucial and worthwhile job, and I knew I couldn't stop now. I was in too deep and, more importantly, I didn't want to get out.

'Don't make any rash decisions,' was all I felt able to say to Jonathan as we huddled on the landing together, feeling devastated and anxious and actually quite used. 'This is just a bad day, a very bad day, but they are not all like this, are they?'

Jonathan slumped against the landing wall and wiped tears from his eyes.

'No,' he spluttered. 'But it's just so hard to bear . . .'

Vicky spent the rest of the evening looking practically

comatose on the settee, staring into space and continually frozen in shock. Jonathan and I did everything in our power to stimulate a conversation, tempt her to eat or drink something or just get her to snap out of her trance, but nothing worked. Eventually, at 9.30 p.m., I fetched her a duvet and a pillow and managed to get her to lie down on the settee for a while.

'Do you want to go up to bed?' I asked eventually, but she didn't reply.

We'd had the television on for an hour or so, hoping that might stimulate Vicky, and when *News at Ten* came on she slowly sat herself up, inching her body up off the settee very cautiously, as if she were a china puppet that needed delicate handling. Then she gradually clicked her head around to me, in the mechanical fashion I'd witnessed before.

'I'm going up,' she said, in the faintest whisper.

'All right, love. I hope you sleep well. I'll walk up with you.'

Vicky edged incredibly carefully out of the lounge and up the stairs to her bedroom. Her eyes seemed so lifeless it was as if she were sleepwalking and was not aware of her movements or what was going on around her.

'Are you sure you're going to be all right?' I asked.

'Yes,' she said softly. 'Night.'

I left her to get herself ready for bed and popped back a few minutes later, tapping on the door gently. There was no response.

'I'm just going to open the door, Vicky, to check you are OK,' I said, as I didn't want to invade her privacy.

Again there was no reply, so I peeped round the door

and saw that Vicky was already asleep, cuddling her duvet. Her head was at the wrong end of her bed and she was still wearing her school blouse and trousers, but I decided not to disturb her and quietly closed the door.

As I tiptoed past Michelle's bedroom on my way across the landing I couldn't help having a look inside. I was expecting the bareness of the room to upset me. Jonathan had told me Michelle had all her bags packed, and I imagined she had stripped out everything she owned. However, the room scarcely looked as if Michelle had left it, which was an even worse sight to take in. Photographs we'd taken on various holidays together were still stuck on her wall, her bed was made with her favourite pink duvet set and pyjamas folded on the pillow, just as she normally left it each morning, and the Winnie the Pooh slippers I'd bought her last Christmas were on the floor, in front of her wardrobe. I picked the slippers up and opened the wardrobe door tentatively. I saw that Michelle had taken the vast majority of her clothes, and that's when it hit me. She'd taken what she needed and what she wanted, and she clearly didn't want reminders of our holidays together, or our gifts. I had no idea what thoughts Maureen had put in her daughter's head; I could only hazard a guess. Somehow, I imagined, she had convinced Michelle that her life with us had not just run its course, but that it was somehow wrong, and something she should cast aside. I didn't know this for a fact, but I supposed Maureen had painted us in a very bad light indeed, because I could think of no other reason Michelle would have treated us this way. I sat on Michelle's bed and allowed myself a little cry, and at that moment Jonathan appeared in the doorway.

'Are you all right, Angela?' he asked.

'Yes,' I said. 'But I think I have an idea how Vicky is feeling. This is like a bereavement, having Michelle disappear like this. What if we never see her again?'

'I know, it's just unbelievable,' he replied. 'I can't get my head around it at all.'

He sat down beside me for a while but it felt like we were torturing ourselves, as we couldn't help looking at the happy pictures of the three of us at the beach, out for meals together and enjoying a birthday tea. We eventually took ourselves off to bed feeling completely exhausted, though neither of us could get to sleep.

I don't think I slept a wink all night in fact, and I eventually got out of bed at 6.30 a.m. on the Tuesday morning and went straight up to Vicky's room. I didn't think for one minute she would be going to school, but I wanted to check on her before I called the receptionist to explain her absence. My knock on Vicky's bedroom door brought no response.

'Vicky, love, can I just come in and check on you?'

I slowly pushed the door open, peeping through the two inch gap I'd created. I could see Vicky was still fast asleep, nestled into her duvet, and so I shut the door quietly and went downstairs. When I phoned the school about an hour or so later I chose my words carefully. I felt very sleep deprived and I certainly didn't want to say the wrong thing or be drawn into any discussion about the death of Vicky's mother.

'There's been a bereavement in the family,' was all I said. 'Vicky won't be coming in today.'

'I'm very sorry to hear that, Mrs Hart. Thank you for letting us know.'

I was just about to hang up when the receptionist unexpectedly asked, 'Does this mean Michelle won't be in either?'

'Oh!, I said, flummoxed. 'I'm sorry, I expect so but, no, I'm afraid I don't know.'

'Right,' the receptionist replied, sounding a little confused. 'So is she staying at home too, or shall we expect her in school?'

'I'm terribly sorry, but I honestly don't know,' I sighed. 'The thing is, I'm no longer Michelle's foster carer.'

'Oh I do apologise. I didn't realise.'

'It's not your fault. It's very recent. Thanks for your help.'

I couldn't get off the phone quick enough. Saying those words, 'I am no longer Michelle's foster carer', really hurt, and I was also strangely embarrassed to say them. I felt like I'd been sacked and people might be talking about me behind my back, wondering what I'd done wrong to have lost such a lovely, sweet girl as Michelle.

Jonathan and I took turns in the shop all morning, and I checked on Vicky every hour, until she eventually got out of bed just before noon. She nodded when I asked if she was all right, and she used the bathroom and changed her clothes, but after that she just sat on her bed in her tracksuit and stared at the wall.

'Vicky, love, you should eat something,' I said. 'Shall I do you some cereal? Or some soup?'

She shook her head and looked away from me, and she stayed in the same state for the rest of the day. I tried to phone Hayley in the afternoon but she wasn't in her office and didn't call me back, and Jonathan and I decided that if Vicky was no better the next day we'd phone the doctor, which we eventually did. Thankfully, we managed to get an appointment for a home visit, as the prospect of man-oeuvring Vicky in and out of the surgery in her zoned-out condition did not appeal at all.

When the GP arrived on the Wednesday afternoon, Vicky was sitting on the settee in the lounge, still wearing her tracksuit, and gazing out of the window at the clouds in the sky. She jumped a little and looked over anxiously when I walked in the room and introduced the doctor, then she looked away from us, avoiding eye contact and shrinking her shoulders back, like she wanted to make herself small and invisible. After exchanging some pleasantries and offering his condolences to Vicky, the GP explained he needed to check her over.

'Vicky, can I look in your eyes?' he asked, taking out a torch-like pen from his medical bag.

'OK,' Vicky said slowly, as if she'd just been woken up from a very deep sleep.

She winced and recoiled when the GP shone the light in her eyes, but she did allow him to continue his examination. He went on to check her throat and ears, took her pulse and blood pressure, asked her to stick her tongue out and tapped her forehead with his fingers, explaining he was checking there was no nerve problem around her head or face.

'I think,' he declared, 'you are simply suffering from severe shock, which is not pleasant, of course, but not unexpected, in the circumstances. There is nothing I can prescribe, but I'd say you're in excellent hands here.'

Turning to me, the doctor explained that I should continue to keep a close eye on Vicky, offer small, digestible portions of food and make sure she drank sufficient water or sweet tea.

'Time is really the only cure for shock like this,' he said. 'It's quite unusual for shock to continue in this fashion for this length of time. As you probably know, most people have a "fight or flight" response to a shocking situation, but not everybody is built the same way and Vicky's response is not unheard of. She will come round when she is ready, and in the meantime you just need to keep doing what you're doing.'

'I'm relieved to hear that,' I replied. 'I was beginning to worry there was something else going on. Vicky has reacted like this before, though never for this long, I have to say.'

The doctor nodded. 'As I say, she'll come round, Mrs Hart, and I can see she is in good hands. Any other problems, don't hesitate to call the surgery again.'

In recent years, stress experts have given the 'fight or flight' response a new name, and it is now known as the 'fight, flight or freeze response'. When I first heard about this a few years ago I was reminded of the doctor's visit that day. As he pointed out, Vicky didn't display the more typical fight or flight response; for her it was clearly the freeze reaction, but it just hadn't been given a label yet. I've also since learned that the freeze response is activated when a person feels there is no hope. If we fight or flee, we believe we can outrun or overpower out attackers, but if we freeze we don't have that belief; we have effectively submitted to the fear and the threat. It follows that Vicky must have felt completely powerless in the face of such shocking news about her mother, and so she retreated into herself, surrendering herself to a state of paralysis.

As for the other occasions when Vicky had frozen, with the benefit of hindsight and the knowledge I've gained since those early days, I believe Vicky had felt so terrified and hopeless when she lived with her mother that freezing had become her automatic default position in times of severe stress. She couldn't fight her mother and she was too young to flee her for many years, so she froze instead. She was literally scared stiff, and now the poor girl was utterly terrified of her mother's death. It was such a sad and pitiful situation for Vicky to be in, and my heart bled for her.

# 12

### *'You don't know how much she terrified me'*

It took Vicky a couple more days to return to anything like normal. As the week went on she managed to eat a few bowls of Rice Krispies and she started to respond a little more every day.

'How did she die?' she eventually asked me on the Friday morning, when we were both sitting at the kitchen table.

'I don't know, sweetheart. I don't think anybody knows yet.'

'It must have been the alcohol, or the pills.'

'Pills?'

'Yes, her "medicine", as she called it. She took all kinds of pills, all the time. Sometimes I had to fetch them for her. She gave me notes, and I had to knock on people's doors and get them.'

I hadn't forgotten Vicky's previous mention of the 'notes' and 'letters' she delivered for her mother, and I'd been hoping she might give more details about this.

'What sort of pills were they?' I asked.

'I don't know. She usually just called it her medicine.'

'I see. And who exactly did she get the medicine from?'

'I don't know. It was always a different house. Sometimes I had to phone a number to get the address. Sometimes I had to wait in the phone box for a call, so I could get the address. Remember I said about knowing all the phone boxes on Izzy's estate? That's because my mother sent me over there to do the same thing sometimes, when she couldn't get what she wanted on our estate. I don't know who the people were. I just did as she told me because . . .'

'Because?'

'Because I had to. You don't know how much she terrified me, Angela. I had to do exactly what she told me, or, or . . . it really wasn't worth arguing, trust me.'

'I'm sorry, sweetheart. What, erm . . .' I wanted to ask what happened if Vicky didn't do as she was told, but I stopped myself, because I was worried about traumatising her.

It was too late, however. The conversation had already triggered bad memories for Vicky. She froze, dropping the spoon she was holding, which bounced off the table and onto the tiled kitchen floor. It made quite a deafening clatter, but Vicky didn't appear to notice, and gazed into space.

'Oh dear,' I said, trying to stay calm. 'Are you all right, Vicky, love, can you hear me?'

She didn't respond at all, and so I put my arm around her and told her to take her time.

'You don't need to be afraid,' I said. 'You're here in the kitchen with me. Can you hear me, Vicky?'

A few moments later she shivered and blinked and slowly clicked her head around, until she was looking me in the eye.

'She still makes me frightened,' she said. 'I don't want to go to the funeral. I don't want to be anywhere near her. I don't have to go, do I, Angela?'

'Nobody can force you to go, Vicky, but I know that sometimes it is helpful to the people left behind, to go to a funeral, I mean. It helps with the grieving process.'

'I won't grieve for her!' she said loudly, suddenly becoming more animated and passionate than I'd seen her in days. 'She hated me! I'm glad she can't hurt me any more!'

'I hear what you're saying, Vicky,' I said calmly. 'And I'm sorry you're going through this. Let me talk to Hayley before you make any decisions, though. We don't even know if the funeral has been arranged yet. I'll try to get some details, then we can work out what to do.'

I'd heard nothing all week from Hayley, so once Vicky had gone upstairs and was out of earshot I went into the hall and called the main office number, as I wanted to get some news before the weekend.

'Hayley's away until next Tuesday,' I was told by a curt receptionist. 'Can you call back then?'

'No!' I said. 'This is becoming urgent. This is not the first time I've phoned. I've been trying to get hold of Hayley all week, actually.'

'I see. Can anybody else help?'

After explaining who I was and why I was calling the receptionist told me it really would be best for me to wait until Hayley was back at work on the following Tuesday.

'But what if the funeral is early next week?' I said, incredulous at being asked to wait a further four days. 'We need some warning and I want some advice. I don't think this is fair on Vicky. She has literally been told nothing, except for the fact her mother is dead. I absolutely must speak to somebody else in the office. Is Stuart Williams there? Or could I speak to the duty social worker?'

'Mr Williams may be available. Hold the line, please.'

I was left listening to a dreadful muzak version of 'Greensleeves' for twelve long minutes, and then Stuart Williams came on the phone.

'Hello, Mrs Hart. I'm sorry you weren't aware that Hayley is on annual leave.'

'No, I wasn't aware of this, and I'm not very happy about it. We've had no news since Monday, and it is almost a week since Vicky's mother died. I really don't think it's acceptable. Vicky has not even been told how her mother died and is now starting to speculate.'

'I see and I'm sorry you feel this way, but I'm afraid no date has been set for the funeral and there really is no more news yet. Had there been, you would have been informed, naturally.'

'I see,' I said, realising I had been a little rash in my judgement of Hayley. Like Tricia, she was a caring and diligent social worker who was also incredibly busy, and was entitled to take a few days off. 'Vicky herself has given me some information, as it happens,' I went on.

'Right. Do you want me to take the details then?'

'Yes, I think that would be a good idea, as Hayley is away.'

'Fine. Please fire away.'

'OK,' I said. 'Vicky has informed me that her mother took a lot of pills that didn't come from the doctor.'

'Thank you, Mrs Hart. I'll make sure this is placed on record. Will that be all?'

'Yes. Thank you. And can you please ask Hayley to contact me as soon as she is back in the office?'

'Indeed. Have a good weekend, Mrs Hart.'

'Thanks. You too.'

I put the phone down and found myself scowling at the receiver. Mr Williams meant well, but I was feeling very protective of Vicky and couldn't help thinking: 'How would you like it if you were in Vicky's shoes? How can *she* have a good weekend?'

In the event, Vicky was very accepting of the fact there was no news; in fact, I think she was relieved that, for the time being at least, she didn't have to make a decision about the funeral, or indeed learn the details of how her mother had died. I was privately wondering whether Brenda may have taken her own life, perhaps accidentally, with an overdose. I imagined Vicky might be having similar thoughts, as this was not beyond the realms of possibility, given what we knew about her mother's behaviour and lifestyle. I said nothing, of course; there was enough going on as it was.

I'd explained to Vicky about Michelle's departure by now, seizing the moment when she was sitting in the lounge watching television one evening during the week. I'd broken the news very gently, because Vicky was still in a semi trance-like state at that point, but I felt I couldn't put it off any longer. Vicky hadn't asked a single question about Michelle's whereabouts, and even when I told her what had happened she didn't seem that surprised, which made me wonder how much she had taken in.

'It's not a good idea,' Vicky had mumbled. 'I don't like the sound of Michelle's mother, or her boyfriend. She should have stayed here.'

That was about as much as I got out of Vicky at first, but several days later, on Sunday afternoon, when we were sitting side by side on the settee after watching a film, Vicky started talking very frankly about Michelle.

'I think Michelle's mum's a bit stupid,' Vicky said.

'That's not a very kind thing to say. Why do you say that?'

'She lets Michelle have sex in the house with her boyfriend, and he's a nutcase as well.'

'Oh!' I said, gasping audibly. 'Did Michelle tell you this?'

'Yes. Her mum encourages her. They did it every weekend you know, when Michelle went round there. She told me everything. Her mum knew and let them. It's so weird! And do you know who her boyfriend is?'

'No! I didn't even know she had a boyfriend, and I

certainly didn't know she was having sex. She's fourteen, for goodness' sake!'

'I know. She made me promise not to say anything when she was living here or I would have told you, Angela.'

'Well I'm astonished, Vicky! So who is the boyfriend? Do I know him?'

'Probably. It's that weirdo, Jeremy Brown.'

'Jeremy Brown? That name rings a bell . . .'

'Yes, he's the brother of that guy Jason who used to DJ at the Saturday disco. You were right about Jason, by the way. He's a total creep. He tried it on with Izzy, you know, but thankfully she told him where to get off.'

I felt like a searchlight went on in my head and I scoured my brain for the few snippets of information I had previously gathered about Jeremy Brown.

'Oh God, Jeremy Brown!' I suddenly blurted out. 'No! He's the one who was questioned for having underage sex! The drug dealer!'

'Well I don't know about the drugs stuff,' Vicky replied, 'but he's the underage sex one. He never got done for it, mind you. I don't know who the girl was he was accused of sleeping with, but I know he got away with it. Anyway, Michelle's mum just lets them have sex in her house so he's laughing now, isn't he? He's allowed to stay the night and everything. I think it's just so weird. He's twenty-four, you know?'

I really couldn't believe what I was hearing, and I wanted to drive straight over to Maureen's house and have it out with her. I started to frantically piece things together, and I began to wonder if Maureen had snared Michelle back with the promise that she would be able to do as she pleased, and live in a house without rules, just because she could, or perhaps because she had an ulterior motive I might never know about. I felt furious with Maureen for being so irresponsible, but most of all I felt very sorry indeed for Michelle. She was still a child, and a very young and impressionable girl at that. What's more, she could be in very real danger of getting pregnant. As if reading my mind, in her next breath Vicky recalled the conversation the three of us had had about teenage pregnancies, when Michelle said she'd like to have a baby when she was young.

'No wonder Michelle went red when you talked about those girls getting pregnant,' Vicky remarked. 'I bet you thought she was just shy; that's probably what she wanted you to think.'

'Well I don't know *what* to think,' I said, recalling how Michelle had commented that if she did have a baby she could put the child in care if she couldn't cope.

'You don't think she's pregnant, Vicky, do you?' I asked, desperately hoping this was not going to be the next bombshell.

'I honestly don't know, but apparently her mum told her that she could live back home if she ever was. She said she could afford to keep her then, because she'd get extra benefits, or something like that.'

'When did Michelle tell you all this?'

'Er, just over the last couple of weeks, I suppose.'

'You knew she was planning to leave?'

'She mentioned it a couple of times, but I thought it was all just talk to be honest. I told her not to. I told her she'd be mad to, but it was like something had changed. I got the feeling her mum had been nagging her about it.'

I wanted to cry, I really did. I didn't know what was true and what was speculation, but whichever way you looked at it Michelle was not in a good situation. If what Vicky had recounted was true, Maureen was failing Michelle in a very reckless and dangerous way.

I shared everything Vicky had told me with Jonathan as soon as I got the chance later that evening, and he looked visibly shaken and upset.

'Do you know what's the hardest thing of all, listening to this?' he said.

'What?'

'It's knowing we can't intervene. We have a duty to report this to Social Services, of course, but beyond that we can't do a single thing to help Michelle, can we? Honestly, Angela, I can't bear this.'

'I know what you mean,' I conceded. 'But look at it like this. At least we have given Michelle two good years. Hopefully her time with us will stand her in good stead for the future, once she's old enough to reflect, and to stand on her own two feet.'

'I think that's a very positive way of looking at things, Angela, but it doesn't help Michelle in the here and now, does it? Really and truly I don't think I can do this any more. It's just terrible feeling so powerless.'

However positive I tried to remain about fostering, I couldn't argue with anything Jonathan said. It was a dreadful state of affairs. I couldn't get Michelle out of my mind. She was a lovely, gentle girl by nature; the thought of her with this man, who may or may not be a drug dealer on top of being someone who apparently slept with underage girls, was abhorrent.

The fact I could do nothing to help but pass messages to Social Services felt wholly inadequate and was hideously frustrating. I called the out-of-hours number and reported everything Vicky had said to the social worker on duty. I wanted to act swiftly, and with Hayley still away this seemed like the best course of action.

'It's logged,' I was told curtly after I'd passed on all I'd heard. 'Thanks for the call.'

'What will happen now?'

'I can't answer that, but your call has been logged and will be dealt with in the appropriate manner.'

'Does this mean Hayley will deal with it when she's back on Tuesday? It's just that I think this requires urgent attention.'

'I'll note your comments and, as I say, your call has been logged and will be dealt with . . .'

'In the appropriate manner? Yes, I got that. OK, thank you.'

I had another sleepless night, and all through Monday I was counting the hours until Hayley was back at work the next day, when I could unload all the questions and worries and alarming details that were cramming my head.

I phoned the office just after 9 a.m. on Tuesday morning and Hayley answered the call immediately.

'Good morning!' she breezed. 'Sorry I missed your calls last week. I was on leave.'

'So I heard.'

'Anyway, first things first. There's some good news. A letter has arrived from Vicky's father.'

'What does it say?'

'Basically, Vincent is delighted we've got in touch and he's very happy to write to Vicky directly, with a view to re-establishing contact.'

'I see. How do we know it's safe for her to be in contact with him? I mean, we don't know him from Adam, do we?'

I wouldn't normally have been so forthright but my patience had been tested over the previous week and I wasn't in the mood to beat around the bush.

'I understand your concerns, Angela. There are standard checks I can make, and the Army has given him a glowing reference, which is reassuring. He left with a bravery commendation, in fact.'

Hayley went on to tell me the name of the town where Vincent lived, which I estimated was about five hours away from us by car, and she then explained the procedure from here on in. Vincent would not be given our home address; all his correspondence would arrive via Social Services addressed to Vicky, and I should encourage Vicky to let me read her replies to him in the early stages, to check she was not giving away any sensitive information that she might later regret, should things not work out.

'I don't suppose you've asked him why he's been off the scene for nearly fifteen years?' I sniffed.

'No,' Hayley replied. 'It's best not to judge though, Angela. Sometimes the facts surprise you.'

'I hope you're right,' I said. 'I'm just feeling particularly protective today, that's all.'

'Why is that?'

'You haven't heard the message I left at the weekend, about Michelle?'

'No. Weekend calls would be dealt with by one of my colleagues and I haven't caught up with them yet. What is it?'

I unloaded everything I'd heard about Michelle's boyfriend and Hayley listened very cautiously.

'You do understand, Angela, that I can't keep you informed of Michelle's situation any longer?'

'I know that, but I'm entitled to pass this information on, aren't I?'

'Of course, just as any member of the public would be.'

'Well as long as you investigate this thoroughly, that's the most important thing. Jonathan and I care very much about Michelle and we would like to know that she is safe and happy and being properly looked after.'

'I will act on this information promptly and professionally,' Hayley said, suddenly sounding as robotic as the weekend duty social worker had. 'I can assure you of that, Angela. At the moment it is hearsay, of course, so needless to say please do not discuss this with anybody.'

'There is no way I would!' I said indignantly.

'Thank you, Angela. And how is Vicky getting on?'

I explained how we'd called the doctor out for advice in dealing with her shock, and I reiterated the information I'd given to Stuart Williams, about the pills Vicky had talked about, as Hayley had clearly not caught up with her manager yet either.

'Most urgently, Vicky is worrying about the funeral now, of course,' I went on. 'Is there any more news?'

'Yes,' Hayley replied. I heard the rustle of papers and she told me it was at the main crematorium, at 10 a.m., one morning the following week. I reached for my diary and to my dismay I realised the funeral was on the same day as Vicky's fourteenth birthday.

'Oh no!' I exclaimed. 'I just don't believe it,' explaining the dilemma.

'That's unfortunate,' Hayley said in a well-meaning tone. 'Now, will that be all for the time being?'

I could tell from the way she spoke that Hayley had been distracted by something, which reminded me of the way Tricia used to behave, and of course the way Stuart 'will that be all' Williams typically conducted himself at meetings. It was as if the pressure Hayley was under had ground her down, sapping her natural bubbliness and compassion. She was clearly extremely busy and needed elsewhere, but I felt I had a hundred more questions for her.

'Actually, no, that's not all,' I replied hastily. 'Do you think Vicky should be encouraged to go to the funeral?'

'She doesn't have to,' Hayley replied patiently. 'It's her choice. It's usually a good idea though, for closure.'

'What if I took her? Do you think that would be appropriate?'

'Entirely, if she's happy with that. I'm sure Lorraine will be there, but she might not want Vicky tagging along with her. Right then . . .'

'Just one more thing before you go! Do we know any more about how Brenda died?'

I was beginning to feel like an over-zealous cub reporter grilling a reluctant interviewee. There was a pause and I heard Hayley rifle through paperwork once more.

'Yes, here it is. Alcohol. She had various drugs in her system too, but ultimately it was alcohol poisoning.'

'So she didn't kill herself?'

'No, well, she didn't commit suicide, if that's what you mean. Her death certificate will say acute alcohol poisoning, or words to that effect. If Vicky wants to know this detail you should tell her. I'm sure you'll handle it well; just remember what I said before. Stick to the facts and don't be drawn into any speculative discussion.'

'Fine. Thanks for your time. Is it OK for me to tell Vicky about her father or will you do that?'

'I'm happy for you to tell her. I'll drop his letter through your door later, I'm passing your house.'

'Great. Thanks.'

When I put the phone down I felt irritated and rather overwhelmed. It didn't seem right that, because of the pressure and time constraints Hayley was under, I'd had to pull the details of Brenda's death and funeral out of her like that. Not only that, the important breakthrough in the search for

Vicky's father had been reduced to a hasty footnote in the conversation. Finding her dad after all this time was a monumental event in Vicky's life, yet because of the number of cases Hayley was expected to deal with she would have to post his precious correspondence through our door on the way to another appointment.

When a large brown Social Services envelope with my name on the front duly landed on our doormat just before 6 p.m. that evening I was even more dismayed when I looked inside and realised that the postmark on Vincent's letter dated back to the previous week, meaning it had probably sat on Hayley's desk for some days while she was on leave.

Inside the brown envelope was a note to me, in Hayley's handwriting.

'Angela, the letter is addressed to me – feel free to read it before talking to Vicky. She can keep this, I have taken a photocopy.'

I walked up the stairs, sat on my bed and tentatively opened Vincent's letter. It felt wrong that I should be reading this before Vicky herself, but I knew it was the right thing to do, as I needed to know what was being said in order to be able to talk to her and guide her through the next steps. Vincent had written on smart white notepaper in neat, black handwriting. It looked as if he had taken great care in preparing the letter, even though it was clear from the timings that he must have replied very quickly to Hayley's initial correspondence.

'FAO Hayley Jenkins' he had written across the top, underneath his address.

> Thank you very much for contacting me. It's very good to have the chance to get back in touch with Vicky, my daughter. I've been overseas a fair bit, but I'm married and settled down now. I wish I had known Vicky was in care before now, but I am glad she is OK and in a good foster home. I have a wife called Carol and my son, Matty, is now 17. Vicky won't remember him, but he remembers her as a baby. Please tell Vicky I would love to hear from her, and I look forward to writing again and sending some photos.
>
> Best regards,
> Vincent Taylor.

Despite the irritated mood I was in, I couldn't help smiling to myself when I got to the end of the short letter. My first impressions of Vincent were good, and he certainly sounded nothing like the 'nasty loser' or 'waste of space' he'd been described as by Vicky's mother. This felt like a ray of sunshine in the midst of a terrible episode for Vicky, but of course only time would tell if my hopes would prove to be correct. We had a long way to go yet, and I knew that whatever happened further down the line it was going to be an emotional ride for Vicky, and no doubt for me and Jonathan too.

## 13

### *'When I was living with her I had to be resourceful'*

'Vicky, love,' I said, tapping on her door. 'Can I come in?'

'Yes,' she said in a day-dreamy voice.

Vicky was sitting hunched and cross-legged on the rug beside her bed, looking through an old *Smash Hits* magazine.

'Hi, love. Listen, I have some good news. It's about your father.'

'My dad? Have they found him?'

'Yes they have, and he's written to Hayley to say he'd like to hear from you.'

Vicky immediately dropped the magazine and straightened her back, giving me her full attention.

'Oh my God! He's alive?'

'He certainly is. Do you want to read the letter? It was addressed to Hayley, so it's been opened.'

Vicky narrowed her eyes and bit her thumbnail.

'Er, yes. I'm a bit nervous . . . it's a shock. Have you read it?'

'Yes, Hayley told me to have a look.'

'Does he sound nice?'

'He does. It's very short, but he says he'll write to you, directly next time, if you want to write back to him.'

Vicky slowly reached out her hand, took hold of the letter and carefully pulled the white paper from the envelope.

'Wow!' she said, reading the words slowly and purposefully.

'So this Matty is like, well, a brother?'

'Yes, so it appears.'

'Oh my God! This is so weird!'

'How do you feel, Vicky? Are you going to write back?'

'Of course! There's loads of questions I want to ask him.'

Vicky was grinning and looked happy. I hadn't seen her smile in over a week, and it was wonderful to see.

'You could maybe send some photographs too, I could help you chose some, if you like?'

'Would you? I wonder what he looks like? I wonder if I look like him?'

Vicky was growing more animated the more the news sunk in, and I was very pleased to see her responding this way.

'I'm going to write to him now. Oh my God, this is actually such good news! How far away does he live? I've never heard of that place.'

'It's quite far, a couple of hundred miles at least, I'd say. All right, love. I'll leave you to it. Good luck.'

*

Vicky was back at school by now, and a couple of days later I took a phone call from Hayley telling me that Lorraine wanted to talk to Vicky about the funeral arrangements.

'Lorraine asked if you could send Vicky over to her flat one night this week, after school,' Hayley said. 'Is that all right?'

'That's fine,' I replied. 'I'd been thinking the sisters needed to see each other, but I didn't want to interfere. I'm sure Vicky will be pleased.'

'Good. Lorraine obviously has her problems, but she can be very sensible too. Hopefully they'll have a good chat.'

When I passed the message on to Vicky she was very pleased and she asked me if she could go over to Lorraine's that same night.

'I've got tons of homework to do, mind you. I haven't really got time to go on the bus. Is there any chance you could give me a lift, Angela?'

'Of course,' I said. 'I'm happy to help. I'll come and fetch you afterwards too, if you like.'

'Thanks. I don't know what I'd do without you. Can I use the phone and call Lorraine?'

'Of course.'

Later that evening, at around 7.30 p.m., Vicky directed me across town to Lorraine's ground-floor flat. I saw the net curtain twitch as I pulled up, and then the front door opened before I'd even switched the engine off. The next moment a very slender young woman stepped out of the flat and walked towards the car wearing a baggy grey jumper, black leggings and fluffy slippers.

'Hi, Loz!' Vicky smiled as she leaped out to greet her sister.

'All right, Vic! Hi! You must be Angela.'

'I am,' I said, leaning across the passenger seat and smiling through the open door. 'Pleased to meet you, Lorraine.'

'I'm pleased to meet you. Er, did you want to come in?'

'No, it's all right,' I replied, imagining Lorraine was only being polite. 'I'll come and collect Vicky later though. What time shall I pick you up, love?'

Vicky looked at her sister and back at me.

'Well, I feel bad having you driving around all night. If Lorraine says it's all right, why not come in? You can meet my nephew! Sure that's OK, Loz?'

'That's fine. James is still wide awake, the cheeky monkey. Carl's out, playing darts.'

The flat was sparsely furnished but it was very clean and pin neat, and the baby was lying in a fancy Moses basket in the middle of the floor, kicking his legs and gurgling contentedly. Vicky immediately crouched beside him, making cooing noises and tickling him under his chin.

'I've missed you, little man!' she beamed. 'Aren't you gorgeous?'

'Now don't you go getting him all wound up before bed, Auntie Vicky!' Lorraine teased. 'Would anyone like a cuppa? I'm putting the kettle on.'

Vicky and I both accepted the offer of a cup of tea, and once it was made the three of us sat very convivially together around the coffee table in Lorraine's small lounge.

'I'm very grateful for all you're doing for Vicky,' Lorraine said to me. 'I've been hoping for the chance to thank you, Angela.'

'It's a pleasure to have her. Jonathan and I are very happy to help; I'm just sorry you've had so much to deal with. It must have been a terrible shock, losing your mum.'

'It was,' she said, turning to her sister. 'How are you doing, Vic?'

'I dunno really. I thought I never wanted to see her again, but now I can't . . . it's weird. D'you know what I mean?'

'Yes, I do. I think you should come to the funeral though. Me and Carl are going, and James of course. I think it's important.'

'I suppose,' Vicky shrugged. 'I don't mind if I'm with you. I won't have to see her body or anything like that, will I?'

'No, of course not. I've dealt with the funeral parlour and all the arrangements. You just need to turn up. You can do that, can't you?'

'Yes, I can.'

I was impressed by Lorraine. Apart from the fact she appeared to be significantly underweight, you would never have guessed she had any issues, and certainly not that she had taken an overdose recently. The flat was clearly very well cared for indeed, and the baby looked very happy lying on his fresh white sheets, sucking on the corner of a soft, satin-edged blanket.

'They've found my dad, by the way,' Vicky suddenly said. 'Did you know anything about this, Loz?'

'No! Wow! That's amazing! Where is he? Are you going to see him?'

Vicky told her sister the scant details we knew, and Lorraine listened eagerly.

'That's great!' she said. 'I don't remember Matty. I was with my dad the whole time when Mum was with your dad, see. I've heard the name though. Maybe Mum just told me about him, or I overheard her mentioning him. I honestly can't remember.'

'So I assume you don't remember Vicky's father either?' I ventured.

'No, nothing at all. Never seen a picture, nothing. I didn't even know his name was Vincent until I saw Vicky's birth certificate recently. Mum never talked about him, except when she slagged him off.'

'I told you, Angela!' Vicky said. 'Mum never had a good word to say about my dad, but I know you're right. We can't just take her word for it. I need to find out for myself.'

I explained to Lorraine how Vicky was going to write to Vincent, and then they would hopefully swap more letters and probably some photographs, and that after that Social Services might arrange a meeting.

'What if he does turn out to be how my mum described?' Lorraine asked, suddenly looking concerned. 'What if he sounds all right in a letter but is this nasty person she told us he was?'

'Social Services are used to dealing with these kinds of things, and Vicky's safety is paramount here. The way it works is that a social worker will travel to meet him first. They'll also do various background checks.'

'Like what?'

'Check that he has no police or prison record, that sort of thing, I imagine. We already know he left the Army with a very good record – a commendation in fact.'

'That bodes well,' Lorraine said. 'Could I come too, if it gets that far?'

Vicky looked at me hopefully.

'It's not my decision!' I smiled. 'It's up to you two, and Vicky's father of course. I can't see there would be any problem, but let's cross that bridge when we come to it, shall we? There's a little way to go yet.'

Before Vicky and I left the flat Lorraine handed me her phone number and asked me to keep in touch, and we made arrangements for me to drop Vicky over on the morning of the funeral. As the sisters were now going together I would not attend, which Vicky said was fine.

'As it's her birthday on the same day I'm going to take her out for a pizza in the evening, if she feels up to it,' I whispered to Lorraine when Vicky nipped to the toilet.

'That's a good idea. I'll get her a present, as soon as I pick up my Giro.'

'OK, Lorraine. That sounds good. I'm so glad to have met you. You take care of yourself, and here's my phone number too.'

I scribbled our home number on a scrap of paper and we all said our goodbyes.

'Thanks, Angela,' Vicky said with an appreciative sigh as we drove away from the flat.

'You're very welcome indeed,' I said. 'It was lovely to meet Lorraine. You're lucky to have a sister like her.'

I felt genuinely relieved and comforted to have met Lorraine. Her life could not be easy, raising a baby in a small council flat and living on benefits as she did, but she was a kind person, and I could see she had Vicky's best interests at heart.

'By the way, where did you sleep, when you were at Lorraine's?' I asked, as the flat clearly only had one bedroom.

'On the settee. Lorraine couldn't stand the mess, but it's hard to be tidy when you have nowhere to put your stuff, isn't it?'

'Yes, it is,' I said. 'Mind you,' I added with a mischievous smile, 'some people find it hard to be tidy when they *do* have somewhere to put all their stuff.'

'Ha ha, very funny, Angela!'


Vicky barely mentioned the funeral again and said nothing at all about her mother over the next few days. When the day finally arrived I arranged for Jonathan to be on duty in the shop, as I wanted to be on hand for Vicky, should she need me, and I was also going to run her over to Lorraine's. Thankfully, when Vicky came downstairs on the morning of the funeral she seemed incredibly together. I hadn't even had to wake her. She'd got herself up in plenty of time and was already dressed in a smart outfit.

'At least my mum taught me to be resourceful,' she

mused, looking at herself in the long mirror in the hall and smoothing her hands down over her slim hips as she did so.

'Yes, I'm very impressed with your outfit,' I said, because I assumed Vicky was referring to the clothes she had picked out. She had put on her smart black school trousers along with her best shirt and favourite jacket, and she'd also blow-dried her hair into a silky shoulder-length bob which made her look very grown up.

'And your hair looks lovely, too. I've never seen you with it down before.'

'Thanks!' she said, staring absent-mindedly at her reflection. 'When I was living with her I had to be resourceful, you know.'

'I imagine you did. I expect you had to do a lot for yourself.'

'Yes, but I mean when she locked me outside. That's what she did, all the time. I'd just be in a nightie and half the time I had no shoes on. I'd have frozen to death if I didn't keep my wits about me.'

'I can't bear to think of you out in the cold like that,' I said.

'She was so cruel, Angela. The older I get the more I realise this. I know it's her funeral today, but I'll say it anyway. She was just so wicked to me. Do you know what? When it became a regular thing to be put outside I got into the habit of hiding clothes behind our bin in the back alley, so that I had stuff to put on to keep warm.'

'Well that really was very clever of you, especially as you were so young.'

'Yes, she could be cleverer, though, when she felt like it. Once, at Christmas, she found the stuff I'd hidden and took it inside when she put me out. I had to get cardboard boxes out of the bins and wrap them round myself to try to keep warm. I had bits of smelly old tin foil wrapped around my feet. And you know what? When she found out I did that she started pouring cooking oil and dirty washing-up water in the bin, so I couldn't take anything out of it.'

'Vicky, that's terribly sad.'

'Yes, I'm resourceful though!' she smiled bravely.

'Here,' I said, handing her a little present. 'This is a birthday gift from me and Jonathan.'

Her eyes shone and Vicky threw her arms around me.

'Thank you!' she said, untying the ribbon, peeling back the spotty purple wrapping paper and peeking inside the jewellery box.

'Oh it's beautiful!' she said, lifting out the necklace.

'The charm is a little guardian angel,' I said. 'Whatever happens in the future, I want you to know that me and Jonathan are here for you. We'll always do what we can to help you, Vicky. You must never feel you are on your own. Remember that, won't you?'

She put it on and stepped back to admire herself in the mirror.

'Thanks,' she said. 'I'll treasure it, always. I won't forget what you've said. Thank you.'

'It looks pretty on you, and it suits you with your hair down.'

'Thanks. Thank you for everything. I'm ready now. Shall we go?'

'Yes,' I said, smiling. 'I'm proud of you, Vicky. Best of luck today. You're doing the right thing.'

Lorraine phoned me just an hour later to tell me the funeral was over. There was no wake, and apparently only a handful of neighbours, including the man from next door, Alf, had turned up along with Lorraine and Carl and the baby, and Vicky.

'Vicky's fine,' Lorraine reported. 'She wants to come home now though. I think she's had enough.'

I told Lorraine I'd be right over, and as I pulled up at the flat she again peeped through the curtains and opened the front door before I'd finished parking up.

'I'm glad you're here, Angela,' Lorraine said, running out to meet me. 'Vicky's gone very quiet. I think she just needs to get back to yours and have a good rest. She saw a picture of Mum that I found in the flat recently, and it shocked her. Vicky said Mum looked very thin and frail compared to how she remembered her. I think it freaked her out. Wait here, I'll get her.'

Lorraine then darted back in the flat and reappeared a minute or two later, steering a pale, shocked Vicky towards the pavement.

'Are you all right, sweetheart?' I asked.

Vicky blanked me as I helped her into the back seat of the car and shut the door.

'I've seen her like this before,' I said quietly to Lorraine, who was standing with her arms folded, looking shattered. 'Have you?'

'Yes, I have,' Lorraine nodded. 'Lots of times unfortunately, when she was at Mum's. But not for a long time, not since she was little.'

'Lorraine,' I said, seeing an opportunity and opening my mouth before I'd thought through what I was about to say. 'Tell me if it's none of my business, especially on a day like today, but I don't know what actually happened to Vicky, at your mother's, and perhaps it would be useful if I did.'

Lorraine looked at the ground, unfolded her thin arms and put her hands up to her temples, as if she had a sudden headache. As she did so I couldn't help but notice that the insides of both her narrow wrists were heavily scarred.

I felt my heartbeat quicken as I registered what this meant; it seemed that Lorraine's previous cries for help must have involved more than an overdose of pills. I was very shocked indeed, and seeing Lorraine looking so vulnerable and upset made me regret asking about her mother.

'I'm so sorry,' I spluttered. 'I really shouldn't have asked.'

Lorraine continued looking at the pavement.

'No, no, I'm sorry,' she started, flicking me a glance from beneath her heavily mascaraed eyelashes.

'No, Lorraine. I really shouldn't have mentioned it. Maybe it's a conversation for another day. I just thought it might help me to care for Vicky, if I knew a bit more, that was all.'

'I wish I could help,' Lorraine said, sounding very apologetic.

'Please don't worry. I just thought I'd ask, as there are no Social Services records . . .'

I was waffling now as I felt so embarrassed at having put Lorraine on the spot like this, today of all days.

'Angela, I would help if I could,' she said finally, 'but I don't know what happened to Vicky, and I feel very guilty about that, because I wasn't there for her, for years and years.'

Lorraine went on to explain that she was ten years old and living with her father when Vicky was born. She went back to live with their mother a year later because of the secondary school she wanted to attend, and she stayed with Brenda for three years, until she was fourteen and Vicky was four.

'I just couldn't take Mum's drinking any more,' Lorraine said, her voice full of remorse. 'But I shouldn't have left Vicky at that age, not with the way Mum was. It was wrong of me.'

'I'm very sorry,' I said. 'But please don't blame yourself. You were a child too, Lorraine. I'll take Vicky home now, and let's keep in touch.'

'Thanks,' she sniffed. 'And thank you again for everything.'

Jonathan and I ended up ordering a takeaway pizza that night for Vicky's birthday tea, as she said she didn't feel like going out. My mother came round with a birthday cake decked out with fourteen candles, which she'd edged with chocolate fingers, Vicky's favourite biscuits. On the top she had written, 'Happy Birthday, Vicky! 14 Today!' in purple icing, and she also brought round some fancy cocktail sticks in the shape of umbrellas and parrots to put in our beakers of lemonade.

It had taken Vicky several hours to come round and start talking and behaving normally again after the funeral, but she seemed to thoroughly enjoy her birthday tea, and she was particularly thrilled with the parrot cocktail sticks, telling my mother all about her love of birds.

'Imagine if you woke up in the morning, dressed in bright colours like a parrot, and you could spread your wings and fly into the sky,' Vicky said.

'I'd love that!' Jonathan smiled. 'I'd fly to Barbados and sit on the beach in the sunshine!'

'Ooh, I wouldn't,' Vicky said. 'I'd just swoop around, looping in and out of the clouds, looking down on all the people.'

'That's a lovely idea!' my mother said.

'Yes,' Vicky replied. 'And if anyone looked lonely or frightened, I'd fly down, sit next to them and sing them a song to cheer them up.'

'How delightful!' my mother smiled. 'Oh, what I wouldn't give to be fourteen again. You have such a wonderful imagination, Vicky!'

We all settled into the lounge after our feast and then Vicky turned to my mother.

'By the way, Thelma, did you hear about my dad?'

'No,' my mother replied. 'I've never heard any mention of your dad. Not a thing!'

Vicky looked astonished.

'I thought Angela might have told you. It's big news. His name is Vincent and Social Services have tracked him down. He's already written to me and hopefully I'll get to meet him soon.'

'Oh what lovely news!' my mother replied. 'Angela didn't tell me anything, but what a lovely surprise!'

I explained to Vicky that I would never discuss any details of her life with anybody, not even my mother.

'Oh! Am I allowed to tell her?' Vicky then asked, eyes widening.

'Yes, love, of course. It's your news, and you can share it if you want to.'

Vicky then repeated all the details she'd gleaned about her father, before asking my mother if she would help her check over the letter she had already written back.

'Of course,' my mother smiled. 'I'd be honoured, Vicky. This is a very important letter indeed.'

Vicky knew that my mother was something of a stickler for grammar and punctuation, as she had helped her with her homework many times.

'Thanks! I want it to be good.'

'And so it shall be!' my mum smiled.

Minutes later Vicky had a piece of A4 paper in her hands that she'd collected from her bedroom and she cleared her throat and began reading aloud from it, which I hadn't expected at all.

'Dear Vincent, slash, Dad,' she read. 'Thank you for your letter. I was very pleased to hear from you. I heard you were a soldier in Northern Ireland. I would like to hear more about your life, and what you have been doing since I was a baby. I will be fourteen when you get this letter. I'm living with Angela and Jonathan Hart, my foster carers, and my sister, Lorraine, lives not far away. She has a baby called James. Do you remember Lorraine? My mother is no longer alive. Please tell me more about Matty. I look forward to hearing from you again.'

Vicky looked up triumphantly when she reached the end of her letter and myself, Jonathan and my mum must have all been holding our breath, because as soon as she finished reading we all exploded with relieved cries of, 'That's great!' and, 'well done!'

'Are you sure it's OK?' she asked.

'Of course it is!' I said. 'Mum, what do you think?'

I looked across at my mother and was taken aback to see tears in her eye. As usual Mum was wearing perfectly pressed Marks & Spencer trousers and a fine-knit turtle-neck sweater, and she had a fancy string of beads around her neck. Her blue eye shadow and rose-pink blusher were immaculately applied, and her dyed brown hair was beautifully set. The tears looked completely out of place on her face; I had never seen her cry before.

'Mum!' I exclaimed. 'It's not like you to be a big softie!' My mum was unerringly stoical and had been brought up to keep a stiff upper lip. I could honestly not recall ever having seen it wobble like this before, even when my father died.

'Goodness gracious me!' she declared, reaching in her

handbag for a cotton handkerchief. 'That's wonderful, Vicky darling. Just pass me a pencil and I'll check it over for you. You might need the odd little comma here and there . . .'

I looked at my mum with pride. She was a much loved and very valuable part of our family, and I realised she had slipped into a grandmotherly role with Vicky very naturally, which was extremely heartening. Jonathan and I shared a knowing smile, as we often did at times like this. It was wonderful that Vicky felt comfortable enough to share this letter with all of us, and I hoped and prayed that she would get the happy outcome she deserved.

# 14

## *'My head hurt a lot when I was little'*

Very sadly, just a week after Vicky's mother was buried, Jonathan and I received the most dreadful news. Our nephew Aiden was being moved into a children's hospice, as doctors could do no more to save him. Then, unbelievably, within days of hearing this news, I took a phone call from my brother Andrew's life-long friend, Timothy.

'Angela,' Timothy said. 'I really don't want to alarm you and Andrew does not know I am calling you, but I feel you ought to know.'

'Know what?' I asked, a feeling of dread descending on me.

'Andrew's been poorly for a while. Has been in denial, I think it's fair to say.'

'What do you mean?'

My mind was searching back to the last time I'd seen my brother. It had been many months earlier, around Easter, when Jonathan and I had been away for a long weekend with Michelle, staying at a campsite about forty miles from

Andrew's home. I didn't see much of my brother; a get-together at Christmas or New Year was typically in order, and we'd meet at big family events from time to time, or on the odd occasion when we found ourselves in the same vicinity.

'What's wrong with him?' I asked nervously. 'I had absolutely no idea he'd been ill.'

'I think you should come over,' Timothy said. 'He's very poorly. It's cancer, I'm afraid, Angela.'

'Good God! Why have I only just found out about this? Does Mum know anything?'

'Honestly, it has all happened incredibly quickly. He didn't want anybody to know, as he thought he might get away with it, you know what he's like . . .'

'What exactly are you saying, Timothy? He's . . . not going to make it?'

There was a long pause.

'He's having palliative care, Angela.'

I honestly could not believe my ears. My brother was a single man who lived an extremely active lifestyle. He regularly took part in long distance races and was a keen fell runner who looked as lean and lithe as a mountain goat. The last time I'd seen him he was talking about doing a big mountain climb for charity, which he went on to complete in the summer, and he looked fantastically fit and well.

Telling my mother was horrendous.

'Andrew, which Andrew?' she said, which shows how unexpected the news was.

'Our Andrew, Mum.'

'Our Andrew? My Andrew?'

'Yes, Mum.'

'But there's nothing wrong with him!'

She said this stridently; looking back, she too was in a certain amount of denial.

'That was my first reaction when I heard the news from Timothy. I think the diagnosis was made very late though, Mum, and it's an aggressive form of cancer, apparently.'

True to form, my mother did not cry. She poured us both a brandy from the decanter she always kept in her lounge, and she raised her glass.

'To Andrew!' she said. 'He's made of strong stuff, and he's not beat yet. Let's drink to his health. May he beat the bugger!'

I sipped at the potent brandy out of politeness; I rarely drink, and when I do I only ever have something sweet and light.

'Mum,' I said. 'We have to face the fact Andrew is gravely ill. We need to go and see him, as soon as we can.'

She collapsed into her favourite armchair, the heavy crystal glass wobbling in her trembling hand.

'I'll cancel my hair appointment,' she said, giving me a subtle nod. 'I was booked in at Jan's for a shampoo and set at 9.30 a.m., but I can manage without.'

I left Jonathan in charge of looking after Vicky and the shop, and early the next morning I drove myself and my mother to my brother's home, which took us almost six hours through some terrible traffic jams. To our absolute shock and horror, we arrived too late. My brother had passed away just fifteen minutes before we arrived, with Timothy and a specialist nurse at his side. Andrew was just forty-seven years old, and my mother was in such a state of anxiety that she had a panic attack when she saw his body, and then insisted I drive us both home almost immediately afterwards.

'Mum,' I said softly, 'it's a long way. Perhaps we should check in to the hotel. Jonathan has made a booking for us.'

'I just want to go home and sleep in my own bed,' she said. 'Please, Angela. Just take me home.'

I felt I couldn't refuse, and we drove back largely in silence, an atmosphere of gloom and despondency hanging in the air.

By the end of October 1989 Jonathan and I had buried my nephew as well as my brother. Aiden was just a few days short of his seventh birthday. It was utterly heartbreaking to see his tiny white coffin and the crumpled figures of his parents, and all the family and friends who loved him.

'Why do good people have to die?' Vicky asked one day. It was early November now, and she had just asked me for some money to buy a poppy at school, for remembrance Sunday.

'Well, death isn't a punishment for bad people,' I replied. 'It comes to us all, unfortunately. Some people are just unlucky, and their lives are cut short.'

'And some people choose to cut their lives short, like my mum. She didn't deserve to live as long as she did.'

'Vicky!' I said. 'It's not nice to speak ill of the dead.'

'I don't care what I say about her. She doesn't deserve any sympathy! I hate her! I wish she died years ago!'

'That's enough!' I said.

'Why? You can't tell me what to say about my own mother!'

'Vicky!' I said exasperated.

She stormed out of the kitchen and up to her bedroom shouting, 'I hate her! She was evil! Don't tell me what I can and can't say about my mother!'

I sat at the kitchen table with my head in my hands, reluctantly acknowledging the fact that I didn't have the energy or the inclination to go after Vicky and have this out with her. If the truth be told, I'd been to see my GP because I wasn't sleeping well and was feeling incredibly stressed. Every muscle in my body seemed to ache permanently and I had a dull pain in my temples that came and went so frequently I'd started to accept it as the norm, routinely taking an aspirin with my morning cup of tea.

The doctor had offered to give me sleeping pills and tranquilisers but I didn't want to go down that route. I knew that some prospective foster carers had been turned down for being on medication but, more importantly, I have never been in favour of taking prescription drugs if I can possibly avoid them. Instead, I'd left the surgery with a fact sheet about stress and relaxation, which I hoped might help. The advice it gave was to take regular exercise, eat healthily and make time for myself, to soak in the bath or indulge in a pastime I enjoyed. When I looked at the well-meaning list I thought, *If only it were that easy! What happens when your loved ones die? Or when your foster child is rude and difficult? A plate of salad and a soak in the bath aren't going to help, are they!*

I was just letting off steam with that thought process, of course. The reality was that with everything that had gone on in recent weeks I hadn't been looking after myself as well as I should, and Jonathan and I had not had the chance to relax and spend any quality time together. I needed to heed this advice, and hopefully it would help me feel better. After Vicky's outburst Jonathan walked into the kitchen to find me still sitting with my head in my hands, and he sank down beside me.

'Are you all right, Angela?'

'Oh, just the usual, Vicky giving me a bit of lip.'

'I'm worried about you. You haven't been yourself at all. I've been thinking long and hard about this. I know you don't want to hear this, but I honestly think we've bitten off more than we can chew here. It's a massive responsibility being a foster carer, and when we've got our own issues, or things go wrong, I'm not sure we can cope.'

I looked up at Jonathan and studied him for the first time in I don't know how long. What I saw shocked me. Jonathan looked gaunt and his skin was grey. The death of his little nephew had hit him very hard indeed, but with Andrew's death, and our responsibility towards Vicky, who was also coming to terms with her own loss, I'm not sure I'd given my husband the attention he needed.

'I'm so sorry,' I said. 'I feel I've neglected you. Things will get better soon, we just need time to get over all that's happened.'

I started to cry, and Jonathan took me in his arms.

'You haven't neglected me. You are amazing. You've looked after me and you've taken care of Vicky and your mother when really you should have been looking after yourself a bit more.'

'I don't want to stop fostering!' I snivelled.

'I know that, Angela. I know how strongly you feel about it, but I think we have to consider it. It's making you ill, on top of everything else.'

'It's not making me ill! I'd have been fine if it was just Vicky's problems I had to contend with, and Michelle's!'

'Yes, but that's my point. Like it or not, we are always going to come up against issues of our own. That's the way life is, and having foster children in our care is a huge responsibility.'

'But what's happened to us recently is completely off the scale and out of the ordinary, Jonathan! We've had the worst time we could possibly have had. Three deaths, all of them so shocking and untimely. This doesn't normally happen to people. It won't happen again, it can't.'

'I agree, up to a point. What we've suffered has been unbelievable by anybody's standards but these things can and do happen. On top of that we're inviting all sorts of additional problems into our lives through fostering, problems we could probably never even imagine.'

'I know, but I love fostering,' I sobbed. 'I love helping the kids.'

'I know that, but is that enough? I'm worried about you, Angela. And what if we have our own kids?'

'Well I can't see me falling pregnant at the moment!' I wailed, as this was something I'd also discussed with the GP, and he'd told me that the stress I was under would not help my chances of conceiving, which did not come as a surprise.

We were still waiting for our appointment at the hospital to discuss our fertility issues and I immediately regretted referring to this. I felt a surge of fear that Jonathan was about to push his point further, and tell me he had made up his mind and wanted to quit fostering.

'Look, Jonathan,' I added hastily. 'I've been thinking. What if we take Vicky to Disney World with us? I'm sure we could change the booking from Michelle's name to hers. I've been thinking about this for a while. She's got her birth certificate from her mother's house now and there's plenty of time, so we could apply for a passport. What do you say?'

'Angela, you are indomitable!' he said, shaking his head from side to side. I could detect the beginnings of a smile on his face though, and I grinned back.

'I'll take that as a compliment! So it's a yes?'

Jonathan paused.

'Of course it's a yes. It's the obvious thing to do, and I

wasn't suggesting for one minute that we should stop caring for Vicky.'

'Thank goodness for that! I'll apply for the passport as soon as I can.'

'Good idea. We all need a break and the holiday will do us all good.'

The weeks leading up to Christmas were fairly quiet, which was a blessed relief. Hayley was efficient in dealing with our request to take Vicky on holiday. She tested the water with Lorraine, who was very accommodating and readily agreed to let us have Vicky's birth certificate for the passport application. We all kept the plans secret from Vicky for the time being so as not to raise her hopes, as we now also needed her father to give his permission, as he was her next of kin.

Vincent and Vicky had exchanged several more letters by now and it had reached the point where Hayley was planning to arrange for a social worker to visit Vincent and his family, with a view to Vicky meeting her father in the early part of 1990. Vicky hadn't shown me her dad's last few letters, but she always told me what he said. Vincent had explained that he had married Carol six years previously. Carol worked as a nurse while Matty was doing an engineering apprenticeship at a local college, and Vincent simply described himself as an 'ex-soldier', not mentioning whether or not he currently had a job. He had split up from Matty's mother when their son was two years old and had been in a fairly new relationship with Brenda when she fell pregnant, which tallied with the little Vicky knew on the subject.

'Things didn't work out between me and your mother,' Vincent told Vicky in one letter. 'We didn't know each other well enough and we found it impossible to live together.'

Vicky seemed pleased with how things were progressing and was looking forward to meeting her father, though she didn't seem to be in any rush.

'Well, I've waited this long,' she shrugged when I asked her how she was feeling. 'I'm kind of nervous too. What if it goes wrong? I want to find out as much as I can, while I can.'

'I think you are being very sensible taking your time like this,' I said.

I wanted to add, 'I'm sure it will all work out fine,' but I knew better, and so did Vicky. We were both aware that the reunion was not guaranteed to go smoothly. It was such a shame that, at her young age, Vicky had been through enough bad experiences to know disappointment may be around the corner. Most kids her age were still filled with the sort of childhood innocence that made them see the world through rose-tinted glasses, but of course Vicky had had those taken from her many years before. It was a great pity, but if things didn't work out, at least she may be better equipped to deal with it than other children.

For our part, Jonathan and I were delighted when we found out through Hayley that Vincent had given his permission for us to take Vicky on holiday, telling Hayley that he hoped it would be possible for us all to meet before the trip. I picked a moment when Vicky had come home with good results from school to tell her about Disney World.

'Look, Angela!' she said. 'I've got my end of term report, and I'm really pleased with it!'

'Let's have a look, sweetheart,' I said, settling down to study it. 'Goodness me. I see you've kept up the A in home economics, and you've got a B+ in English! That's wonderful.'

The rest of Vicky's results were a mixed bag, but it was the progression, not the grades, that I was interested in. Vicky had missed a lot of school throughout her childhood, and when she first came to live with us her results were all below average. However, her attendance had improved dramatically and she was now reaping the rewards. Vicky had been working hard at home too, and I was thrilled her efforts were paying off.

'Vicky is an enthusiastic pupil,' her home economics teacher had written. 'She is a pleasure to have in the class.'

The physics teacher was clearly a little less impressed.

'With more focus and a lot less cheek and chatter, Vicky could do very well in the public examination,' he had written.

'Ha ha!' Vicky laughed when I read that remark out. 'He's such a geek! He expects us all to learn in silence!'

'Vicky!' I scolded. 'Now don't spoil things by being cheeky. On the whole this is a wonderful report. Well done!'

'Thanks, Angela. You know, I'm really enjoying the cookery. I think I'd like to be a chef when I'm older, or do something related to food and catering.'

'Really? I thought you wanted to work in a bird sanctuary?'

'Well, I'd like to do that, but I don't think there are many jobs around like that. I think I stand more chance of working in catering, and I think I'd be good at it.'

'That sounds sensible,' I replied. 'But you should keep your options open. Have you ever visited a bird sanctuary or an aviary at the zoo, by the way? There might be more of them than you think. And I've been doing a little bit of thinking . . .'

I smiled broadly and raised my eyebrows, goading Vicky to ask me what I was up to.

'What? Angela! You're not taking me to visit an aviary are you? Oh my God, I'd love that!'

'Well, as it happens I do think you deserve a big treat for all your hard work. Jonathan and I were wondering, would you like to come to Disney World with us, at Easter?'

'What? Really?' Vicky leaped over and flung her arms around me. 'Oh wow! That would be awesome!'

'That's what I was hoping you would say. I've done some research, and they have exotic birds at several places near the park in Florida. You can even hand-feed some of them.'

'Oh my God! How awesome would that be! I'd love to come! Thank you so much! Er, does it mean I'll have Michelle's ticket?'

'Yes.'

'Oh. It's a shame she can't come, isn't it?'

'I know. I miss her. Do you see her around at school?'

'No, haven't seen her for ages. If I do I'll tell her you said hi, shall I?'

'Yes, you do that. But don't tell her about Disney, mind you! That wouldn't be fair, would it?'

'No, of course,' Vicky smiled. 'But I can tell my friends, can't I? They'll be so jealous!'

After missing the youth club and Saturday disco for several weeks in the aftermath of her mum's death, Vicky's busy social life was now back on track, and once her homework was done she was out most evenings, or Izzy and some other friends came to our house to listen to music. Occasionally, I'd catch Vicky nipping into the garden for a cigarette.

'Sorry, Angela,' she'd say. 'I'm doing my best, you know.'

Vicky wasn't embarrassed, just apologetic, as she knew how disappointed I was on her behalf that she was still smoking. The music concert she wanted to go to, that was meant to be her motivation and reward for quitting, had unfortunately been and gone months earlier.

'I know you're trying hard,' I said one time. 'Perhaps you could make it your New Year's resolution to stop once and for all?'

'I could,' she said, 'that's if I haven't stopped before then. You never know.'

Vicky put on her American accent and gave me a salute. 'I will make it my mission to succeed, Mrs Hart!'

'Glad to hear it,' I laughed. 'You know, I think your physics teacher got you spot on.'

'What d'you mean?'

'With more focus and a lot less cheek and chatter, Vicky could do very well!'

The following week, when Vicky was helping me with the deliveries, she went very quiet after opening a Christmas card from one of our regular customers. It had a robin on the front, and after staring at it for a while Vicky started to tell me more about why she liked birds.

'My love of birds started with that robin, you know?' she said wistfully.

We had climbed back into the van after making the latest delivery and were both struggling to keep warm, as it was freezing cold that day.

'I remember you said robins were your favourites, but was there one particular robin you liked?'

'Yes, there was one who was always there, you see, outside the back door.'

Vicky was talking quietly and slowly, and it was obvious she was referring to when she lived with her mother.

'He was always outside the back door, at your mum's?'

'Yes,' she said, shivering as she spoke. 'When I was out in the cold, I'd talk to him, and he'd come bobbing up to me and always looked like he was listening.'

'What did you say to him?'

'Probably all kinds of nonsense! Too much chatter and cheek, no doubt!'

She paused and added thoughtfully, 'But usually stuff like: "You look pretty with your red breast, Mr Robin." Then I'd imagine he replied to me, "You look pretty too!" and I'd say, "Don't be silly, Mr Robin! I'm wearing an old nightie! My hair is all messy and red, but it's not pretty like the red on your chest!"'

Vicky was staring out of the windscreen now, seemingly drifting away.

'Your hair was red?'

'It was blood. My head hurt a lot when I was little.'

'I'm very sorry to hear that. Do you want to tell me what happened, to make your head hurt?'

Vicky sighed and shook her head. 'Do you think they will have robins in Florida, Angela?'

'I don't know, love. I think they will be mostly tropical birds over there.'

'He was my friend, Mr Robin. You know, sometimes it was just like I only had Izzy and Mr Robin. They were the two people who were always there for me.'

'I really am sorry to hear that, Vicky.'

'Sorry, Angela. You must think I lose the plot sometimes!'

Vicky laughed half-heartedly and blew hot breath onto her cold hands, turning the air in front of her a cloudy white.

'I don't. As I've always said, you can tell me anything.'

'Yes, but then you have to tell Hayley, don't you?'

'If I think it's important to your case, to your wellbeing.'

'Exactly. I can't be bothered with it. My mum's dead now, so what's the point? Anyhow, maybe I won't need a social worker for much longer. Guess what?'

'What?'

'My dad has said that I might be able to go and live with him, you know, if things work out once we've met up and everything!'

'Oh!' I gasped, taken aback to hear this. It was the first thing I'd heard from Vincent that had worried me. Surely it was too soon to be talking about such a move? As far as I knew the latest plan was for us to visit him in February, a couple of months before our holiday. He had jumped the gun, in my opinion, though I kept very quiet.

Vicky started to smile, oblivious to my reaction and the effect this may have on my feelings.

'I take it you are pleased about that?' I said kindly.

'Well yes, obviously! I know he lives a long way away, but he is my dad, isn't he? He's family.'

'He is. Did he say anything else?'

'Only about his disability.'

'I didn't realise he had a disability.'

'Nor did I until his last letter. But you know my mum said he had a disease?'

'Yes, I remember you mentioning that.'

'Well she lied, but that doesn't surprise me. My dad only has one leg, you see, but that's because he was injured in the line of duty, serving as a soldier in Northern Ireland. He's a hero, not a loser.'

'Good heavens! That's quite a thing to be untruthful about.'

'I know. I told you my mother was evil. Look, Dad's sent a photo of himself.'

I took hold of the photograph Vicky had pulled from her

coat pocket and had a close look. Vincent had a broad, open smile and blond hair, and in the picture he was giving a thumbs up sign while sitting in his wheelchair, with one leg of his tracksuit bottoms folded beneath him. He was a handsome-looking man, and he had a vague look of Vicky, with grey-blue eyes and a slender nose.

'Well I never!' I said. 'How do you feel, seeing his picture?'

'Great, I suppose,' she shrugged. 'It feels a bit weird too. I mean, he's my dad! I never thought I'd meet him, ever. And I thought he was horrible, but he's not. It's a shock, but a good shock.'

# 15

### *'I don't want to talk about it
### or think about it or ANYTHING!'*

Christmas was low-key but very enjoyable. With the losses we'd all suffered in the previous months, the celebrations were fairly muted. There were no big parties and get-togethers, and all the various branches of mine and Jonathan's families chose to spend the day with their nearest and dearest. This suited us fine. The shop was always busy right up until Christmas Eve, and I was very happy to have a quiet day at home with Jonathan, Vicky and my mum. Lorraine was going to her father's for Christmas dinner and had arranged to see Vicky on Boxing Day, when the sisters would swap presents at Lorraine's flat.

On Christmas morning Vicky, Jonathan and I all mucked in to peel the vegetables and potatoes, and Vicky insisted on making Yorkshire puddings to go with the turkey, which my mother was quite put out by when she arrived mid-morning.

'You can't have Yorkshire puddings with Christmas

dinner!' she protested seriously. 'It's roast beef and York-shire puddings and that's it – you can't change tradition.'

'Oh yes you can, Thelma!' Vicky teased. 'I'm making them anyway, but you don't have to have one.'

'Angela, what have you got to say? Surely you agree with me?'

'You know what, Mum, I quite fancy a Yorkshire pudding actually!'

'Well, honestly!'

When the moment came to serve up, Vicky made a big show of leaving my mother out when she served up her delicious-looking golden Yorkshires.

'Don't worry, Thelma!' she teased. 'I'll have two. They won't go to waste.'

'Well they do look rather good, Vicky. Perhaps I'll have one after all. Just that small one there would be lovely . . .'

'This one?' Vicky teased, lifting up the one my mother had her eye on. 'On no! You couldn't possibly! You can't change tradition!'

We played board games after lunch and watched *Mary Poppins*, which is one of my all-time favourite films. I'd made up a stocking for Vicky that included various items of clothing, some new trainers she'd asked for, a stationery set, a guide book on Florida, two recipe books, a couple of cassettes and a pair of cosy pyjamas with a toucan on the front. She put the pyjamas on in the early evening and curled up on the settee next to me.

'Thanks for a lovely day, Angela,' she said sleepily. 'I do love you and Jonathan, you know.'

My heart leaped. After all that had happened in the last few months, those few words made everything seem right in the world. Jonathan caught my eye, and I gave him a big, satisfied grin. Despite it being incredibly busy in the shop recently, on top of all the extra work at home the run-up to Christmas created, my stress levels had fallen significantly in the last few weeks, and somewhere along the line I realised my muscles and head had stopped aching and hurting as they had done. I felt bathed in peace and goodwill as I sank into the cushions beside Vicky. She had bought me a big box of chocolates, and I opened them up, took one and passed them around.

'I thought you were watching your weight, Angela,' my mother said, very annoyingly.

'Mum! It's Christmas Day!' I said indignantly.

She raised her eyebrows to the ceiling, and then Vicky said, 'Life is for the living!' as she tucked into a strawberry cream as ostentatiously as she could.

Vicky was right. If this year had proved anything, it was that you never know what is round the corner, and you need to seize at happiness and clutch it tight whenever you get the chance.

In the new year Jonathan and I had several appointments at the hospital, to try to discover why I had not fallen pregnant in all the time that had passed since we had stopped taking precautions. It was soon established that Jonathan's fertility was not in question, so therefore the problem lay with me. I was prepared to take whatever news came my way and, once again, I found myself thinking back to the bereavements we'd suffered the previous year and counting my lucky stars. I was alive and I had a good life. If I couldn't have children I would accept it was not meant to be, and I would not let it spoil all the goodness I had in my world.

'You're amazing,' Jonathan said when I told him how I felt. 'A lot of women would not respond like that, and you're such a maternal person too.'

'I know, but maybe that's a blessing. Maybe that's why we're fostering. Perhaps that was meant to be, because someone up there knew before I did that I couldn't have kids and set me on this path.'

Jonathan shrugged. We are not churchgoers and neither of us are sure if there's even a God, so my philosophical speculation didn't spark much of a discussion.

'Who knows,' he smiled. 'The Lord moves in mysterious ways – possibly!'

I underwent a series of tests that ultimately revealed I had a fairly common condition affecting my ovaries, which meant they weren't working as effectively as they should.

'Does this mean I will never be able to get pregnant?' I asked the doctor who delivered this news, fully expecting him to say yes.

'No, not at all,' he replied. 'The tests show that your reproductive system is not as efficient as it should be, but there is no reason you can't get pregnant. Technically, it could happen, but then again it might not, but it is entirely *possible*.'

'Really?' I said. 'Well that's wonderful. Thank you,

doctor. And is there anything at all I can do to improve my chances of conceiving?'

'No, Mrs Hart. Just keep trying. And the very best of luck!'

It seems so old-fashioned now, but in those days it simply wasn't the norm to interfere with what Mother Nature intended, and I wasn't offered any kind of treatment to help increase my odds of falling pregnant.

'Tell me honesty, Angela, how do you feel?' Jonathan asked afterwards.

'Fine,' I said. 'Honestly, I feel exactly the same as I have done all along. If it happens it happens, and I won't be devastated if it doesn't. What about you?'

'Relieved,' he said. 'I thought the news could have been much worse, and I think that would have been tough. I'd love us to have kids of our own, and I really hope we do. It's great news.'

When we got home that afternoon we were both in a really good mood. We'd asked Vicky and my mum to look after the shop for a couple of hours while we were at the hospital, and by the time we got back they'd closed up and were preparing the evening meal together, using one of Vicky's new recipe books.

'Welcome to our rest-o-rante!' Vicky announced in an exaggerated Italian accent. 'Tonight we have a spaghetti bolognese for your delight! With ze garlic bread!'

It smelled wonderful and tasted even better, and for pudding we were presented with tiramisu.

'Da-dahhh!' Vicky announced when she placed the delicious-looking desert in the centre of the table.

Jonathan and I applauded and my mother looked very proud indeed.

'I think Vicky's going to be an excellent little cook,' Mum said.

'Going to be?' Vicky responded, pretending to be annoyed. 'I'm already ze greatest chef zis house has ever known!'

We all started laughing, and there was a wonderful, warm atmosphere as we enjoyed the meal and all cleared up together.

'What's the best meal you've cooked, Jonathan?' Vicky asked, which made me and my mother chuckle rather uncharitably, as he wasn't renowned for his culinary skills.

'Ooh, let me see. I can make a mean English breakfast,' Jonathan said.

'Bacon and eggs! Any idiot can make that!'

'Less of your lip, Vicky!' he retorted. 'I can do a lovely jacket potato with beans and cheese if I put my mind to it too. That's if the microwave hasn't been blown up by one of my trainee chefs, of course . . .'

'I can't believe you've brought that up again!' Vicky said, rolling her eyes dramatically. 'That's just a rubbish thing to do!'

'Rubbish!' Jonathan said. 'Did somebody say rubbish? Oh yes, there it is! I'll just go and put that in the bin outside.'

With that he picked up a squealing Vicky and jokingly

carried her outside, dumping her on top of the dustbin in the passageway running up the side of our house.

'No don't throw me out!' she said, enjoying the game. 'I promise I'll stop being lippy!'

'It's too late for that!' Jonathan said. 'I've done it now! Now stay there and don't come back, d'you hear!'

We'd had some good news from Hayley this week too, which no doubt added to the upbeat mood in the house. Another social worker had made the initial visit to Vicky's father to prepare the ground, and we now had a confirmed date in the diary for February, when were all invited for lunch with Vincent, Carol and Matty. Vincent said Lorraine was very welcome too, and she had jumped at the chance to come with us.

Vicky's relationship with her sister appeared to have improved no end since their mother's death. Lorraine seemed quite happy for Vicky to pop in unannounced on her way home from school, and Lorraine would typically give me a quick ring to tell me Vicky was there, always sounding chirpy and pleased to see her sister. In hindsight, I wonder if Lorraine had suffered from post-natal depression following James' birth. Nobody ever said as much, though in those days the condition was nowhere near as widely recognised as it is today. Whatever the truth, Lorraine seemed to be in a much better place than she had been, and it was really good to hear her sounding so well.

'How do you feel about seeing your dad, now we have an

actual date?' I asked Vicky when the subject came up one evening.

'I don't know really. When I first heard about it I was so excited, but now I'm a bit nervous. What if it doesn't work out? What if I don't like him, or he doesn't like me? I keep thinking all these things, I can't help it.'

'That's perfectly normal. It's going to be a big day in your life.'

'I know. I'm so glad you're going to be there, and Lorraine. I couldn't do it on my own, I'd be terrified! Well, not terrified, but really nervous.'

Vincent had suggested that if Vicky felt comfortable enough after we'd all spent the afternoon together she was welcome to stay for the week, as we were visiting at the start of half-term. Vicky was keen on this idea to begin with, but as time went on and the reality of it sunk in she started to worry about being so far from home, on her own.

'Look, Vicky,' I said. 'You don't have to do anything you don't want to do. It's up to you. You must do what you feel comfortable with, and you don't have to make any decision until you get there.'

To be honest, as February drew closer, I was starting to feel incredibly nervous myself. I'd been so focused on offering Vicky support that I hadn't taken stock of my own thoughts and feelings for a while, but in a quiet spell in the shop one afternoon I had the chance to mull things over. I was concerned for Vicky's emotional wellbeing first and foremost, of course. I could not begin to imagine what it would be like to meet your father for the first time at the age of fourteen, and I sincerely hoped it would be a positive experience for her, both on the day of the reunion and in the long term. If things went well and Vicky did end up living with Vincent, would this be the best outcome for her?

I thought about the effect all this might have on Lorraine too. It had been established by now that she was not in a position to take her sister back in. Her flat was too small and she was still on some medication to help keep her depression at bay. Vicky had accepted this at the last review meeting, which Lorraine attended, and there were no hard feelings at all. In fact, Vicky had told the meeting she now wanted to stay with us, believing it was in everybody's best interests. Nevertheless, Lorraine clearly wouldn't want her sister to move halfway across the country, and I didn't want her to suffer any kind of relapse with her depression or mental state. The sisters had lost their mother so recently. They needed each other, and though Lorraine appeared to have made an excellent recovery in recent months and was looking so much healthier, having also put on some weight, she clearly had her issues and was an emotionally vulnerable person.

As for myself, I couldn't imagine not having Vicky around, even for a week, and I would miss her terribly. She had been with us for more than six months now and was very much a part of the family. Losing her full time was unthinkable, especially on top of Michelle's departure.

Despite only being passed for two placements, Hayley had asked me and Jonathan to take in a couple of very young children on a short-term placement after Michelle left. It was not unusual for the rules to be bent a little like this, if Social Services had nowhere else to place the children. Had we accepted to take both youngsters in at the same time, Hayley would have needed to go back to the panel that passed us for fostering to request an extension to our placement limit, but in the event this was not necessary. We were relieved that the breakdown of Michelle's placement had not put Social Services off using us as carers, but Jonathan and I had decided that with everything that had been going on in our lives it would not be wise for us to take too much on.

Now, though, I knew in my heart that the very first thing I would want to do if Vicky moved to her dad's permanently would be to pick up the phone to Hayley and tell her I was prepared to take on another child or two. Whether Jonathan would be in agreement I really didn't know, but that was what I dearly wanted to do, if it came to it.

'Penny for your thoughts!' Jonathan said all of a sudden, placing a mug of steaming tea down in front of me.

'Oh! The joys of being a foster carer!' I said, taken unawares.

'What are they?' he grinned sarcastically.

'Very funny!' I smiled. 'Joking apart, never knowing how long the kids are going to stay is the worst thing in the world, isn't it? I know we've said it before, but it doesn't get any easier, does it? That's what I was thinking about. It's so tough!'

'You're telling me,' Jonathan said. 'What will be will be,

Angela. We can't control the future but we'll cope. We always do.'

'I know you're right. And I know I've said it before, but it's tougher for Vicky than us. That's what we need to focus on.'

Just before closing time things very unexpectedly got a little tougher, when one of my friends popped into the shop, looking rather reticent.

'I know you've had a lot on your plate, Angela,' she started. 'But I had to tell you this. I hope you don't mind.'

'What?' I said, thinking to myself that this felt like déjà vu and Vicky must have been up to some of her old tricks again, making a nuisance of herself in the town.

'I'm afraid there's a rumour going round that Vicky has been hanging around with all kinds of boys, and Jonathan has gone mad and hit her, and thrown her out the house.'

'Pardon?' I said, stunned. 'Where on earth has this come from?'

'It's like this. You know my next door neighbour is good friends with the couple next door to you?'

'No. Which couple? Our neighbour is an old lady, living on her own.'

'No, not Mrs Dodds! The ones on the other side, across the passageway.'

'I don't even know them!'

'Well, they claim they saw Jonathan threatening Vicky and throwing her out of the house, telling her not to bother coming back.'

'You are joking?' I said, suddenly realising what they'd witnessed.

'No, I'm not.'

'Well Jonathan was,' I replied.

'Pardon?'

'He was joking. Honestly, this is just ridiculous!'

I explained the whole charade about Vicky being thrown into the rubbish, which I must admit really didn't sound anything like as funny as it had been on the evening of our Italian meal.

My friend sympathised and apologised for being the bearer of bad news.

'Don't worry. I appreciate it. I will have to phone Social Services. Thanks for letting me know.'

I reported the whole story to Hayley as soon as I possibly could. She logged the incident after my initial call, and had had a brief word with Vicky about it. That was the end of the matter as far as they were concerned. Afterwards, I discussed it with Vicky.

'I just don't believe it!' Vicky said. 'How many times was I out in the cold with hardly any clothes on, getting knocked around, for years and years, and nobody did anything? When Jonathan is just joking around with me, all this happens. It's so stupid!'

'Knocked around?'

'Oh God! Never mind!'

'But I do mind! Vicky, please talk to me about what happened to you. It might help.'

'It won't! I don't want to talk about it or think about it or ANYTHING!'

Of course, now I had to phone Hayley back and pass on Vicky's remark that she'd been 'knocked around for years and years'.

'I see,' Hayley said quietly. 'She was clearly at risk. It seems unbelievable that we have no file, no records.'

'I agree,' I said. 'Tricia thought it was just human error, that Vicky's file got lost or mislaid. It's such a shame because it feels like there are so many pieces of the puzzle missing. I don't for one second doubt a word Vicky has said, by the way.'

'No. Me neither. You've done the right thing in not pushing her though, Angela. We will just have to hope she will talk to you again when she feels up to it. Would you say she's opened up a bit more since her mother died?'

It was a good question, and I wasn't immediately sure of the answer. I thought on my feet though; I was pleased Hayley was taking the time to ask about Vicky's emotional state and I didn't want to waste the opportunity to chat further.

'Well, I think the way she talks about it has changed, though she's still not giving much away,' I found myself responding.

'In what way?'

'There's less fear, I think. I can see it still frightens her to think about the past, but she knows she's not going back there, to her mother's, so I think the terror she used to feel has subsided a little.'

'That makes sense,' Hayley said. 'Poor Vicky. It's dreadful to think of her being terrified. Anyway, at least we've made good progress with her father.'

'Absolutely. By the way, has he shed any more light on the past at all?'

'The notes I've had from the social worker who visited him don't tell us anything we don't already know about Vicky's history, though I'm sure you will find out more when you visit. I hope so.'

'So do I, though perhaps we're being optimistic. Vicky was very young indeed the last time Vincent saw her. Still, at least we've found him and the meeting is imminent. Let's hope it goes well.'

The week before we were due to visit Vicky's father, Jonathan and I were asked if we could take in a five-year-old boy for respite care, just for a few days while his mother was having a minor operation. It had been almost a year since we'd accepted a child on a very short-term placement like this – though of course that was what we thought we might have been doing with Vicky – but Jonathan and I both agreed it was something we could now manage, and wanted to do. We also hoped it might be a good distraction for Vicky in the run-up to meeting her dad.

'Guess what? We've got a little boy called Steven coming to stay with us for a few days,' I told Vicky. 'He's only five.'

'Really!' she smiled, but then her face fell. 'What's happened to his mum? She's not dead, is she?'

'No, love. She's having an operation and there's nobody else who can look after him.'

'Ah! Bless him. I'll help.'

The curly haired little boy arrived very early in the morning, as his mum needed to be at the hospital at the crack of dawn. Hayley carried Steven into the house, still in his Batman pyjamas, and he appeared to be half asleep as I greeted him and invited Hayley to bring him into the kitchen.

'Have you had any breakfast, Steven?' I asked.

He scowled at me through squinting blue eyes from beneath his fringe of ginger curls, and didn't reply.

'I'm going to have a bowl of cornflakes. Would you like some?'

'I want Mummy!' he muttered. 'Mummy!'

'Well, Mummy has to be away for a few days,' I said. 'Isn't that right, Hayley?'

The placement had been rather hastily arranged on the phone and I had been given scant details. I wasn't sure if it had been explained to Steven that his mum was in hospital, and I didn't want to say the wrong thing.

'Yes, that's right!' Hayley chimed. 'Steven's mummy has been feeling poorly, so she is going to be looked after by the kind doctors and nurses in hospital, who will make her feel better. Here's the paperwork and Steven's school and contact information, Angela. I'll be off then!'

I left Steven sitting at the kitchen table, kicking his legs and looking thoroughly miserable as I saw Hayley to the door.

'It's a routine operation,' the social worker said quietly before she left. 'All being well Mum will only be in overnight, but she'll need a couple of days' rest at home. If there are no complications Steven will go home on Friday, after school.'

'Right, that's good. Anything else I need to know?'

'No, I don't think so. You've got the address of his school and all his uniform is packed. Best of luck.'

When I returned to the kitchen Vicky had appeared, wearing her toucan pyjamas, and she was crouched down in front of Steven.

'Do you know what this bird is called?' she was asking him.

Steven had stopped scowling and was looking intently at the colourful toucan on Vicky's pyjama top.

'Parrot!' he said, looking very pleased with his answer.

'No, nearly! Try again.'

'Birdie!' he then beamed jubilantly.

'Good try but that's not a type of bird, silly! Shall I tell you?'

Steven nodded and gave Vicky a beautiful wide smile.

'It's a toucan! Can you say that?'

'Too-can, too-can, too-can,' Steven repeated.

'Very good, Steven! You're clever, aren't you?'

He smiled proudly.

'Looks like you two have already met then!' I said. 'That's good. Well then, Steven. I'm having my cornflakes now. Did you decide if you'd like some?'

He looked at me suspiciously, then at Vicky.

'I'm having some!' she said.

'Me too!' he said excitedly.

'You can-too but toucan can't,' Vicky replied, quick as a flash.

I couldn't help laughing, and I was impressed by Vicky's wit.

'Goodness me, Vicky, you're a natural!'

'Well, some of us have it and some of us don't,' she shrugged cheekily.

I asked Vicky if she wanted a lift to school that day, as I thought it would help Steven if she came in the car with us.

'All right,' she said. 'Will you be picking us up too?'

'Well, if you like. Steven finishes twenty minutes before you so that should work out fine.'

'Result!' she said, rubbing her hands together gleefully.

I had a bit of a struggle getting Steven into his school uniform and shoes, because when Vicky disappeared into the shower he became all grumpy again.

'Want Mummy!' he repeated.

'I know, love. It won't be long before you can see Mummy!'

'Want Mummy!'

'Oh I do like your lovely red jumper! What's the name of your class? I heard all the classes are named after different animals in your school.'

'Want Mummy!'

When Vicky reappeared on the landing he instantly cheered up and she distracted and entertained him brilliantly.

'I hope you're not one of those people who snores, Steven!' she said. 'Because my room is right there and I will be able to hear you, and I don't like snoring!'

With that she started oinking like a pig, and Steven copied her, giggling his head off as he did so. The two of them got louder and louder, making each other laugh. It was heart-warming to see.

Clearing out Michelle's old room had been a horrible job. I had placed the photographs and other items she left behind in storage boxes, and I'd left them in the room for a long while, not really knowing what to do with them, but Steven's stay prompted me to move them into the loft and give the room a good airing and dusting. I had no idea if I would ever see or hear from Michelle again, but I couldn't have thrown her things away; it would have been too final and too upsetting. Now her old room was being put to very good use, and it finally felt like we had moved on, in a positive way.

Steven's stay passed really quickly and without incident. He was well behaved but very quiet when he was with me, and he asked about his mum constantly. By contrast, the pattern we'd established on the first morning continued, with Vicky entertaining him marvellously whenever she was with him. This was a great outcome, as not only did Steven stop asking about his mum when Vicky was around, but she was clearly enjoying her success with him.

'Don't worry, Steven, funny Vicky is here!' she'd say, giving me a cheeky look when she found me struggling.

'Is Angela being boring again? Boo for Angela!'

'Boo!' Steven would say, giggling.

'Now that's enough, you two!' I'd caution, pretending to be cross.

On his last morning Steven had PE, and I had instructions to send him in with his kit. The shorts, T-shirt and plimsolls were in the holdall he'd arrived with, but there was no kit bag and so I fetched a plastic bag to put them in.

'What's he doing with that?' Vicky exclaimed when she came down the stairs and saw Steven standing in the hall holding the carrier bag, exactly as I'd asked him to.

'His PE kit is in there, why?'

'He can't take a carrier bag like that!'

'What's wrong with that? He hasn't got a kit bag . . .'

'No, Angela! You can't let him go out like that! He can't turn up at school like that!'

'All right,' I said, realising from Vicky's somewhat extreme reaction that this was not a point to argue.

Steven was looking a bit bemused and I didn't want him to get upset, but it was Vicky I was more concerned about. She had flushed pink and was really very agitated.

'OK, Vicky, have you got a spare bag he could use? I don't think I have anything suitable.'

'Yes, I'll get my old swimming bag, hang on.'

Vicky bolted up and down the stairs at record speed and reappeared with a red and blue nylon bag with drawstrings.

'Look, Steven, do you want to use my bag?'

He nodded shyly.

'Good, give me that carrier bag, come on, that's it, put it all in here. There!'

Vicky breathed a sigh of relief once the PE kit had been transferred to the swimming bag, and then she marched into the kitchen and very pointedly threw the plastic bag in the bin. 'There!' she said, sounding as if she had averted a catastrophe.

If something like this had happened right at the start of my fostering career I might well have become irritated, or I may have stood my ground, thinking what a silly fuss this was over nothing. I had learned a lot, however, and clearly this scenario had touched a nerve.

'So, er, what was all that about this morning?' I asked Vicky when the two of us were putting the dishes away together that evening, and Jonathan was playing snap with Steven in the lounge.

I'd wagered with myself that Vicky was going to say something about the fact she had first arrived at our house with a carrier bag containing her clothes, and that she didn't want Steven to be reminded that he was in foster care, albeit for such a very short time.

'My mother always sent me out with carrier bags like that,' she said. 'Not just for PE either.'

'You didn't have a school bag?'

'No, never. But she also sent me out with carrier bags at night, with her letters and stuff in.'

'Oh, you mean the letters you gave to people in exchange for the pills and medicines?'

'Yes. It sounds weird, doesn't it? Like I said, I'd have to knock on doors and hand over letters, and I'd have to collect bags of pills for her. I was always paranoid that people could see what I was carrying around because the carrier bags were always the thin white ones that came from the off-licence. They were practically see-though and I was scared my friends might see me and ask me what I was up to, because nobody but Izzy knew what my mum asked me to do.'

'I see. Were they all for your mum? It sounds like a lot of pills.'

'When I think about it now, it's obvious the pills weren't just for her, but I thought they were at the time, because why else would she go to all that trouble to get them? Sometimes I was out every night of the week, all over the estate, or over at Izzy's estate. I'd have a huge bag full, sometimes two bags. They looked like the sort of pills you got from the chemist, in tubs and packets. Looking back I never saw my mum take that many pills. She can't have been taking all that lot. She'd have been dead years earlier if she did.'

'It's quite a mystery, isn't it?'

'Mmm. Sometimes she had men coming over, and they would bring stuff in bags too.'

'More pills, you mean?'

'I think it was booze mostly. She always called the men her "gentlemen callers". I hated it when they were there, because she'd be more drunk than usual. I used to go to the library to get out of the way, and I'd read for as long as

I possibly could, until the library shut. I'm not surprised my dad didn't stick around very long, the state she was.'

'Well, just be careful. We don't know anything about what your mum was like when she was with your father, do we? I guess we mustn't jump to conclusions.'

'I think you're too nice, Angela! She was always drunk and horrible for as far back as I can remember. I've got loads of questions for my dad, absolutely loads. What happened to Steven's dad, by the way?'

'I honestly don't know,' I said, though I wouldn't have shared this information with Vicky even if I did.

'Vicky!' Jonathan suddenly called from the top of the stairs. 'Have you finished down there?'

'Nearly! On the last few glasses!'

'Good!'

'Why?'

'There's a certain young man who doesn't want to play snap with me any more. He wants to play with you.'

Vicky rolled her eyes dramatically.

'All right, I'll come up in a minute!' she said, pulling a face as if she were a harassed housewife juggling a dozen chores and kids.

'And I suppose I'll have to pretend he beats me too!' she said to me affably.

'You've got it!' I said, giving her an encouraging smile.

'Thanks for listening to me, Angela,' Vicky replied. 'It means a lot. I've never said most of those things about my mum to anybody.'

'Well I think that's quite normal, love. It can take years

and years to talk about the past when it has been so upsetting, and some people bottle things up forever. I'm glad you feel you can talk to me.'

'At least somebody wants to talk to you, Angela!' she said, raising her eyebrows and giving me a knowing look.

It took me a moment to realise this was a cheeky dig at the fact I'd struggled to establish much of a rapport with Steven.

'Now, now, there's no need for that!' I said as she scampered up the stairs.

That was classic Vicky, I thought, as I stood in the kitchen alone. There she was, reliving the haunting troubles of her past one moment, then catapulting herself back into the present with a mischievous joke the next.

I heard Steven squeal with delight as Vicky entered the lounge upstairs and I felt a surge of optimism about what lay ahead. She was a wonderful, spirited girl, and she was certainly due some good fortune.

'Come on, Vincent,' I found myself thinking. 'Please don't let her down.'

# 16

## *'It was our mum who did this'*

The day had finally come when Vicky was going to meet her father.

'I don't want to go,' she declared, as she picked at her breakfast of scrambled eggs, bacon and beans. Her suitcase was packed in the hallway, filled with clothes to last the week in case she wanted to stay for half-term. We were due to pick Lorraine up in half an hour and Jonathan had planned our route and was making a last-minute check of the traffic news on Ceefax.

'I'm sure you're just feeling nervous, sweetheart,' I said, locking the kitchen window and busying myself at the sink with a few bits of washing up.

'It's not that,' Vicky replied. 'I mean, it's not about today, about meeting him. It's about everything else.'

'How do you mean?'

'Well, I'm happy here with you and Jonathan. I'm worried about messing things up.'

'Vicky, love, it's understandable you've got all these

thoughts in your head. What you must remember, though, is what I've already said: nobody is going to force you to do anything you don't want to do. If we simply have lunch and you come away and don't see your dad again for a while, that's fine. If you decide to stay for the week, that's fine too. We'll just have to take one step at a time.'

She pushed her barely touched breakfast away.

'That's just it! I don't know what's going to happen and I just want to KNOW! NOW!'

'Well, there really is only one way to find out,' I said, trying to keep my voice as calm as possible. 'Come on, go up and brush your teeth and we'll get going.'

'Urgh! It's so annoying! I bet you're just hoping I get on with him and go and live there, so you can get rid of me!'

She stomped out of the kitchen. I knew Vicky well enough not to rise to this unreasonable accusation. She was just letting off steam, and I knew she didn't believe this for one second.

Lorraine was also in a jittery state when we collected her, and the two sisters sat in the back of the car looking out of sorts and awkward in each other's company.

'How's James?' Vicky asked.

'Fine. Carl's really good with him. They're going to the park.'

'That's good.'

'Yes. I'll miss him today! I've never left him for this long. So how long did you say the journey is, Jonathan?'

'I reckon five hours, Lorraine, if we don't hit any traffic problems.'

'I thought so.'

Vicky tut-tutted loudly.

'What's that for?' Lorraine said. 'You should be grateful Angela and Jonathan are going to all this trouble. It's very good of them to drive us all this way.'

'It's not the journey I'm moaning about. The longer the better as far as I'm concerned! It's that you're complaining about leaving James for one day. Vincent left me for fourteen years. Why am I even bothering with this? Mum was right. He's a loser.'

Jonathan and I swapped a glance and waited to hear what Lorraine would say.

'Maybe he is,' she said. 'But maybe he isn't. At least you can find out for yourself, once and for all.'

'Yes, it might be just the once,' Vicky huffed. 'You're not wrong there.'

The sisters then sat in silence for quite some time, and Jonathan put Radio 2 on to help improve the atmosphere, which it did, fractionally. Vicky had brought a book along and she eventually read a few chapters while Lorraine leafed through some women's magazines she had in her handbag.

We eventually stopped to stretch our legs and use the facilities at the motorway services when we were about an hour-and-a-half away from Vincent's home. The break seemed to do everybody good.

'Do you know what his house is like?' Lorraine asked.

'No idea,' Vicky replied.

'What if he lives in a big mansion?'

'Ha ha, what are the chances of that, Loz? It would be funny though, wouldn't it? What if he's rich? What if he's a millionaire?!'

The mood had certainly lightened, and once we were on the final stretch of the journey an air of excitement and anticipation began to creep into the car. I felt charged with a mixture of emotions. My nerves were on edge and I had so many doubts and concerns about what might happen, but I was also eager to discover what the rest of the day would bring. They say that blood is thicker than water, but would the old adage prove to be true in Vincent and Vicky's case, or had too much water passed under the bridge for father and daughter to re-connect?

'I think we're very nearly there!' Jonathan declared as he indicated left into a large housing estate situated close to a busy dual carriageway. 'Can you read out the last few directions, Angela?'

I felt my pulse quicken, and when I flicked my head to the back of the car Vicky and Lorraine had both sat upright and were peering out of the windows attentively. The housing estate we entered was incredibly run down. The pebble-dashed houses were all very small and many looked neglected. Unfortunately the weather seemed to suit the scene perfectly; it was dull and overcast and there was a cold nip in the air.

'Next right,' I said to Jonathan.

'Right!' he said cheerfully.

His demeanour reminded me of the day we'd pulled up at the tatty council offices for Vicky's initial review meeting, when she was terrified her mother might turn up, and Jonathan was doing his best to gee her up. We were heading deeper into the estate now and, disappointingly, the further we ventured the worse state the houses and gardens seemed to be in, and the more depressing the landscape appeared. One house had a rusting fridge outside the front door and bulging bin bags strewn on the front garden. A child in a jumper and a nappy played with an upturned shopping trolley beside the concrete porch of another home, and there was a group of grey-faced youths standing under a vandalised lamppost, all of them smoking rolled up cigarettes and dressed in scruffy shell suits.

'Next left,' I said. 'Then it should be at the end of the cul-de-sac.'

My eyes were on stalks as we headed down Vincent's road. I was praying his house would look more inviting than the majority of the others we had seen, and thankfully it did.

'That's it!' I said, pointing to one of two semi-detached bungalows standing at the end of the cul-de-sac.

Jonathan pulled up and we all took a moment to gather ourselves together.

'It's bigger than my place, anyhow!' Lorraine said.

'Should have realised he'd have a bungalow,' Vicky commented.

'Oh yes, the wheelchair,' I replied. 'Of course. Come on then! We've made good time. Thanks for driving, Jonathan.'

Vicky climbed out of the car looking extremely wary, and I longed to throw my arms around her. The rundown estate appeared to have sapped away some of the hope and eager expectation she seemed to have felt earlier, and her shoulders were now drooped and her chin was on her chest.

'Come on then,' Jonathan said brightly. 'Let's go!'

We all shuffled up the ramp leading to the front door, and it opened before we had chance to knock.

'Hello! I'm Carol!' the lady standing before us exclaimed. 'Come on in! It's freezing out there!'

'Thanks!' I said, as she stepped back into her wide hallway and repeated, 'Come on in!'

'I'm Angela,' I said, going first. 'And this is Vicky, Lorraine and my husband, Jonathan.'

'Hello!' everybody responded.

Carol was slightly built and had thin, fair hair styled in a short bob. She was wearing a cream blouse with a crocheted pink cardigan over the top, some navy blue slacks and a pair of mules.

We all shuffled slowly forward. 'Shall we take our shoes off?' I asked.

'No, no need!' she said. 'Just come in.'

We followed her through a door on the left of the hallway that led into the lounge, and there was Vincent, sitting to the right of us in his wheelchair, smiling broadly.

'Hello!' he said in a strong Scottish accent, scanning our faces before zoning in on Vicky. 'So you must be Vicky! Well, well, well. Come and say hello to your old man!'

Vicky stepped towards him tentatively.

'Hi!' she said quietly, raising her hand as if to give a little wave.

'No need to be shy! Come and give me a hug! Say hello properly!'

Vicky reluctantly obliged, giving Vincent the quickest, lightest hug she could get away with before retreating back into our little group.

'Sit down, everybody!' Carol said kindly, gesturing towards a burgundy velour settee that stretched along the length of the wall on the left hand side. From her accent she appeared to be from the local area. Vincent's thick Scottish brogue had come as something of a surprise; I'd wrongly assumed he was from our region, where Vicky was born.

There was an elaborate brass fireplace facing us and the entire wall around it was covered with slate tiles, some jutting out to make shelves that contained brass ornaments of horses and dogs. In pride of place, in the centre of the mantelpiece, stood a gleaming medal in a large velvet-lined display box, which I imagined must be Vincent's Army commendation.

'I'll put the kettle on,' Carol said. 'Who would like tea, or coffee?'

Jonathan and I said we'd love a cup of tea, Lorraine asked for a glass of water and Vicky said she didn't want anything.

'Are you all right, love?' I said.

Vicky had sat herself next to me on the settee and was looking like a rabbit caught in the headlights, staring across the room at Vincent.

He was wearing a rugby shirt that was stretched around his wide stomach plus red tracksuit bottoms, with one leg folded beneath him, just like in the photo he had sent. Somehow, he looked different to the picture though, and at first I couldn't put my finger on why. He had the same blond hair, grey-blue eyes and slender nose of course, but now he looked absolutely nothing like Vicky, as I had first thought he did. Had that been wishful thinking on my part, I wondered? Had I been searching for something that wasn't there, trying too hard to make a connection?

'So then, Vicky, tell me about yourself!' Vincent said. 'It's so great to meet you after all this time!'

Vicky continued to stare at him, but she didn't reply and to my dismay I realised she had gone into one of her frightened, semi-frozen trances.

'I'm sorry, Vincent,' I spluttered. 'This happens sometimes. It's when Vicky is a bit, er, uptight.'

Vicky was sitting statue-still and unblinking when Carol returned with a tray containing three large mugs of tea and Lorraine's glass of water.

'You sure I can't get you a glass of water or anything, Vicky?' Carol said, trying to catch her attention. 'Or we've got Coke or squash?'

'Sorry,' Jonathan interjected. 'As Angela was just saying to Vincent, Vicky goes very quiet like this sometimes.'

'Oh! I'm sorry.'

Carol looked again at Vicky, and we all followed her gaze. Vicky was white, deathly still and her eyes were glazed and unblinking.

'Can I do anything to help? Are you sure she's all right?

I'm a nurse, as I think Vincent has told Vicky in one of the letters. Shall I check her over?'

'Honestly, she'll be all right,' I said. 'It happens from time to time. I think it's probably best to let her come round herself.'

When I'd finished speaking Vincent let out a loud sigh and then he held his head in his hands.

'Christ! What have I done to my girl?' he said.

I looked at him in alarm. His outburst was unexpected, and I wanted to say, *Please don't blame yourself*, but the words wouldn't leave my lips.

'It's not your fault,' Lorraine suddenly said. 'It was our mum who did this. She did this to Vicky, not you.'

Vicky's began to click her head towards Lorraine in the machine-like fashion I'd witnessed several times before.

At the same time Carol went to Vincent's side and put her arm around him.

'Don't go getting yourself all upset, babe,' she said. 'You know it's not good for you.'

When Carol spoke those words a penny dropped and I realised why Vincent didn't look the same in real life as he did in his photograph. It was the expression deep in his face that made him look so different. The glossy picture he sent had captured him with a twinkle in his eye, but in the flesh he had a slightly haunted look about him; the type I'd seen before in soldiers who'd served in places like Northern Ireland.

*Oh my God*, I thought, *he could be just as traumatised as Vicky.*

'How do you know?' Vicky said quietly to Lorraine. She spoke so softly Lorraine had trouble hearing her.

'What?'

'How do you know it was Mum's fault?'

'Are you defending her?' Lorraine replied, sounding shocked.

'No. I just want to know the whole story. I want to know the other side.'

I gave Vicky a reassuring look.

'As you can imagine,' I said to Vincent. 'Vicky has lots of questions.'

'Let me tell you, so have I,' he said, wiping a tear from his eye.

Before we knew it, Vincent had launched into an astonishing monologue that had us all on the edge of our seats.

'I want you to know the full story, Vicky. It's what you deserve, no more no less. *I'd* want to know the full story if it were me, I surely would. So here we go, here's what happened.

'When I met your mother I was fresh out of the Army. Didn't know where my life was going, what I was going to do with myself. Matty was a wee bairn, and his mammy buggered off and left me. Couldn't cope with a "cripple". Aye, that's what she called me. A cripple! I'd served for Queen and country in Belfast, for Christ's sake! I could have died. I was bloody lucky to only lose a leg. Anyway, she upped and left and there I was, in a wheelchair, with one leg and a wee lad to look after. I was living in your neck of the woods then, and thank God the local authority gave me a flat and some home help. That's how I met your mother. She was friendly with one of the lasses who helped me out. I met the pair of them in the pub one night, when Matty was with a babysitter. Bam! That was that. She was a proper livewire, your mammy, I'll give her that. She was singing in the pub. I don't mean entertaining; she was just having a good sing song and a knees up with her mates, and towards the end of the night she came over and chatted me up. "You look like a fella who needs showing a good time," she said.'

Vincent paused for breath for the very first time since he'd started telling his story and I cut in. It was a gut reaction.

'Are you sure it's appropriate for Vicky to hear all this,' I interjected, as I was concerned about what was coming next.

Vincent completely ignored me and Vicky didn't tear her eyes off her father to even glance in my direction. I looked at Jonathan as if to say, 'What are we going to do?' and he shrugged half-heartedly as Vincent cleared his throat, took a deep breath and began another monologue.

'And show me a good time she did! She was a bloody good laugh, and a real tonic; just what I needed. She didn't even care that I only had one leg – how lucky was I? It wasn't long before your mam was staying over at my flat all the time, as it was hard for me to get out, with Matty being such a young bairn and me being in the wheelchair. Anyhow, we'd only been together for a couple of months when your mother told me she was expecting. Was I over the moon? You bet your life I was! I felt like I'd been given a second chance in life.

'Your mammy was no saint, mind you. I thought she'd change her ways with a wee one on the way, but she didn't. No, not Brenda. She seemed to get wilder, going out every night and drinking and smoking as much as she always had. I should have realised she wasn't the best mother in the world, what with you, Lorraine, living with your daddy. Brenda had told me she had shared custody with her ex, but if that was true she never did her half. I never even met you, Lorraine, the whole time I was with your mother.

'As the pregnancy went on we started arguing over her drinking but Brenda wouldn't change her ways, oh no! I hoped things would get better once the baby came along, but I'm sorry to say it didn't. She would prop you up in my arms with a bottle of milk, Vicky, and go out to the pub, coming in at all hours, steaming drunk. This went on for a couple of months, and then one night I left her in the flat with you and Matty while I called round to see the bloke next door. He was into fishing, and he was going to take me over to the local lakes. I'd gone round to make some plans. I was only out for twenty minutes but when I got back Matty was roaming around in a dirty nappy and you, Vicky, well, it breaks my heart to say it, but you were screaming blue murder in your cot. There was no sign of Brenda until the early hours of the next morning, when she fell in the door stinking of booze again.

'That was it. I told her we were over and I was going to apply for custody of you, but she went nuts. She told me she had found a new fella who had his own house, and that I stood no chance of winning custody, being on my own and disabled as I was. We weren't even married and so she was right; everything was stacked against me. I didn't give up though, Vicky. I want you to know this. I tried to get custody. I tried as hard as I possibly could, but I was turned down flat. Even then I didn't give up. I asked Social Services to put you on the "at risk" register, and I said that if ever there was a problem they must contact me, as I would take you in. Nobody ever contacted me, though, which I figured was a mixed blessing. I assumed Brenda must have sorted herself out, or I would have known about it. That's what I told myself for year after year. My Vicky is all right. She has to be, or Social Services would have been knocking on my door.'

There was a long pause, and you could have heard a pin drop.

'Now I'm told there were no records anywhere about my fight for custody, or my request to put you on the "at risk" register. It's absolutely criminal! I've spent the last fourteen years thinking you were all right; you had to be all right. If you weren't Social Services would have got in touch, right? That's what I've always believed, always. Now I find out my paperwork must have been lost or thrown away like old chip paper! I might as well have not existed! Social Services might as well have not existed! And we've lost all these years . . .'

Vincent dissolved into floods of tears, and his loud sobs reverberated around the room. We all sat silently, as if out of respect for Vincent's feelings, and to mourn the loss he was clearly feeling.

'Fourteen years!' he repeated, shaking his head from side to side. 'Fourteen years!'

As he said 'fourteen years' for the third or fourth time, a gangly teenager appeared in the doorway.

'Er, everything all right? I, er, thought I'd better pop in and say hello.'

'This is Matty, everyone,' Carol said.

'Hello, Matty,' myself, Jonathan and Lorraine said politely. Vicky just stared at him. She looked like she'd just stepped off the biggest, scariest roller coaster you could imagine, and was feeling disorientated, nauseous and slightly shell-shocked.

'Your dad's just been filling everyone in,' Carol said to Matty. 'Obviously, it's quite emotional.'

'OK,' he said, looking Vicky up and down. 'Well, it's good to meet you all. I'll, er, come back down when the food's ready.'

'He seems like a lovely lad!' I remarked, trying to lighten the atmosphere but cringing to myself at how crass this probably sounded.

'So I was right, we'd never met,' Lorraine muttered. 'I knew I would have remembered.'

Piecing everything together, Lorraine was aghast at Vincent's story, and she turned to me and asked in an irritated manner, 'How could Social Services not have kept records?'

'We'll never know exactly what happened,' I said. 'Perhaps they did and they got accidentally lost or destroyed . . .'

'I think that's a generous viewpoint, Angela,' Jonathan said, which took me by surprise. 'It wasn't as if it was one phone call that wasn't logged, or a tip-off from a stranger that was mishandled or overlooked. This was Vicky's father making a clear request.'

It was unlike Jonathan to find it hard to bite his tongue, but he clearly couldn't help himself. I caught his eye and gave him a 'that's enough' look, and saw him button his lips together.

'Are you all right, love?' I said to Vicky.

She nodded very slowly.

'Are you all right, Dad?' she said, looking over at Vincent.

His head shot up and he looked at Vicky with a look of love and relief on his face.

'Yes,' he said. 'What's done is done, I suppose. What's the expression? No use crying over spilt milk?'

His bravado in the light of what we'd just heard reminded me of the way Vicky behaved at times, pulling herself together with impressive speed. It was humbling, and I glanced towards Vincent's medal on the mantelpiece. Carol saw me.

'Commendation,' she said. 'Vincent is a very brave man indeed. He doesn't like talking about it.' She paused then added pointedly, 'He went through a lot, you know.'

'You wouldn't guess I was brave, would you?' he said, attempting a smile. 'Can you get me a tissue, baby?'

Carol fetched some tissues from the kitchen.

'Anyone else?' she said, passing them round as if they were a box of chocolates. We all took one and dabbed our eyes or blew our noses. It had been a very moving reunion indeed.

'Well, I hope you're all ready to eat something?' Carol said, clasping her hands together and looking at us hopefully. 'I've made a huge potato salad, there are two types of quiches, plenty of cold meats and we've got rhubarb and apple crumble for pudding.'

Vicky looked at me with a look of amusement on her face, which I was very glad to see.

'Ah, Vicky's a dab hand at making rhubarb crumble,' I said.

'No way!' Vincent exclaimed. 'Crumbles are my signature dish. I love them.'

'No way!' Vicky echoed. 'With custard not cream?'

'Of course! Custard every time!'

Carol showed us through to the dining room and the meal was a great success. The food was delicious and our hosts had clearly gone to a lot of trouble. The conversation shifted to the usual kind of chatter you'd expect when new groups of people meet. We found out Vincent was a keen fisherman and worked part time doing administration work for the British Legion, which he thoroughly enjoyed. Carol was an auxiliary nurse at the local hospital, and they'd met when Vincent was undergoing physiotherapy there. She had no children of her own and was in her early forties, the same age as Vincent. Matty didn't say much but he politely answered the few questions directed at him and excused himself as soon as he possibly could after the main course, explaining that he wasn't into puddings.

'I'm off to the gym soon,' he said, 'so I'll leave you all to it. Nice to have met you.'

As soon as Matty left the room Vincent asked Vicky if she was going to stay for the week.

'Yes, I think I'd like that,' she said without hesitation, which I wasn't prepared for. I could sense that Jonathan and Lorraine were as surprised, pleased and reticent as I was.

'Great!' he said. 'I'd like to spend more time with you. We've got a lot of catching up to do.'

Vicky smiled. 'I know,' she said. 'I'm glad I found you.'

# 17

## *'It's not fair! It's torture!'*

'I think I'll just phone up and make sure she's feeling all right,' Lorraine said.

We'd pulled over for fuel and Lorraine was making a beeline for the telephone box near the petrol station.

'I'll come with you,' I said.

Jonathan nodded. 'Send her my love.'

We'd only left Vicky forty minutes earlier, but it felt like days. My heart was aching for her. She'd looked happy – excited, even – as we'd said our goodbyes, but I wondered how she was feeling now, once she was at her dad's alone, in a strange town, staying for a whole week with a family she had only just met. Lorraine had started crying in the back of the car as soon as we turned out of Vincent's estate. It was such a bleak-looking place, and despite the fact Vincent and Carol had been so welcoming and their home was warm and comfortable, it really didn't help matters that their neighbourhood was so uninviting.

'Oh my God!' Lorraine had sniffed. 'What have we done? We can't leave her there, can we?'

'She'll be fine,' I said, holding back the tears. 'And I've told her that we will collect her any time she likes if she wants to come home early. She just has to pick up the phone.'

This was true, but I was really struggling to come to terms with the situation myself, and I knew my words gave none of us any comfort.

Listening to Vincent's story had been shocking. He could have been reunited with Vicky so much earlier, if only records had been kept and warnings heeded. What was it going to do to Vicky when she'd had chance to digest all this information? To know she could have escaped the terrible life she had with her mother if only a few basic files and pieces of paperwork had been dealt with properly would be extremely difficult to cope with. The very thought of it made me burn with sorrow and regret, but how was it going to affect Vicky? She had been the one put out in the cold in her nightie and sent out dressed in ill-fitting, second-hand clothes. She had been the one living with a drunken mother who was seemingly more concerned with her pills and alcohol and her 'gentleman callers' than her daughter's wellbeing. And it was Vicky who was knocked about and had a sore head, the details of which I had yet to uncover.

'Vic! Are you all right?'

Lorraine had obviously got through to her sister and I was standing outside the phone box, holding the door ajar so I could hear half the conversation.

'Oh that's good. I'm glad about that . . . What's that? Oh that's nice. Really? Oh that's good too. Now just remember what Angela said. Ring us any time, you, d'you hear? . . . All right, Vic. Look after yourself. There's the pips. Bye . . . And you. Bye. Bye.'

'She's fine,' Lorraine nodded to me, hanging up the receiver.

'Of course she is!' I said bravely.

'Oh Angela!'

Lorraine hugged me and sobbed into my shoulder.

'Now don't go setting me off!' I said. 'Come on! She's absolutely fine. What did she say?'

'Nothing really. They've got a cat called Hugo who doesn't like visitors, but she's just met him and says he's lovely. He's got different coloured eyes apparently, like David Bowie.'

'Oh that's good. She'll love that.'

'Also, Vincent has got a pigeon loft in the back garden. He likes birds, like Vicky. Funny that, isn't it?'

'It is! It certainly is!'

When we set off again Lorraine eventually had a snooze in the back of the car, and I inevitably found myself picking over Vincent's words, and the way he had told his story.

'Do you think Vincent's had some kind of therapy?' I whispered to Jonathan after mulling things over in my mind for a while.

'What, because of losing his leg?'

'Well, yes, but I was thinking more in terms of what he must have gone through, mentally.'

'You mean psychotherapy, or something like that?'

'Well I don't know what they call it. It was just a bit unusual, the way he got everything off his chest in one fell swoop like he did. It was like he's used to doing it; a lot of people would be tongue-tied, but he was the opposite. It was quite astonishing, really, wasn't it, the way he just rattled it all off, hardly pausing for breath?'

'Mmm, I think you might have a point, Miss Marple!' Jonathan smiled thoughtfully. 'We have to be careful though. We don't know exactly what he went through, do we? Or what he was like before the . . . before he lost his leg.'

'I know,' I said. 'I don't want to criticise him, but I wonder if he thought of the effect it would have on Vicky, to have everything told to her like that? I mean, *I* found it shocking enough. What about Vicky?'

Jonathan flicked me a glance and nodded. 'I'm not sure he considered that, or he would have taken things slower, wouldn't he?'

'I think so. And Carol definitely made a point of mentioning his commendation, and saying he'd gone through a lot. I think that was her way of telling me that Vincent's way of doing things needs a little bit of understanding.'

I phoned Vicky every day, and to my relief she seemed to be having a whale of a time. Her dad had shown her pictures of himself in his Army uniform which she was very impressed with, she loved playing with Hugo the cat, and Carol had driven them to the local country park, where they'd walked around a lake and Vicky had pushed her dad in his wheel-chair and fed the ducks.

'Funny how Dad likes birds!' Vicky laughed.

'Isn't it just!' I smiled. 'And it was funny about the crumble as well, wasn't it?'

'I know. He's also taught me a good trick to help me cut out smoking,' she said, adding that Vincent had also been a smoker since his teens, but had managed to stop when he left the Army.

I knew Vicky was still having the odd cigarette. Her New Year's resolution to quit had lasted less than a week, and so I very much hoped Vincent's input might make a difference.

'What's his secret then?'

'Well, he buys a quarter of pineapple cubes and a quarter of cola cubes from the corner shop, and whenever he fancies a fag he has one of those instead. I've tried it, and it works!'

'Well I never! That's great. Er, have you wanted a cigarette often?'

'Quite a bit.'

'So have you been feeling a bit stressed, or homesick?'

'No, not really. I mean, I miss you and Jonathan, obviously, and Lorraine and everybody really, but I'm really enjoying myself. It's just a bit funny being in a strange place, with no friends.'

Her frankness reassured me, though I still had plenty of doubts and worries. Everything seemed to have happened so fast, and I desperately didn't want things to go wrong, for any of us. When the week was over I drove back on my own to pick Vicky up, as Jonathan needed to be in the shop and there had been no offer from Vincent's side of any help with transport. I didn't mind. The goodbye hug she gave her dad was very different to the one when she'd first arrived, and I was pleased to have witnessed it. Vicky flung her arms around Vincent enthusiastically, showing genuine affection.

'See you soon, Dad!' she beamed. 'Thanks for everything.'

Carol was as pleasant as she had been when we first met, offering me a cup of tea and asking if I wanted a sandwich.

'No thanks. I've brought a packed lunch to have on the way back,' I said. 'But that's very kind.'

It was only when Carol called Matty to say goodbye that I detected a little tension. Matty very reluctantly appeared from his bedroom at the back of the bungalow, and said an extremely curt goodbye to Vicky, before turning on his heel.

'What was all that about?' I asked Vicky when we set off.

'I don't think he likes me,' she said. 'I heard him asking Carol when I was leaving, and he knew I could hear.'

'Oh, that's a shame. I suppose it must be quite a big thing for him, though, suddenly having you arrive on the scene. He's been the only child all this time.'

'He was nasty,' Vicky muttered.

'In what way?'

'When we were on our own in the kitchen one morning he said I shouldn't trust my dad.'

'Did he? Why?'

My heart sank, and I was very afraid of what Vicky might say next.

'He said he's got mental problems, not just physical ones. And he asked me if I believed the story about him fighting for custody. I told him that of course I did. Why would he make that up?'

'What did Matty say to that?'

'He said, "If he wanted you that much, I think he'd have tried harder to find you."'

'And what did you say back?'

Vicky took a deep breath.

'I didn't answer him. I wasn't going to waste my breath.'

With that she plugged in her earphones and listened to a cassette on an old Walkman that her dad had given her, which she was thrilled with. I decided to leave her to it; I was confident Vicky knew she could talk to me again whenever she felt ready.

'Can I go back at Easter?' Vicky asked when we finally got home.

'Yes, love, if your dad and Carol are happy to have you.'

'Yes, they are. They said I can stay whenever I want. Would you be able to drive me there again?'

'I'm sure that can be arranged. We're in Florida for a fortnight but you get nearly three weeks off as it happens, as there are also a couple of staff training days added on to the end of your Easter break. I'm sure we can fix something up. You're not worried about Matty?'

'Nah, he's just jealous. I saw his face when Dad gave me the Walkman.'

'Oh dear, that's unfortunate.'

'He can like it or lump it as far as I'm concerned. I don't even care if there's some truth in what he says. The important thing is I've found my dad now, and I'm not going to let anyone spoil that.'

Vicky and I had a meeting with Hayley following her week away. She reiterated everything she had told me, saying she was very happy with how things had gone, but omitting to mention what had happened with Matty.

'Would you like to live with your father full time?' Hayley asked.

'Yes,' Vicky said emphatically, her eyes widening. 'Am I allowed to?'

I felt my throat go dry.

'Yes. Your father has told us he's happy for you to move in, whenever you want.'

'What, really? You mean now?'

'Well, we would have to find you a school place first, so I can't give you an exact date. Realistically, it is likely to be at the start of the summer term.'

'After Easter? That's a long way off. Mind you, at least I'll still get to go to Florida!'

Vicky grinned and looked at me.

'That's great, isn't it, Angela?' she said.

'Wonderful,' I replied, though needless to say it wasn't great for me, not at all. I would miss Vicky dreadfully, and I also had misgivings; I felt it was too soon for Vincent to make such a big decision, though of course it wasn't my place to say so. My opinion didn't count, and I was not going to rock the boat by sharing it. Hayley was the professional here, and if she and her well-trained colleagues in Social Services were supportive of this plan, who was I to argue?

Before she left Hayley asked if she could have a quiet word with me, once Vicky was out of the room. For a second I naively wondered if she was going to check how I was feeling about the situation, or canvas my opinion about Vincent taking Vicky in. I was wrong.

'I have some news about Michelle,' Hayley said unexpectedly.

I could tell from the look on her face that this was not going to be good, and I braced myself.

'Is she all right?'

'She is pregnant,' Hayley announced.

'No!'

'Yes, I'm afraid so. The baby is due in a couple of months. Did you know anything about this?'

'No, I didn't!' I said indignantly, suddenly realising that Hayley wasn't telling me this to keep me updated, but rather because she was required to do so. I felt judged, in fact, and my gut reaction was to stand up for myself.

'As you know I did report that I had heard Michelle's mother was allowing her to sleep with her boyfriend on her weekend visits, but I only found out about this after her placement with us had broken down.'

'Michelle fell pregnant when she was living with you, Angela,' Hayley said sombrely. 'I'll make a note that you had no knowledge of this, and I'll be in touch about Vicky leaving. The term times are different where her father lives, so we might need a bit of luck with finding a school place.'

Hayley fished her car keys out of her bag and stood up.

'Hang on,' I said, reeling at all the news. 'Vicky has got her exams next year, so we need to make sure she can continue with the same subjects, and the same exam boards. You can't just put her in any school!'

'We'll do our best to find the most suitable school place for Vicky, of course, but as I'm sure you know our priority is to return her to her parent. It may be a case of Hobson's choice.'

My heart tightened in my chest. Vicky had made such good progress at school, and I really didn't want her education to suffer. I didn't want Vicky to suffer in any way whatsoever. I felt fiercely protective of her and also very upset at the prospect of losing her.

'And Michelle?' I gasped, exasperated. 'What's going to happen now? Is she staying with her mother? Is she keeping the baby?

'I can't tell you that, Angela,' she said, giving me what seemed to be a slightly disapproving look.

I wasn't sure if Hayley was intimating that my question was inappropriate or, worse, that she was being openly critical of the fact Michelle had fallen pregnant while under my care. Either way, I was left feeling rattled and uneasy, and with an uncomfortable knot in my stomach. After Hayley drove off I caught a look at myself in the long mirror in our hallway. At a glance I looked the same as usual. My dark brown hair, parted on the side, fell in natural waves to my jaw line, just as it always had. My make-up was minimal; the dab of blusher, scant coat of mascara and lick of lip gloss I applied each morning were barely visible, which was exactly how I liked it. I somehow looked different though, but I couldn't quite put my finger on it.

*Something's changed, Angela*, I thought to myself as I stared back at my reflection.

I'd gone through so much since becoming a foster carer, and particularly since Vicky's arrival. My general appearance had stayed the same, of course, but something had changed within me, and Hayley's visit had just made me realise it. The brisk way Hayley had dished out the alarming news about Vicky's relocation and Michelle's pregnancy had upset me. I knew she was only doing her job, and that she had to conduct herself in a professional manner, but I could have cried, and the old me *would* have cried. Now, however, despite feeling hurt and shocked I could feel a powerful rush of determination coursing through my body. I wasn't going to crumple in the face of yet more blows; I was in too deep, and I was not giving up, however testing this was. I raised my chin and put my shoulders back proudly as I looked myself in the eye. There was a steely spark there that I didn't have before. I'd learned so much, and I'd toughened up; that was what had changed since I'd embarked on this journey.

Fostering wasn't about me and my sensibilities. If I'm very honest, at the start I had wanted to enjoy the rewards of caring for kids as much as I wanted to care for them. I still wanted the benefits, of course, because nothing beats the satisfaction gained from helping a child, but now I understood very clearly that in order to earn the rewards I needed to be able to take the kicks in the stomach and the stabs to the heart. That's the name of the game in foster care, and I knew that now, without a shadow of a doubt.

'Please don't even think about telling me this is the final straw,' I said to Jonathan as soon as I told him about Hayley's visit.

'What are you talking about?'

'I know what you are going to say, but I've made my mind up, Jonathan. We went into this to help kids. We thought it would be a heck of a lot easier than it is, but d'you know what? We still want to help kids, don't we?'

'Yes, of course.'

'That's agreed then. Just because it's harder than we thought, we mustn't stop. Otherwise we'd have been doing this for selfish reasons.'

Jonathan thought long and hard about what I'd said. He was still catching up with Michelle's latest news, and the fact Vicky was making plans to live with her dad, so it was an awful lot for him to deal with. I wouldn't normally put him on the spot like this, but I guess it shows how passionately I felt about what we were doing, and where I wanted our lives to go next.

'Will you stand by me?' I asked bluntly. 'I want to carry on fostering, come what may.'

'I can't say that yet,' he replied. 'Let's wait until Vicky has left and see how we feel.'

I knew he was right to be cautious like this, but I also knew I was not going to change my mind. Fostering was my destiny. I had never felt more certain of anything in my life.

Vicky got herself a boyfriend in the March. He was called Scot, and she'd known him for a couple of years through the youth club. My mother, of all people, was the first to know as she bumped into the two of them holding hands in town one Saturday.

'Aren't you going to introduce me to your companion?' my mother had said, which prompted Vicky to blush, roll her eyes and mutter, 'This is Scot, this is Thelma.'

'Before your mum tells you, I have got a boyfriend, and his name is Scot,' Vicky announced to me when she got home that afternoon.

'Oh that's nice, love,' I said. 'What's he like? When do I get to meet him?'

'He's coming over later, after dinner, if that's OK?'

'Great! What are you doing?'

'Just staying in my room, listening to music.'

'OK.'

This was all new territory to me, and I discussed it with Jonathan.

'Do you think it's OK to let them go upstairs together?' I asked.

'Well, I think Vicky's a sensible girl. We know what she thought about Michelle on that subject. I guess we should just make sure we check on them.'

'Agreed,' I said. 'The last thing I want to do is fall out with her now, but her health and safety comes first, needless to say.'

My mother was coming round later that evening too. She had taken delivery of several boxes of belongings from my brother Andrew's home, and had asked me to help her go through them. It wasn't a job I was looking forward to; I was dreading it, in fact. When the doorbell rang, about half an hour after we'd finished our Saturday treat of fish and chips, without thinking I said to Vicky, 'Oh that'll be your gentleman caller.'

Vicky stopped dead in her tracks, dropping the tea towel she was holding onto the kitchen floor.

'Are you all right?' I asked.

It was as if she'd been struck by a thunderbolt. Vicky had a terrified look in her eyes and stared straight through me.

'Vicky? What on earth's happened, sweetheart?'

The next moment Jonathan and my mother appeared.

'Look what the wind blew in!' Jonathan joked.

'Oh! Mum! I thought it was Vicky's boyfriend at the door.'

'Sorry to disappoint!' she replied, looking at Vicky. 'Oh, what's the matter?'

'Vicky?' Jonathan said. 'What *is* the matter? Can you hear me?'

Looking at my mum I began to explain that this had just happened, and that Vicky had frozen just a moment before.

'I said to Vicky "that'll be your boyfriend at the door" and then this happened,' I said.

Vicky began turning her head ever so slowly in my direction, clicking it round, half inch by half inch.

'That's not what you said,' she said almost inaudibly, when her eyes were finally in line with mine.

'Well I'm really sorry, love, that's what I meant to say.'

Vicky had gone grey and all expression had fallen from her face.

'What exactly did you say then, Angela?' my mother asked, looking concerned and confused.

'Well, like I say, I said . . . oh, I remember now. I said: "That'll be your gentleman caller."'

Vicky gasped when I repeated those words, and I suddenly realised my mistake. Brenda's visitors had been referred to as gentleman callers. My remark must have triggered a memory, and I could have kicked myself for being so careless. It was not even an expression I normally used; I think I must have only said it because I had my mother on my mind, as it was the kind of thing she might say.

'Vicky, love, I'm sorry. Come and sit down.'

I cupped both my hands under her elbows and guided Vicky to a kitchen chair.

'Just take a deep breath,' I said. 'Just breathe.'

I indicated to my mother and Jonathan that they should leave us to it, and I heard them climb the stairs to the lounge. As soon as we were alone, Vicky focused her gaze on me expectantly.

'You look a bit better, love,' I said. 'You're doing fine. We can sit here for as long as we need to.'

'When will it stop!' she suddenly blurted out.

'You've been through so much, it's no wonder you're a bit het up.'

'Het up?' Vicky repeated, sounding quizzical.

'You know, jumpy, on edge.'

'I know what it means!' she snapped. 'But it's more than that, Angela.'

Vicky fell silent and I didn't speak either, wanting her to take her time, and not wishing to antagonise her further.

Eventually Vicky broke the silence.

'I thought it would get better, but whenever I'm reminded of her I'm still terrified. It's like she's haunting me.'

'Well she's not,' I said quite firmly. 'Your mother can't touch you or speak to you or send you outside or do any of the things she used to do.'

'That's what I've tried to tell myself. I thought I could even wear my hair down after she died, but I can't even do that! I'm still scared. It's not fair! It's torture!'

I thought about the day of her mother's funeral, when Vicky had blow-dried her hair into a bob. It had been the one and only time she had worn her hair down, but she'd tied it up ever since.

'I thought it looked lovely when you wore your hair down,' I soothed.

'I like it down. I wanted to do it nicely tonight, with Scot coming over, but I couldn't, just couldn't. It's all her fault!'

'I see. Can I ask you, Vicky, what was it that your mother said, or did, involving your hair?'

Vicky put her hands over her face.

'That horrible man next door, Alf, he knew what she did.

He heard, he saw. When I saw him at the funeral I thought I was going to be sick.'

I had heard on the grapevine that Alf disappeared immediately after Brenda's death, only turning up again briefly for her funeral. The gossip was that his involvement in whatever pill dealing went on was about to catch up with him, and he'd done a moonlight flit. Whether this was true or not I wasn't sure: I heard bits of tittle-tattle in the shop all the time, and not all of it was accurate.

'I'm very sorry to hear this, Vicky, I really am.'

'It's not your fault. As for the gentleman caller thing, well . . . those men she had over were such creeps. One time do you know what she said to me?'

'No. Go on.'

'I was wearing a short skirt and when I crossed my legs she said I was flashing my knickers on purpose. She said I was trying to show off to her gentlemen friend! Angela, I was about seven. I didn't know what she was talking about. The man was frightening. He laughed his head off and his breath stank, and he only had about three teeth in his head, all of them black and yellow.'

'Oh, Vicky, love. Come here. Can I give you a hug?'

She nodded and I gave her a cuddle.

'I'm so sorry I used that phrase. It was very careless of me. I hate to see you frightened.'

She gave her body a little shake, which I took as my cue to move away from her.

'I'll be all right. Far worse things have happened to

people. Scot will be here in a minute, I'd better sort myself out.'

Vicky helped herself to a handful of tissues and I told her she was very brave, and that if she wanted to finish telling me about her hair, or anything else for that matter, she could, any time she wanted.

'Thanks, Angela,' she said, wiping her nose. 'Please say sorry to your mum and Jonathan.'

'No need,' I said. 'They both understand.'

'I'm lucky to have you,' Vicky said. 'I'll miss you when I'm gone.'

# 18

### *'I used to live in a scary house'*

In the last week of the term before the Easter holiday, Jonathan, Vicky and I attended another review meeting with Hayley and Stuart Williams. We'd been told that a school place had become available for Vicky within the catchment area of Vincent's home, and now plans were being made for her to move in with her father after our trip to Florida. It felt like things had happened incredibly fast, but Vicky didn't seem fazed by the changes in her life.

'This is a bit different to last time!' she had said cheerfully when we pulled into the scruffy out-of-town Social Services car park once more. The litter and graffiti hadn't changed, but Vicky was like a different girl.

'Isn't it just!' I smiled, thinking back to that awful day when Vicky's mother failed to turn up.

Vicky had been on quite a high ever since we received the news that she could move to her dad's, and it seemed she couldn't wait for the next part of her life to begin. With our holiday also imminent, she was positively buzzing.

Once again Vicky, Jonathan and I sat in the stuffy waiting room, just as we had done several months earlier. The water cooler was still out of order and the same tatty collection of magazines was on the table, but the atmosphere was completely different.

'Do you know, in my wildest dreams I could never have imagined all this would be happening to me!' Vicky said. 'Last time we were here, I just wanted to die.'

'Don't say that, sweetheart,' I said, as the thought of Vicky ever feeling so low was upsetting. 'I can't bear to think of you being miserable.'

'Sorry, Angela. But I'm not miserable now, am I? It's all worked out.'

Once the review began Vicky beamed as she confirmed to Hayley and Stuart Williams that she was happy to move schools and live with her father and his family.

'Is there anything at all that is worrying you?' Hayley asked.

'No,' Vicky replied. 'I can't wait.'

'Anybody else want to add anything. Angela?'

'No, I don't think so, other than to say that Jonathan and I have thoroughly enjoyed having Vicky staying with us.'

'Aww!' Vicky remarked. 'That's so kind of you!'

'Well it's true, Vicky,' I said. 'You're a lovely young lady.'

I was still worried about how things would turn out for her, but of course it would have been wrong for me to voice such thoughts, and in any case my opinion wouldn't change a thing. The move would be a monumental change for Vicky, and I hoped that the bond between father and daughter would be enough to compensate for the compromises they would all inevitably have to make.

I had spoken to Lorraine several times as the plans took shape, and I knew she was going through similar mixed feelings.

'I'm happy for Vicky but worried too,' she put it simply, when I asked her how she was. 'I think she's very brave. I'm not sure I would do it, if I were in her shoes.'

'I agree. She's gutsy. At least that's a characteristic that will stand her in good stead if things don't turn out as well as we all hope.'

Thankfully, Jonathan and I had the holiday to organise, which kept our minds off things. We were hiring a relief manager to look after the shop while we were away and she needed to be shown the ropes, plus we had all the packing and lots of planning to do for the trip. It was many years since Jonathan and I had been to Florida, and we spent several evenings poring over the brochures for Disney World. We'd visited the Magic Kingdom and Epcot theme parks last time and we definitely wanted to return to those with Vicky, but we also wanted to see Dolphin Cove, Sea World plus the Universal and MGM Studios, as they were then called. There was also the tropical aviary I'd researched, which was a bus trip away from our hotel, and was a must-do.

'Is there anything else you particularly want to do or see?' I asked Vicky one night.

'Not really, just the birds,' she replied with a shrug.

'Can I go over to Scot's house? Izzy and a few others are going too.'

'Yes, you can, love, as long as you are home by 9.30 p.m.'

'OK. By the way, how long are we away for exactly?'

'The holiday is fourteen nights, Vicky. We get back four days before you move to your dad's.'

'Oh. That's a long time. I wish it was just a week.'

I didn't rise to this. It was a typical teenage remark and I didn't let it bother me. Vicky was clearly very keen on Scot and they'd been spending a lot of time together. I knew Vicky wanted to come on holiday and was grateful for the opportunity, but of course she wanted to see Scot and her friends too, before she moved away.

'Well, it's all booked now, and there's no point in going for less than a fortnight. There is so much to do.'

Vicky tut-tutted and walked out.

'OK. See you later.'

I raised my eyes to the ceiling.

'Kids!' I said.

'Unbelievable!' Jonathan responded. 'She has no idea what a treat she's in for.'

'I know,' I laughed, feeling a surge of excitement. 'I can't wait to see her reaction to the rides and attractions. It'll be absolutely brilliant. Florida here we come!'

Vicky had never been abroad or even stayed in a hotel before, so everything was an adventure, right from the moment we left England. She was thrilled by things I didn't anticipate, like the tray of food she was handed on the flight to America, and the air conditioning and fluffy white bath-robes we had in our hotel room at Disney World.

'It's like being in a film,' she said more than once.

It was blazing hot in Florida and we did a lot of walking and queuing every day, but Vicky never complained, not once. She got soaked to the skin at Sea World when we rather mischievously encouraged her to sit on the front row to watch the killer whale in action.

'You knew that would happen, didn't you?' she laughed accusingly as I took photos from several rows behind. 'I'll get you for this!'

Jonathan and I had seen a very similar display on our previous visit and loved it. We only returned so that Vicky could enjoy the experience too, but we were taken aback by our own reactions. It was an absolute joy to watch her having so much fun, and our eyes were on Vicky as much as on the show. Space Mountain was another attraction we revisited.

'I think it's one of the best rides here,' I said to Vicky. 'I think you'll really like it.'

'What happens?'

'I can't tell you that. It'll spoil the fun. Come on!'

Vicky screamed her head off but absolutely loved it, so much so that she was prepared to wait another hour to have a second turn. The haunted house was the only attraction that didn't go down well. Vicky was really scared, particularly when we were confronted with a spooky room where a candle-lit seance was supposedly taking place.

'Argh! Fire!' she screamed in terror, covering her face with her hands.

Vicky came off the ride looking as white as a sheet.

'Oh my God, what were we thinking of?' Jonathan whispered. 'Do you think she'll be all right?'

Vicky looked scared stiff, and we had to gently guide her to a bench and sit with her for about twenty minutes until she came round and fully composed herself.

'Sorry, love,' I soothed. 'I didn't think you'd be that frightened or I would never had taken you on there.'

'It's not your fault,' she said quietly. 'Haunted houses just aren't my thing.'

Her expression softened and she eventually gave me a smile and attempted a joke.

'I think it's because it was too real,' she said, giving a little shudder. 'I used to live in a scary house, remember!'

'Yes, love, but it wasn't full of ghosts and skeletons, was it?' I replied, desperately trying to come up with a light-hearted reply but not doing very well.

'Nah! It was worse than that!'

Jonathan and I shared a forlorn look and declared that it was high time for an ice cream. Thankfully, I think our trip to the tropical aviary more than made up for this low point. Vicky was in raptures as we explored the hot, jungle-like walkways, spotting all kinds of brightly coloured birds and listening to their funny squawks and beautiful songs.

'Hello!' Vicky said, whenever she got close to a bird. 'Aren't you pretty?'

She then stayed very still, as if patiently waiting for a

response, but of course most of the birds just shook their tail feathers or flew away without giving her a second look.

'They're lovely, but they're not as friendly as Mr Robin,' Vicky concluded.

The holiday was a wonderful success, and the three of us returned home looking sun-kissed and brimming with tales. My mother listened enthusiastically as we described our adventures and showed her the scores of photos we had printed at Boots.

'What was the highlight?' Mum asked.

'The aviary!' Vicky said, without hesitation. 'And I liked the bathrobes in the hotel. It was like being in *Dallas*.'

My mum laughed. 'I didn't expect that reply!' she said. 'You're easily pleased, Vicky. Was there anything you didn't like?'

I imagined the haunted house would have flashed into Vicky's mind, but she gave an answer I didn't anticipate at all.

'I missed home,' she said. 'I'm not sure I like being so far away. It's weird.'

This remark gave me mixed feelings. I was pleased Vicky was happy in the home life we'd created for her, and indeed that she even called our house home, but of course I couldn't help worrying once more about how she would cope when she moved away. If two weeks in Florida with us had made her feel homesick, how would she manage starting a new life hundreds of miles away?

I found it heartbreaking when we had to start packing

up Vicky's things in the days after our return home, but I tried to hide my feelings, as I didn't want to upset her. Fortunately, Vicky didn't seem in the least bit perturbed, but I wondered if this was immaturity.

'It's like packing for another holiday when I've just got home from one!' she said as she piled her belongings into two large suitcases and a couple of holdalls I'd given her. 'I'm going to put this one on the wall in my room at my dad's,' she added, placing one of our holiday snaps inside a book to keep it flat.

The photo showed Vicky, Jonathan and myself at Sea World, all posing for the camera and laughing. It was taken shortly after Vicky got soaked by the whale and she was huddled between us, doing her best to get us both as wet as she possibly could.

'That's great,' I said. 'Let me see if I can find you a little frame for it.'

I stepped out of Vicky's bedroom and stifled a sob. I was finding this very difficult, but I knew I had to be strong, for Vicky's sake.

My mother came over that evening, bringing a cake that she'd decorated with the words 'Good Luck, Vicky' which also moved me, and the next day I took Vicky over to Lorraine's so the sisters could say their goodbyes.

Lorraine insisted that I went inside the flat, even though I was adamant that I didn't want to intrude.

'Don't be silly,' Lorraine said. 'You're like family now, Angela!'

Again I found myself experiencing mixed emotions. It

was a lovely thing for Lorraine to say and I knew she meant it, but the sentiment just made it even harder for me to deal with Vicky's departure. I did feel very much a part of Vicky's family, but as a foster carer I had no idea if I would remain so as time went on. Vicky was young and adaptable, and I had to face the fact that she might very well lose touch with me and Jonathan as she established a new life with her dad.

Vicky sat in Lorraine's lounge with her little nephew on her lap, and she did 'Round and Round the Garden' on the palm of his chubby little hand. James was eight months old now, and when Vicky got to the bit in the rhyme where she tickled him under the arms he giggled raucously. Lorraine started crying.

'Sorry!' she said, scuttling to the kitchen and dabbing her eyes with a piece of kitchen towel. 'Oh my God, he's going to miss his Auntie Vicky!'

'I'll be back!' Vicky beamed. 'Don't you worry, little man!'

The journey to Vincent's the next day was inevitably tough. Lorraine didn't come with us this time. Jonathan drove and we went through a bit of a charade, trying to treat it like any other car trip, though of course it wasn't.

We were both putting on a brave face and, if Vicky was feeling in any way upset or anxious, she did a great job of covering it up. She was bubbly and chatty the whole way, talking about getting a new school uniform and wondering what her bedroom would look like now, as Carol had promised she would have it redecorated before Vicky moved in.

'We're here!' she shouted triumphantly when Jonathan

drove onto the estate, and then Vicky jumped out of the car the moment it stopped, skipping up to the bungalow and pressing the bell enthusiastically.

When the front door opened Vincent was in the hallway in his wheelchair, looking very pleased and really quite emotional, and he welcomed Vicky with open arms. There was no sign of Matty, but Carol was there, and she told Vicky she was delighted the day had arrived at last.

'Me too!' Vicky said. 'I can't believe it really. It's like a dream!'

We didn't stop, and even when we said goodbye Vicky didn't show a flicker of concern or sadness.

'I'll see you soon,' she said brightly. 'Thanks for driving, Jonathan!'

She gave him a salute then hugged us both, and thanked us for all we'd done for her.

'You're more than welcome,' Jonathan told her.

'Bye, love,' I managed. 'Now keep in touch, do you hear? Let me know how you're keeping.'

'Course!' she said. 'See ya! Wouldn't want to be ya!'

I smiled fondly. This was typical of Vicky, switching to cheeky mode as her default position. I knew she would have her worries underneath this confident facade, but I only hoped that they would dissipate quickly as she settled in and got to know her newfound family.

Vincent and Carol reassured us that Vicky would be allowed to use the phone whenever she wanted to give us a call, and they invited us to ring any time. It was all quite surreal. When I spoke to one of my friends about it some time later, she said it sounded like the first time she dropped her daughter off at university.

'I was holding back the tears but she was ecstatic!' my friend said. 'I didn't want to cry in front of her, but once I'd driven off and turned the corner it was like the floodgates opened!'

There certainly was a similarity, as I cried my eyes out as soon as we'd pulled off the estate. However, there was an added dimension to our situation, one that my friend and I were acutely aware of but neither of us wanted to articulate. The fact was, this was not like dropping your own child off at university. For a start, Vicky was only fourteen, but more importantly, she would not be coming home with a bag of dirty laundry at the end of term. No, it wasn't the same at all, because the harsh reality was that there was a possibility I might never see Vicky again, and there was absolutely nothing I could do about that. All I could do was hope and pray that she was happy in her new home, and that even if we didn't see her again, she would keep in touch.

# 19

*'Everything is different'*

It was incredibly quiet in the house without Vicky, and I missed her a great deal. She phoned on the first Sunday afternoon after she'd left and told me all about her new school.

'I've got a trial for the netball team next week,' she said. 'And I really like my home economics teacher. They're doing the same syllabus so I'm well happy!'

'That's good, love. And how are you getting on with everybody at home?'

'Good, thanks. My dad's got lots of stories to tell. Do you know, he used to work on a fish farm, before he joined the Army, and he's a really good cook?'

'That's great to hear!'

'Yes, he and his workmates used to take so much fish home that he learned how to cook it in every possible way! He's already taught me how to make kedgeree. My cookery teacher was well impressed when I put that on a breakfast menu I was working on.'

'That sounds great. I'm so pleased things are working out.'

'So am I! I miss everyone back home, but I'll be able to visit in the summer, won't I?'

'Of course, love. I'm looking forward to it already. Now don't forget, ring me any time you like if you want a chat. Look after yourself.'

'Thanks, Angela. You too. Give my love to Jonathan and your mum.'

We had a similarly upbeat conversation the following Sunday, and this time I had some news for Vicky.

'We've got a little girl coming to stay next week,' I said. 'Her name's Melanie and she's nine. She'll be with us for a few weeks, just to help her mum out.'

'Ah! That's nice,' Vicky said.

'Yes, I'm very pleased. Jonathan and I had been wondering whether to have a little break from fostering, but it's been way too quiet in the house for my liking!'

Vicky laughed and so did I, but what I said was no joke. Though Jonathan and I had enjoyed having a week or so to catch our breath after Vicky's departure, we both admitted we felt there was something missing from our lives, without having any kids at all in the house. One night I'd made a huge cottage pie and, after Jonathan and I ate less than half of it between us, we both looked at what was left.

'Did you think you were catering for more?' Jonathan said kindly.

'Habit,' I said. 'I like having more people round the table. What do you think?'

After several long and searching conversations we both agreed not to make any rash decisions about our long-term future as foster carers. However, to my delight we settled on continuing to make ourselves available to take in kids on short-term placements, which is how we came to agree to have Melanie. This seemed like a good compromise. Jonathan did not want to commit to fostering indefinitely but he was very happy to provide respite care. This also suited me for the time being. I didn't feel ready to commit to a long-term placement so soon after Vicky, but my feelings hadn't changed and I was more determined than ever that I wanted to carry on fostering.

'Er, exactly how long is Melanie staying?' Vicky asked.

'Two-and-a-half weeks if all goes to plan. It's just respite care.'

'Oh that's good,' she replied wistfully.

'Is everything all right, Vicky?'

'Well, it's like this, Angela. I do like it at my dad's but I'm not sure I want to stay here forever.'

'Oh, I see. It's very early days. Is something wrong?'

'No, not really. I mean, I don't really like Matty, or should I say Matty doesn't like me. He hasn't made me feel welcome, which isn't very nice.'

'I'm sorry to hear that. Has something else happened?'

'No, nothing like that. He's just a bit off with me generally, that's all. He makes it obvious he'd rather I wasn't here.'

'I see. I suppose it's a big adjustment for him too. What about your dad and Carol? How are they?'

'Absolutely lovely. I really like them and they are very

kind. I can't believe the things my mum told me about my dad. He's the opposite of the way she described him.'

'I'm very glad to hear it. So is something else bothering you?'

'Everything is different. I'm just such a long way away from home. I miss Lorraine and James, I miss all my friends and I miss you and Jonathan, and your mum. The girls at school are OK, but they all have their groups and have grown up together. I've got a different accent to them and I just feel like I don't belong.'

'It's a huge change, Vicky, so I'm not surprised you're still settling in. I'm sure things will improve in time. Have you spoken to your dad about how you feel?'

'Yes. He's brilliant. He told me he's had some training in talking about problems, because he had to go through a lot of counselling when he lost his leg. He helps counsel other soldiers sometimes, and he's a great listener and a really easy person to talk to. He's told me everything I'm feeling is normal and, like you, he says it will take time for me to settle, but . . .'

'But what, sweetheart?'

'But I'm really not sure it's what I want. I've met my dad now, and I know I can visit him whenever I want, but I think I'd rather live with you.'

'OK, Vicky. I hear what you're saying and you need to talk to your dad and your social worker about this, but I would recommend you give it a bit more time, and don't make any impulsive decisions.'

'OK, Angela,' she said. 'I'll try my best.'

\*

Vicky struggled through the summer term at her new school feeling incredibly homesick and, after visiting us in the holidays for three days, she said she missed her dad but had made up her mind that she wanted to move back.

'Can I live with you again?' Vicky asked me outright on the last night of her visit.

'I'd love to have you back,' I replied immediately, though I quickly added that it wasn't just up to me.

I didn't want to give Vicky any false hopes and had no idea if this were possible. I also wasn't entirely sure how Jonathan would react, but in the event he didn't think twice about having Vicky back, if it were possible. We both agreed she felt like one of the family and, after discussing her situation with Social Services, it was decided that Vicky could come back for the start of the autumn term, as long as her old school or a suitable alternative could accommodate her.

Vincent was incredibly understanding throughout, telling Vicky that if she changed her mind she could return to live with him at any time. Hayley was very supportive and helpful too. In the event she secured Vicky's place back at her old school at lightning speed and dealt with all the necessary paperwork extremely efficiently. In the meantime, Jonathan and I fostered two more young children after Melanie's short stay, both of them for a week or two of respite care. They filled the house with noise and clutter and were fun to be around, but it wasn't the same as having a teenager in the house.

'I enjoy looking after the little ones, but it's very different to having Vicky here, isn't it?' I had said more than once.

'Definitely,' Jonathan agreed. 'I never thought I would say this, but I miss the challenges involved in having a teenager in the house. I think it suited us.'

We didn't know it at the time but this was a prophetic conversation, because a few years later Jonathan and I went on to train as specialist carers for teenagers. For the time being, however, we continued to make ourselves available as short-term respite carers, while also welcoming Vicky into our home and lives once again. It was a great joy to have her back.

After the few months spent apart we could see that Vicky had come on in leaps and bounds since we first met her, which was very satisfying indeed. The swaggering slip of a girl who'd arrived at our door in the oversized purple tracksuit, swinging her carrier bag of clothes, was now fast approaching her fifteenth birthday. She was quite the young lady, and her youthful cockiness had turned into impressive poise and self-confidence.

'I'm extremely grateful to you and Jonathan,' she said as she unpacked her suitcases in her old bedroom. 'I'm not sure I would have come back if I couldn't stay with you again.'

'Well we are thrilled to have you here,' I told her. 'We missed you so much.'

'I missed you too! You gave me my first proper home. My mother's house was never a home. I'm so happy to be back.'

I never stopped worrying and wondering about the level

of abuse Vicky had suffered at the hands of her mother, but the more experienced I became as a foster carer the more I understood that I couldn't ask. It had to come from Vicky, and I resigned myself to the fact that maybe she would never tell.

Vicky's return was a great success. She lived with us for almost two more years, during which time her episodes of freezing and going into shock reduced and became much less severe. She left us again when she had finished school and was nearly seventeen, and we have kept in touch ever since.

Vicky didn't talk about her mother for more than twenty years, but one day she did open up, completely unexpectedly. By then Vicky was in her thirties, married to her lovely husband, Keith, and their two daughters were aged nine and eleven. Vicky had brought the girls over to our house for a visit when I made a remark about their beautiful long hair.

'What lucky girls you are!' I said. 'I don't think I've ever seen such pretty hair!'

Both of Vicky's daughters had flowing blonde hair that was clearly very well cared for, and it was glistening in the sunshine as they bounded around my garden, playing with our pet rabbits and guinea pigs. Ever since the girls were born I had noticed that Vicky was very particular about their appearance. They were always immaculately dressed, and if they got the slightest mark on their clothes Vicky would change them immediately. You didn't need to be a genius to work out why, and even though I sometimes worried that Vicky may be overcompensating because of her neglected background, ultimately I was very proud of her and would never have criticised her parenting skills. She was a caring and devoted mum, and she could not do enough for her daughters.

'I could never have my hair long and loose like that,' Vicky said wistfully, in reply to my compliment.

'You always had yours in a ponytail, didn't you?' I said, glancing at the neat pixie crop she had had ever since she became a mum.

'Yes. That was because of my mother, Angela. I had it down for her funeral though, remember?'

'I do remember, very clearly. And afterwards you told me you couldn't wear it down after all.'

'That's right. I didn't tell you why though, did I?'

'Not really, no.'

There was a momentary pause and Vicky looked me in the eye, holding my gaze as she spoke softly but purposefully.

'My mother used to swing me around by my hair, Angela, when she was drunk. There was no warning. She'd suddenly make a grab for me, and then I'd be bouncing off the walls and the banisters and the furniture. I tied my hair up so it was harder for her to snatch hold of it when I tried to run away, but she usually still managed to get me.'

I felt like a door had been opened into a world I hadn't been allowed into before, and I was gripped with sorrow.

'And so . . . that is the reason you always tied it up?' I said, trying to take in what I'd heard.

'Yes, and because if she grabbed my hair when it was loose it hurt more, and it ripped out more easily.'

'That's just dreadful,' I whispered.

'I know. Even when she was dead I was still scared of having my hair down. I felt like I always had to be looking over my shoulder.'

'Oh, Vicky. That's very sad.'

'Sad? That's one word, Angela. Cruel, I'd say. She was evil, pure evil. It wasn't until I had my own kids that I realised how bad she was.'

We sat in silence for a few moments, watching the girls, who were now picking daisies.

'Can I ask, why didn't you tell anybody, Vicky?'

'I was too scared, Angela. It was as simple as that. She threatened to kill me if I told anyone, and I believed her.'

I remembered how Vicky had said to me, many years before, that she thought her mother might murder her. It was heartbreaking to even think about how scared she must have felt.

After a few moments, Vicky went on to tell me that when she was eight years old she had found her mother surrounded by flames in bed. Brenda had knocked over a candle when she was drunk and Vicky had to beat out the fire.

'She told me it was my fault, and after that I was always afraid that my mother might kill us both, if not with fire, by some other means, like cutting us with broken glass in the way she cut her fingers, only worse. I thought she was mad enough to do it, especially as she hated me so much.'

Vicky made a sound halfway between a snort and a laugh and, as I had seen her do many times before, she then swiftly pulled on a brave face and attempted to lighten the atmosphere.

'My God, Angela, do you remember that haunted house we went in, in Disney World?'

'Oh dear, I do indeed. You were petrified!'

'I know, but it wasn't the ghosts and skeletons that frightened me. It was that freaky psychic woman with the candle. Remember her? She was meant to be doing some kind of spooky seance. Honest to God, Angela, I thought it was my mother coming back to haunt me! How daft was I?'

'Not daft at all. In hindsight it wasn't a very good idea to take you into a haunted house! I've always felt guilty about it.'

'You? Guilty? You have absolutely nothing to feel guilty about, Angela! You gave me the only childhood I ever had.'

Squeals of delight came from the bottom of my garden, and Vicky and I both looked over to see her daughters putting daisy chains in each other's hair.

'Look at them!' Vicky said proudly. 'I haven't told them yet, but Keith and I are planning to take them to Euro Disney. It's something I've always wanted to do, as I loved our Disney trip so much. We've finally saved up enough money and we're going to go next Easter!'

'Euro Disney, hey? Oh Vicky, that's great news! They'll love it, and you and Keith will too!'

'I know. I think the girls are both at the perfect age to enjoy it. I can't wait to see their faces when we tell them! Thanks, Angela.'

'What are you thanking me for?' I asked, puzzled.

Now it was Vicky's turn to look a little perplexed.

'None of this would be happening without you, Angela. I was unwanted and unloved when I first came to your house. You made me feel welcome and loved when I didn't think anybody cared. I wouldn't be the person I am today if it wasn't for you.'

# *Epilogue*

It has been a privilege to see Vicky blossom into a wonderful wife and mother, and she has also achieved well in her chosen career. Looking back over the years, I feel very proud of her success.

Social Services placed Vicky in 'supportive lodgings' a few months after she had finished school at sixteen-and-a-half. This was common practice for teenagers in care in our region in the early nineties. The houses were council-owned properties shared by several youngsters, and typically supervised by a local foster carer or warden who made regular visits and was on call should any problems arise. Supportive lodgings were meant to provide a stepping stone, but in retrospect it was not the best idea to place a lot of teenagers under one roof with few boundaries and a great deal of freedom. Vicky shared her house with four teenage boys who held frequent parties and often had the police or council officials knocking at their door, investigating complaints from neighbours about the noise.

'It's a bit untidy,' Vicky remarked when I took her to the house for the first time. 'I don't mind my own mess but I hate other people's.'

The kitchen and bathrooms were grubby, the lounge carpet was threadbare and stained and Vicky's room had mould growing up the wall underneath the window.

'Come on!' I said. 'Let's do our best.'

I had given her some bedding and towels and I helped her to make the bed and unpack. I also placed a vase of her favourite flowers on the windowsill, which she really appreciated. I was naturally upset leaving her there, but Vicky was already turning into a very capable and independent young woman and I felt sure she would be fine. I told her she could visit us whenever she wanted to, and that she only had to pick up the phone if she needed anything, as we were just a ten minute walk away. Somehow, even then, I knew we would always keep in touch; we had a bond that I think we both felt very strongly.

Vicky had maintained a very good relationship with her dad and it was comforting to know that not only did she have Jonathan and I nearby to support her, but she could turn to her father for help if need be. Vincent had continued to tell Vicky his door was always open should she ever want to stay, and she and Lorraine were closer than ever too.

After exceeding her predicted grades in most of her exams, Vicky secured a place at the local technical college, where she embarked on a two-year catering course. I invited her round for Sunday lunch every week, and she arrived on the dot of noon without fail each time. My mother was now suffering from rheumatism and arthritis and no longer wanted to entertain, so she would come over too, and we always had a good time, often playing board games together for hours on end. On many occasions Vicky asked if she could stay over, and several times she asked if I could help her out with money. I never refused her a bed for the night if we had the space, even though Jonathan and I had continued to foster, taking in many other children and teenagers. I didn't give Vicky any cash though, instead offering to do her washing or giving her some groceries, as I felt this was more helpful to her in the long term.

'Don't you trust me?' she would say, giving me a cheeky look.

'I do, Vicky, but you're still very young and learning to stand on your own two feet. When I was sixteen and seventeen any money in my pocket went on a new top or a record. I want to make sure you're eating properly and looking after yourself.'

'Boring!' she always teased.

'I only have your best interests at heart, Vicky,' I said one time.

'I know, Angela,' she replied. 'And I am very glad you do. I don't know where I'd be without you.'

After finishing her catering course, Vicky took a live-in job at a hotel about seventy miles away. Once again I told her to keep in touch, and I knew that she would.

'As if I wouldn't!' she said. 'You're my family.'

Vicky phoned several times a week and visited often, even spending Christmas with us for many years to come, which we all thoroughly enjoyed. Lorraine had another baby and would often come over with her two boys when Vicky visited. She and her husband had been re-housed onto the estate where Vicky lived as a child and unfortunately, even after all this time, Vicky was still terrified to venture anywhere near her mother's old house. This is still the case to this day. Lorraine completely understood and so the sisters would often meet up at my place, which was always a joy for me. It was wonderful to see how far they had both come. Lorraine was fit and well and clearly loved being a mum, just as Vicky did.

There is a supposed truism I've heard repeated many times since I started fostering, the one that suggests children who have suffered neglect or abuse typically choose one of two paths, either continuing the cycle or completely breaking free. I agree with this observation to a point, and Vicky was certainly a very positive example of a survivor, as the life she created for her family was so very different to the one she endured as a young girl. Her friend Izzy is another success story, incidentally: like Vicky, she married a good man and became a mother of two, and she now runs a successful business in our town.

Sadly, over the years, I heard that Michelle had found it much more difficult to break away from her past. She had placed her baby daughter in care after falling out with her mother and had ended up in a homeless hostel when she was just eighteen. She cut Jonathan and I out of her life completely after she left us so abruptly, which was a source of pain to us for a very long time. Michelle eventually married, very unhappily, then divorced, and her daughter went on to have a baby when she was still in her early teens. Thankfully, I've heard more recently that Michelle has finally found the happiness she deserves: she is a doting grandmother and has settled down with a new partner who treats her well.

Vicky was in her twenties when she met her husband, Keith, through work. They eventually found jobs together at a busy seaside hotel, which happened to be close to the resort where Jonathan and I had taken Vicky on her first ever caravan holiday. We met her there a few times when we were on our travels, and it was always good to see her. Vicky invariably looked happy and healthy, and we would have a great time together, reminiscing about the day she threw ice over Jonathan, or the trips and barbecues we shared at the coast.

Keith is a kind and caring man, and when he and Vicky eventually married and had their two girls we were guests of honour at both the wedding and the christenings, which were very memorable occasions. Vicky continued to visit regularly even once she was a very busy mum, which I really appreciated.

'Angela, I would never, ever come back without coming to see you,' she said once, when I thanked her for making the effort. 'You are the reason it's even possible for me to come back.'

'That's kind of you to say,' I replied. 'But I only did what any foster carer would have done.'

'No,' she said. 'That's not true. You have done so much

more. You could have waved me off at the age of sixteen and never seen me again, but you didn't.'

I've had so many people say to me over the years that they couldn't possibly be a foster carer, because they would find it too upsetting to say goodbye to children over and over again. That always raises a wry smile, because in my experience fostering is not short term at all. It's a life-long relationship, if the foster child wants it to be, and I have kept in touch with many of the fifty children I have fostered over the years.

After that day in the garden, when Vicky told me about her mother's cruelty, she began to reveal more secrets of her past, bit by bit and often when I least expected it.

One winter's afternoon, out of the blue, she told me that her mother would get drunk and have sex with her 'gentlemen callers' during the daytime, not caring what Vicky saw or heard. Alf, the next-door neighbour, would take Vicky's mother upstairs for what he called his 'payment in kind' after delivering alcohol and pills, or bags of second-hand clothes for Vicky.

Another time Vicky told me that even though she was afraid of being put outside in the dark, in her nightie, and of being dispatched around the estate in the cold at night, she was infinitely more afraid of being in the house alone with her mother.

'Sometimes I could just look at my mother the wrong way and she'd snap. She didn't need an excuse, but sometimes she would invent one anyhow. "You're late!" she'd shout, because if I'd gone out to the library or to see a friend she always told me to be in before it was dark. I always did my best, but sometimes dusk would be falling, which my mother used as an excuse to lose her temper with me.'

The secrets keep coming, to this day. Quite recently, Vicky and I took the girls to the cafe in the park. Vicky finished her glass of Coke and then went very quiet and contemplative.

'You know what, Angela? Sometimes my mother would finish her drink, smash the glass and start cutting her fingers, telling me I had to watch. "Look what you made me do!" she'd say. "I never wanted you! Look what you've done to me!" When her fingers were bleeding she'd threaten to cut her wrists, or cut me. "Come here!" she'd yell. "Get here now." I remember telling you some of this before, Angela, but I didn't tell you the whole story. I'd have to go over to her because if I didn't I thought she'd slash her wrists, but as soon as I was close enough she'd grab my hair and drag me across the floor. Afterwards I'd have sores on my scalp and red streaks in my hair, but I didn't know if the blood was hers or mine.'

Vicky always tries to end such conversations on a positive note, usually by thanking her lucky stars that she has survived and created such a lovely life for herself. In all the years she has never discussed with me how she felt about her father's custody battle with her mother or his attempts to put her on the 'at risk' register. Vincent passed away a few years ago, but even his death did not prompt any such discussion from Vicky. I still wonder what she thinks about her missing files, and how their loss inevitably altered the course of her life, but Vicky has never referred to their disappearance, and she has never expressed any bitterness or regret. Despite the knocks she had in life, she is a naturally sunny person with a generous heart and a kind spirit – a lesson to us all, in fact.

'What you've achieved is nothing short of remarkable,' I said to Vicky the last time she spoke about her past.

'Thanks, Angela,' she said, a wide smile spreading across her face. 'I could say the same to you! You turned my life around, and I will never be able to thank you enough.'

Vicky was not the first of my foster children to say something of this nature to me, and this is the reason I have carried on, year after year, and am still a foster carer today, with Jonathan continuing to support me every step of the way.

The compliment was incredibly special coming from Vicky though. My heart swells with pride each time I see her or think of her, and I feel very fortunate to still be part of her life, watching her flourish.

If you liked *Terrified*, you'll enjoy Angela's next book,

# The Girl Who Just Wanted To Be Loved

OUT JULY 2016

### *Say hello to Bluebird*

Bluebird publish inspirational lifestyle books,
bringing you the very latest in diet, self-help and
popular psychology, as well as parenting,
career and business, and memoir.
We make books for life in every sense: life-enhancing
but also lasting; the ones you will turn to
again and again for inspiration.

Find out more about the exciting books we have coming soon:
**www.bluebirdbooksforlife.com**
**www.facebook.com/bluebirdbooksforlife**
Follow the Bluebird team on Twitter **@booksbybluebird**
We'd love to hear about your favourite **#booksforlife**

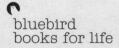

bluebird
books for life